ENGLISH IMAGINARIES:
Six Studies in Anglo-British Modernity

ENGLISH IMAGINARIES:

Six Studies in Anglo-British Modernity

Kevin Davey

Lawrence & Wishart
LONDON

Lawrence & Wishart Limited
99a Wallis Road
London E9 5LN

First published 1999

British Library Cataloguing in Publication data.
A catalogue record for this book is available from the British Library.

ISBN 0 85315 868 1

Photoset in North Wales by
Derek Doyle & Associates, Mold, Flintshire.
Printed and bound in Great Britain by
Redwood Books Ltd, Trowbridge.

Contents

Introduction:
Where next for the
Anglo-British?

The publisher and socialite Nancy Cunard defends her black lover from High Society racism in the early 1930s; novelist and playwright J. B. Priestley helps to break the electoral truce during the Second World War; rock guitarist Pete Townshend of the Who smashes his guitar in the mid-1960s. Twenty years later the fashion designer Vivienne Westwood masquerades as the prime minister; poet David Dabydeen transcribes a painting by Turner; the artist Mark Wallinger puts a race-horse into training and calls it *A Real Work of Art.*

On the surface, a disparate set of events spread throughout the century. What they have in common is that they were each stages in an unfolding transformation of the English imaginary, essential steps towards the modernisation of Britain. These actions all helped to establish new nodal points in the discourses on our national identity, challenging the dominant racialised representations of Englishness and creating new spaces in which new identifications could be made. All still have much to tell us about who we are becoming.

This book draws on the work of the french psychoanalyst Julia Kristeva, and the Italian Marxist Antonio Gramsci, to analyse a range of reflexive and future-oriented explorations of Anglo-British whiteness. Each of the six individuals studied sought to articulate the English imaginary with a new multiracial and democratic modernity. *English Imaginaries* contains stories forgotten or unfamiliar that I feel are relevant to today's anxieties and should therefore be retold. It is not a book that attempts to identify new roots for British or English radicalism. Rather it looks at a number of exploratory routes that have gone beyond the dominant Anglo-British identifications of their time - as well as at some of the costs incurred by embarking upon them – and the progress they have made towards a modern English Imaginary.

These stories reveal the national importance of improper behaviour. They celebrate transgression, parody, reversal, sexual experiment and downright bad tempered dissent as important parts of our heritage. The essays suggest that it is our cultural outriders, rather than our politicians, that have been, and remain, more responsive to the challenges of the world in which we now live. They also indicate that just as the colonial imaginary of the Anglo-British was not all pervasive and unchallenged before the war, it has not completely disappeared in the years since. Although whiteness has gone through a number of transformations, the Anglo-British national imaginary moves at a far slower pace than its critics and, indeed, many of its institutions.

I was born in a tied cottage in Constable country, in Suffolk. Consequently, I became aware, at a very early stage, of the artificiality of the dominant representations of England. For the last decade I have lived and worked in the most ethnically diverse borough in Britain, Hackney in northeast London, a place where Cool Britannia is, at best and for very few, what happens on a Saturday night. Here, the unemployed and low paid majority live their weekdays in a very different nation to the New Britain celebrated by new Labour.

The cultural politics of New Labour seeks to accommodate all traditions and social partners into a project of renewal for the United Kingdom, aggregating them into a mathematical majority, treading on tip-toes around the English national imaginary. I believe the upshot, to date, is far short of hegemonic.[1] And I fear the result, if the hierarchical structure and whiteness of the Anglo-British imaginary is not fully addressed, and its unity, memory and alterities are not brought to public consciousness and renegotiated, will be temporary and reversible.

This set of readings of the work of six individuals is not definitive. It is produced for a particular occasion – the arrival of the English at a major intersection on the highway of modernity, allowing them to choose between a number of routes forward, sideroads that will slow down their progress, and the foolhardy option of retreat, whether to Little England or the stubborn fantasy of the left that the Keynesian welfare settlement can be restaged in one country. The choices are the result of Labour's victory at the polls in May 1997. Although a general direction has been set, dilemmas about the Europeanisation, democratisation and deracialisation of Anglo-Britain are far from resolved.

These essays do not assume the fixity of the texts or the authors discussed, nor do they offer any final verdict on their work or character. Indeed, most of the texts and individuals addressed are, and remain, highly self contradictory and ambivalent. My readings simply address a problem that is present in each of their lives and work – the viability and future of Anglo-British whiteness in the modern world, and the need to renegotiate the English imaginary.

I have avoided comparable figures who have been extensively written about, hence the choice of Cunard instead of Eliot, Pound or Lewis; Priestley instead of Orwell; Dabydeen instead of Rushdie or Naipaul; Wallinger rather than a more prominent young British artist. Given Kristeva's argument that 'in the imaginary, maternal continuity is what guarantees identity', it came as no surprise that in at least four cases – Cunard, Priestley, Townshend and Dabydeen – lost or absent mothers inaugurated their contestation of dominant representations of the Anglo-British motherland although I was unaware of this when I selected them. All six have a renewed relevance in the period of crisis, renewal and transformation that the Anglo-British are now undergoing. These mini biographies try to link political discourse on the incomplete modernisation of the British state with the use of concepts developed to theorise the processes by which identifications, individual and collective, are achieved.[2] They draw in particular on the notion of abjection developed by Julia Kristeva.[3]

The marginalisation of aesthetic high modernism in Britain, and the replacement of Europe by America as the homeland of modernity and the avant garde, and hence the vector for utopic longings in the immediate postwar years, is a crucial part of the historical context.[4] Modernism questioned the certainties of modernity, including its affirmation of centred and unified identities, both national and personal. While Cunard attempted to draw on some of its energies in her attempt to disarticulate the racialised psychic and social suturing of Anglo-British power, Priestley resisted the theses of modernism in the name of popular pleasures and the demotic. Both responses could be, and were, articulated to a project of democratisation and deracialisation. As British decolonisation increased in pace, Pop Art made the hierarchy differentiating high and popular cultures unsustainable, setting the scene for subsequent developments in rock music, fashion and British art and for the wider crisis of reproduction of the Anglo-British colonial imaginary that ensued. Thus opened the period of Townshend's upgrading of Rock to Opera, Dabydeen's blackening of the canonical artefacts produced by Hogarth, Conrad and Turner, and the detournements of historical costume and painting traditions undertaken by Westwood and Wallinger. This period witnesses a crisis of the national imaginary that is far from over.

Today iconoclasm and hybridity are frequently forgiven if they provide product differentiation or diplomatic opportunity. Some of these figures have been recognised by the arts and political establishments as major contributors to Britain's changing image at home and abroad. Their opposition helped to shape subsequent hegemonies: J B Priestley, whose radically democratic antipathy to state socialism contributed to the emergence of authoritarian populism, was awarded the Order of Merit in 1977. Vivienne Westwood, who by helping to engineer punk and by questioning national authenticity on the catwalk, threw Thatcher's vision of England's nature and destiny into sharp relief, received an OBE in 1992. The vision of Pete Townshend, whose dogged concern with youth subcultures has long thrown up difficult questions about the inclusiveness of the national community, was endorsed by the Princes Trust in 1996. In each case an evolving and increasingly fragile Anglo-British state honoured itself by claiming these talents as its own, forgiving those that once transgressed against it.

'Since the English do not exist', the Neoist Alliance jokes, 'we won't bother to reinvent them'.[5] In fact their many and conflicting identifications, ethnic and civic, will not be wished away so easily.

There will be no significant political change without the further transformation of our national identifications and the way these are articulated with other aspects of our lives. We must urgently attend to the archaic and anachronistic narratives, articulations, alterities and abjections, the many conscious and unconscious horizons of the imaginary Englands that deny our new social reality. We must break down the inflexible and exclusive identities and narratives of the Anglo-British, destroying forms of racialised cultural protectionism and pre-empting the revival of an English fundamentalism.

When we have become, as Kristeva argues, strangers to ourselves, we will be better able to acknowledge the others with whom we cohabit in our cities and regions, in the two Unions – British and European – and in the wider world. One of the pleasures in this process of reflexive revision is the discovery that the past identifications of the English have not been as homogeneous and inflexible as they are sometimes represented, that postcolonial impulses were apparent during colonialism, just as colonialist attitudes have stubbornly persisted into the present. We will continue to make our own history and new identifications, in inherited circumstances and with new and received materials. For it is always time for the Anglo-British, whoever they think they are, to think again.

NOTES

1. Kevin Davey, 'The Impermanence of New Labour', in Mark Perryman, (ed), *The Blair Agenda*, Lawrence and Wishart, London 1996, pp76-99.

2. In particular Perry Anderson, *English Questions*, Verso, London 1992; Tom Nairn, *The Enchanted Glass*, Radius, London 1998; Anthony Barnett, *Iron Britannia*, Alison and Busby, London 1982 and *This Time: Our Constitutional Revolution*, Vintage, London 1997.

3. Julia Kristeva, *Powers of Horror*, Columbia University Press, New York 1982.

4. The best accounts are Serge Guilbaut, *How New York Stole the Idea of Modern Art*, The University of Chicago Press, Chicago 1983 and Anne Massey, *The Independent Group: Modernism and Mass Culture in Britain, 1945-59*, Manchester University Press, Manchester 1995.

5. *Life/Live: La Scene Artistique au Royame Unie en 1996 de Nouvelles Aventures*, Musee d'Art Moderne de la Ville de Paris, Paris 1996, p230.

1

England: an imaginary country

In one of Tony Blair's first speeches as leader, to the Labour Party conference, there is a remarkable invocation of a future in which all forms of difference, division and separation have been overcome. He envisioned a nation for all the people: 'Where your child in distress is my child, your parent ill and in pain, is my parent; your friend unemployed or helpless, my friend; your neighbour, my neighbour. That is the true patriotism of a nation.'[1] The promise of a utopic overcoming of loss, separation and inequality resonates throughout a diverse polity which has seen most of its institutions and traditions disorganised by Thatcher's neo-liberal modernisation of Britain.

For the Anglo-British are today divided, uncertain and at odds about their future. Once they were simply 'the English', with the Home Counties as their core, the dominant partner within a multinational state whose overarching identity, Britishness, concealed the hierarchy, the extent and the heterogeneity of England's evolving empire. The Scots, the Welsh and the Irish may have dual identifications, but for the Anglo-British, Britain serves as another name for the ambitious and self confident England that has existed as a nation state since the fourteenth century.[2] The Royal Standard which flies over English palaces, and the flag of the Union which was later unfurled over England's unmodernised parliament and a fifth of the globe, together symbolise the augmented power of the English over the inequitable diversity, difference and impurity of the subjects of the Crown. Colonial Anglo-Britain regarded black immigration into its homeland, and any nationalism other than its own, as a threat to its self conception of continuity, rootedness and homogeneity. Its longstanding, if battered, self esteem was briefly restored by Thatcherism.

That Greater England, symbolised by bowler hats, stiff upper lips and horsewhips, is no more. Decolonisation, migration, and a globalised economy and culture have transformed its civil society. A modernising Labour government, the imminent devolution of the Union and the cautious resumption of European integration, under the banner of a people's Europe, will further hasten its demise. Blair's invocation of a new unity addresses an anxiety but cannot furnish a closure. New forms of othering and identification, redefining new commonalities and differences for the English, will take place alongside his attempt to refurbish the nation. Culture will outperform politics in the race to produce new narratives and representations of nationality and modernity.

An identity is an unstable, aspirational point of identification, an attempt to position oneself, or construct a group – in relation to others – through ever-changing representations of a shared or distinguished culture, history, memory or set of utopic longings. Governments intervene in but cannot dominate these attempts to negotiate and regulate conflicting, collective, representations that increasingly mismatch national territories. There is no singular, univocal, national essence or identity, old or new, simply waiting to be uncovered, not even to a conjuror government eager to unveil and display a new Britain. Instead, discourses of national distinction, dispersed in many domains, from economic policy to rock music, are one of the many 'incessant fields of recoding that secure identities'.[3] Difference and adaptation are the ontological and historical condition of each and every polity. Notions of identity, authenticity and essence, where they do gain a footing, have to be created, buttressed and recreated. Where this activity is feverish, as in England today, the greatest dangers and opportunities can be found.

The elements of the changing identification that concerns me here, Anglo-British whiteness in its many modes, were formed relationally, in cultural and historical distinction from three subordinate British nationalities as well as diverse constructions of its European rivals, insubordinate classes and colonised black others. When it was not busily offering itself up, incognito, up as the overarching canopy of Britishness, it was this constantly changing and inequitable distinction and alterity that constituted the shifting collective identity of the English.

THE PECULIARITIES OF THE ANGLO-BRITISH

For nearly forty years there has been a debate on the British left about the specificities of Anglo-British history in the modern period, and the restricted national and political identities that have emerged from it.[4] The results of that historical and political enterprise must now be reviewed in the light of a new understanding of how the process of identification operates.

This discourse of the left addresses the political and economic consequences of the empire and the early capitalisation of agriculture and industry which resulted in Britain's early dominance of international trade, shipping and finance. The industrial bourgeoisie, it concluded, was made in the image of the landed aristocracy. As a result, when faced with the potentially damaging influence of the French Revolutionaries, the British propertied classes held together and succeeded in mobilising a national identification which countered French constructions of modernity – nipping democratic republicanism in the bud and preserving the patrician state. Britishness, according to Colley – whose account needs to be modified to reflect the dominance of the English within that multinational configuration – has therefore been predominantly protestant, parliamentary and yet monarchist, its preferences imperial and Francophobe.[5] As Tom Nairn demonstrates, in Britain, a surrogate nationalism based on the monarchy was erected against a modern European nationalism based on the people.[6] The political and administrative staff of this multinational state, in the main, viewed expressions of non-English ethnicity with anxiety. The Anglo-Britishness of its lead partner was a racialised configuration, an imagined white nationhood.

Today Anglo-Britain contains many peoples, not one. The English are no longer unitary, univocal or complete. A tentative relaxation of migrant transnational affiliations, together with the effects of racist opposition, have produced, among others, the emergent social identities of British Muslim and black British. Both have good prospects for consolidation.[7] This development provides few grounds for complacency, as the emergence of these connected but distinct communities has far-reaching political implications for Anglo-Britain. As Ricoeur reminds us, 'many peoples means many centres of sovereignty'.[8] And the institutions of Britain's devolving Union are, as yet, far from pluralist and participatory. In addition, these identifications provide the occasion for countervailing ethnic and national closures, such as those threatened by Middle England, or enacted by the rural activists of the countryside campaigns, whose political confidence Labour has to retain if it is to stay in office.

A residual white Englishness, which has long struggled to shore up its fractured identity, must be helped to unlearn its privilege, to adjust to the global flows and circuits of capital and culture, and the transnational social forms that regulation will increasingly take, and to construct new relationships, real and imaginary, with its cohabitees and neighbours in England, in Europe and across the globe. Instead, the longstanding claims of Englishness to superiority and distinction are being co-opted by the Labour government into its own ambition to become 'a shining example to all of what a modern state should aspire to'. First, the speechwriters beat out the bad news on their keyboards: the Anglo-British must renounce the illusion of regaining their past greatness. Then they tap in the compensatory good: Britain is going to become the best, a world beater, a beacon, no less than the model nation for the twenty first century. By courageously relinquishing a previous inflection of superiority, Britons 'can regain our standing in the world'.[9]

Blair's 'enlightened patriotism', is either a sleight of hand or a stroke of brilliance. But one thing is sure: it has swept aside the necessary task of English self examination, delegating most of that reflexive labour to the Millennium Dome. This position displays a superficial understanding of the processes of national identification and dangerously underestimates what might be at stake in the new ever-increasing challenges to the inherited English imaginary. Time will reveal the limitations and, I fear, the folly of the Labour approach.

For any new social arrangements to work, and inclusive if provisional identifications to form, England's national imaginary must be brought up to date.[10] Anglo-Britain is no longer imperial, nor a great power, nor homogeneous. Westminster now oversees a number of ethnicities in a flexible Anglo-British service centre for global capital. It is an important source of design, advertising, telecommunications, banking and software services.

Previously dominant Anglo-British identifications, some of their core elements reproduced over centuries, can no longer be sustained. Pioneering industries, which developed global markets, have passed away. The BBC is now three television channels among three dozen, the Church of England one sect among many, and the National Health Service is no longer a universal first resort. The old unifier of the monarchy has lost its authority and glamour. Our inherited political

9

institutions have been compromised by years of sleaze, sectionalism and low levels of participation. They have been augmented, and to a great extent displaced by, the pooled transnational sovereignties (IMF, GATT, EU, UN) which increasingly regulate our economy, law and citizenship. Blair's devolved Union and modernising populism is a desperate attempt to relegitimate the British state and the very practice of national politics.

After many centuries, the Anglo-British are beginning to recognise their diasporic and contingent nature. As they acknowledge that their strategies of inclusion may no longer be effective for a range of regional and national identities, and that their imaginary exclusion and abjection of black and European Others is no longer sustainable, boundaries which were based on former identifications and differentiations are dissolving. The English are experiencing with a new intensity long-standing fears of engulfment, evanescence and separation. It is at this English anxiety that Blair directs his reassurances about the possibility, once again, of community.

In the political domain, England's future is now figured as a choice between dispersal, federation or nativism. The Anglo-British can become modern deracinated Europeans; a regional and regionalised partner pooling and devolving its sovereignty; or a redistinguished nation with a devolved parliament within the Union.

As if the end of one historical regime of difference and othering were not painful enough, the Anglo-British fear the proliferating warnings that a localised national identification, however modern, may be an anachronism. For a new postnational spectre, deterritorialisation, is haunting Europe. Time, space and identity are linked, our theorists tell us: who we are is linked to where we think we are. And the contemporary relationship to time and space is fast changing, dispersing and compressing imagined communities with new systems of transport and telematics, often accompanied by celebrations of the postnational, the globalisation of fields of activity and the emergence of deterritorialised identities.[11]

Economies and imaginaries have not been susceptible to national management for a long while. Just as regional trading blocs and global institutions regulate the space in which transnational corporations operate, so too do representation and identification exceed the space, and bypass the superintendence of, the nation state. If we take Paul Virilio seriously, we can no longer even be certain about the reality of public and domestic space. 'The Old Continent', he argues, is 'fading before the "immateriality of telecontinents" built up of the unending dataflow between Europe and America'.[12] Contemporary panics about postmodernist theories, the possibility of community, and new art practices are all fuelled by the anxiety about national identity.

COOL BRITANNIA

Putting on a brave face amidst this turmoil, the government briefly celebrated Cool Britannia – an attempt to articulate Anglo-British national identifications, ethnic diversity and the output of the cultural industries. Memories of the 1960s, when a long postwar period of Americanisation was reversed by the British invasion, a transatlantic contraflow of musicians and fashion designers, are being relived with enthusiasm. 'Now, together, we have reclaimed the flag', Peter Mandelson confidently informed an audience of Asian businessmen.

> It is restored as an emblem of national pride and national diversity, restored from years as a symbol of division and intolerance to a symbol of confidence and unity for all the peoples and ethnic communities of a diverse and outward-looking Britain.[13]

Urban and multiracial, the nightclubs, galleries and sports fields of Cool Britannia are a marked departure from the Powellite England of timeless tradition, white nationhood, and distinction from Europe. But Cool Britannia masks a new configuration of power. It is not as radical or irreversible a departure as is often claimed.

First, it is clearly the case, as Ford and Davies argue, that 'London started to swing when the City told it to, when culture became strategically linked to inward investment'.[14] Secondly, there is the possibility that the contraflow is actually a normal and phased feature of the Anglo-American marketplace for music and the arts. Has everyone forgotten the American 'Anglomania' that featured early in the Thatcher years?[15] Cool Britannia may even be non-indigenous. The current prominence of English (and, it is often overlooked, American) designers in French couture can be explained using French factors alone – the unresponsive nature of its hierarchical educational system, a lengthy apprenticeship requirement which produces uniformity, the effect of recent economic stagnation on morale, the recruitment of the exotic, which is central to the fashion cycle – without any reference to British genius. Can the soundtrack to Cool Britannia be understood as a national phenomenon? Is it not in fact a popular rather than a national-popular cultural practice, stirred by the Black Atlantic and shaken by the vibrations of Eurostar?

The idea of Cool Britannia was briefly an important element in the unifying discourse offered by an aspiring hegemonic alliance of new Labour and the City. If it accommodated difference, it also found room for those in Labour's diverse coalition who did not consider the transformation and deracialisation of the state, the society or the national imaginary to be urgent.[16] This was achieved by placing 'Pomp and pageantry alongside "cool Britannia"'as Chris Smith put it when he set out the prospectus for a government which wishes to ensure that 'a proud sense of cultural identity leads to a proud sense of national achievement'.[17]

As an attention-seeking gesture, it has been successful. The Anglo-British were so decisive a shaper of the identities and prospects of other nations in the imperial-industrial era, that it should not be a surprise that, when its identities and structures convulse, the world watches, cheers and wants to join in. Nor should it be surprising, given their track record, that the English decide to make the best of the crisis by calling themselves a beacon.

Pomp, pageantry and Cool Britannia structure a moment of opportunity, but it is also one of danger.[18] Although Anglo-British colonialism ended between 1945-70, and race relations laws were soon enacted, England's colonial imaginary, traumatised by loss and uncertain of its future, did not evolve as punctually as the state might have liked. An IPPR survey in early 1997 revealed that white Britons of all classes still feared that British identity was threatened by ethnic minority residents.[19]

Cool Britannia is at best an aspiration, at worst a misrepresentation. Its messages about Anglo-British hybridity and modernity are not voiced throughout the culture as a whole. Certainly there are high levels of residential integration and inter-marriage between racial and ethnic groups in urban England. Wiggers – white youth who have cultivated West Indian accents – crowd the capital's clubs. The multicultural tears which were shed at the death of Diana, the people's princess, prompted a number of commentators to claim that a definitive break in national identifications and assumptions about the racialised nature of Anglo-British community had occurred.[20]

Yet despite Blair's claim that 'Britain is a multi-racial society that works' there are still high levels of white racial violence, black underachievement and disproportionate levels of black unemployment.[21]

Judges, senior civil servants, senior police officers, cabinet ministers and most of the decision makers in major companies and non-governmental organisations are almost exclusively white.[22] A large number of white Anglo-Britons still support a variety of repatriation strategies for non-whites.[23] The Labour Party has its own anxieties about swamping and it has acted to prevent Asian dominance of local constituency parties.[24] And a Labour Foreign secretary has fought to retain border controls at a time when most of his European partners would prefer to abandon them. Contrasting the Party with the non-governmental domains of fashion, music and art, Martin Jacques concludes that 'Labour is not a part of multicultural Britain'.[25]

Fanon wrote that 'colonialism is not a thinking machine'.[26] But the changing relationship of the Anglo-British to their self-contrasted black others indexed here, and in the essays that follow, suggests otherwise.

NEW LABOUR – ON THE RIGHT TRACK?
Does new Labour invoke a culturally homogeneous, and therefore racialised national community? Paul Gilroy and Jonathan Rutherford think so.[27] But Anthony Barnett considers Labour's use of the tried and trusted icons of Anglo-British nationalism to be a sign of misplaced and excessive caution. In Barnett's opinion, Powellism no longer matches the mood of the electorate and its advocates will pay dearly for their anachronism at the ballot box.[28]

The truth lies somewhere between, or beyond, these positions. If laments for empire and suggestions of black racial inferiority are absent from Labour's discourse, it remains the case that the party's normative pronouncements on the family, crime, drugs and employability address racialised suburban and Middle-English anxieties about the inner city, and draw on a cultural differentialism that has some commonality with the Tebbit 'cricket test'.

It would be naive to expect anything different, for cold calculation accompanies Cool Britannia on Labour's triumphal march through the national imaginary. After all, the party had to mobilise the former Conservative voters of Middle England, with whom it struck a deferential deal, in order to secure office. Coded references to the 'beautiful people' and generous helpings of the iconography of the threatened island nation – the apparently natural defences of the white cliffs of Dover and the Anglo-British bulldog, a direct appropriation of the imagery of the 1987 Saatchi and Saatchi campaign on behalf of the

Tories – ensured that notions of racial incommensurability and 'ethnic absolutism' could be articulated with the more inclusive elements of Labour's discourse.[29]

By contrast, fighting to regain its footing on the Conservative right – a problem long identified by Paul Gilroy – the identification of the Anglo-British national culture, past, present and future with the practices and histories of one race persists in an undiluted form. 'Youngsters of all races born here should be taught that British history is their history, or they will forever be foreigners holding British passports', argued Lord Tebbit, in a racialised broadside against tolerance that emphasised cultural difference as the key incommensurability between blackness and Britishness:

> Multiculturalism is a divisive force. One cannot uphold two sets of ethics or be loyal to two nations, any more than a man can have two masters. It perpetuates ethnic divisions because nationality is in the long term ... about culture.[30]

Tebbit warned that the white cultural foundations of nationhood had to be reinforced if Britain was not to fragment, like Yugoslavia, or be taken over by the European Union. Where once there was identity, now dismemberment and abjection threatened. Devolution was already converting the United Kingdom into 'bite sized morsels to make easier eating for our federalist masters in Brussels'. Tebbit's views were dismissed by the new Conservative leadership which did not believe that his views, or an older national imaginary as affirmed by Margaret Thatcher, would return them to power. 'There were those who would not admit it', she famously said, shortly after the Falklands war, 'people who would have strenuously denied the suggestion but – in their heart of hearts – they too had their fears that it was true: that Britain was no longer a nation that had built an empire and ruled a quarter of the world. Well they were wrong. The lesson of the Falklands is that Britain has not changed and that the nation still has those sterling qualities which shine through our history'.

This archaic inflection of Anglo-British distinction has had its day. But William Hague's advisers are also unlikely to recommend a return to the reassurances offered by John Major, Margaret Thatcher's successor as Prime Minister. He appeared to believe that Anglo-British culture and institutions had negotiated an extended exemption from modernity, preserving the nation's schools, sporting preferences, suburbs, tastes and religious beliefs from change:

> Fifty years from now ... Britain will still be the country of long shadows on county grounds, warm beer, invincible green suburbs, dog lovers, and – as George Orwell said – old maids bicycling to holy communion through the morning mist. And, if we get our way, Shakespeare will still be read – even in school. Britain will survive unamendable in all essentials.

Even the Conservatives now recognise that the idea of a singular and unchanging heritage is untenable and ethnocentric, and, perhaps more importantly, a barrier to a growing and differentiated black and Asian vote. After Lord Tebbit's outburst, William Hague quickly offered 'patriotism without bigotry' as a new definition of Conservative multicultural nationalism. In a major breach with Powellite and Thatcherite tradition, he later inaugurated a new Conservative constitutional agenda which endorsed the devolution of the Union on condition that an English assembly be established and electoral reform of the Commons be abandoned.

An English parliament would incubate the new strain of English nationalism – twinned with an enduring Euroscepticism – which has emerged in the Conservative Party. Many people are opposed to an English parliament because it would dwarf the Scottish and Welsh assemblies and, on historic voting patterns, would be dominated by the Conservative Party. But it should not be dismissed out of hand: an English parliament might also provide a valuable forum for renegotiating Anglo-British whiteness, especially after electoral reform.

The colonial imaginary remains closer to the heart of contemporary arguments about Englishness than the applause for Cool Britannia suggests. Until Labour has fully uncoupled the historic linkage between the nation and Empire, the national culture and race, the celebrations will be premature. This stubborn articulation deep in the English imaginary must be transformed as the necessary accompaniment to the changing of our political institutions.

NEW LABOUR AND THE NATIONAL-POPULAR

For Gramsci, the national-popular consisted of the symbolic forms that condensed and projected the role of the people in the creation and the maintenance of the nation. As we shall see, there are difficulties with this concept now that the unitary nature of identities, the individual and the collective, can no longer be presumed. But the national-popular is still crucial to any analysis of national identification and to political strategies seeking hegemony.

In Britain the national-popular has rarely referred to the origin of the existing form of the state, more usually to its development, partial democratisation and the shared experience of war. The story of modern Englishness is therefore frequently a story without a beginning, for that beginning – particularly the short-lived assertion of popular sovereignty over the monarch and the yoking of abrasive nations – is perhaps too radical an opening to sustain the outcome which ensued, a constitutional monarchy and Anglo-British ascendancy. As a result it has often been argued that Britain suffers a political dissociation of the national and popular. Thatcher sought to fuse them back together by exploiting a new war experience, the weight of the Conservative's southern English majority in a disproportionate electoral system, an anti-statist rhetoric that resonated deeply among many social groups ill served by a failing welfare state, and an economy scarred by corporatism. Britain, and Britons, it seemed, could be great again.

This new articulation endured for the best part of two decades, until the welds of national and popular were once again cracked, this time by the poll tax, high unemployment, rising taxes and not-so-great economic management. In 1997 Tony Blair took office, promising a healed community and a degree of control over the national imaginary. His future-oriented narratives offered the British people a role in the construction of a modernised and inclusive Young Country based on flexible labour markets, lifelong learning, a transformed welfare state and a devolved Union.

During the same period in which the opposition to the Conservatives grew, and a winning social partnership was brokered by Blair's modernising nationalism, many of the nation's former regimes of truth became reflexive. By the 1980s, critical intellectuals had produced genealogies of the discipline of English which revealed it to be a form of elitist cultural nationalism which had been deployed against the powerful currents of democracy, popular culture and cultural markets that are central to modernity.[31] The new heritage industries operated in a similar fashion, offering nostalgic narratives to cover the failings of the neo-liberal modernisation of Britain being pursued by the Thatcher regime. These tales did no go uninterrupted by the left.[32] By the 1990s the new discipline of postcolonial studies was investigating the racialised formation of the West, and of Englishness and its representations.[33] The gulf between these reflexive debates on the national-popular and the cultural politics adopted by New Labour, provides the intellectual and political context for this book, and its main cause of concern.

Stuart Hall reminds us that it is important to distinguish between the popular, which often draws on the culture and experiences of other nations, and the geo-political idea of the national-popular: 'The national-popular has some powerful elements in it, but it also has some worrying ones too.' As a concept it contains:

> a more political approach to the question of the popular, because the national-popular becomes an object of national political strategy. So you can use it to think about the terrain of operation of the state. Nonetheless, it also inserts us into a curious argument ... the idea that you could create an idea of the national-popular conception of the UK which wouldn't have anything to do with anywhere else.[34]

A spatially confined, non-relational approach to the process of identification would dissociate politics from a society involved in globalised cultural transactions. 'If you go down that path too far, thinking that the privileged object of politics must be the nation – the national-popular, rather than the popular – what a bag that puts you in'. It is the bag into which New Labour has leapt with a grateful smile. Labour's spin doctors and strategists have displayed a very strong inclination to shape and manage the process of national identification.

They are determined to halt any slide of meaning around Anglo-Britishness, and link the activities of the cultural industries to the wider political project of renewal. This is the common purpose of the Department for Sports, Media and Culture, the Task Force for the Creative Industries, the forthcoming National Endowment for Science, Technology and the Arts (NESTA) and The British Council. It will not be an easy task. Cool Britannia caught a chill less than a year into the project as a result of the government's welfare to work policies and its instrumental use of celebrities.[35] Contestations over the social and national identifications made possible by those living and working in England's cultural industries are likely to be a volatile frontline throughout the Labour administration.

ENGLIGHTENED PATRIOTISM

Neither Labour nor the Conservatives dare dispose of the residual narratives of white Anglo-Britishness, for they do not share Barnett's confidence that the era of Powellism is over. Nor do they believe that it is wise to base their political strategy exclusively on the new ethnicity of a younger generation.

Anglo-Britain's younger citizens do not perceive national identity to be important.[36] And where Englishness is salient, it is not identified with the nation state. Two thirds of young people now say they are English rather than British. But their Englishness consists of an affective attachment to the England football team, the national anthem and two television soap operas, Coronation Street and Eastenders.[37] The same survey revealed that the monarchy, Britpop and parliament all rated poorly. Soon after, a British Social attitudes survey concluded that 'young people are certainly less in awe of traditional British institutions'.[38]

Although other aspects of an individual's habitus will be experienced as more pertinent to the process of identification than the institutions of state, national identifications are still important points of connection between the social identities of younger and older Britons, and are vital to the brokering of the social partnerships and coalitions of political support required for modernisation. As such, they feature significantly in all political strategies aspiring to hegemonic status. This is why politicians increasingly associate themselves with the processes of national distinction and identification produced in the cultural domains of fashion, art, and music. Why else would morally zealous, family-minded ministers risk their reputations by spending their evenings, and sharing their photo opportunities, with drug-taking popular musicians and gender-bending fashion designers?

The construction of the Millennium Dome at Greenwich is the most obvious attempt to articulate diverse, and sometimes transnational, cultural practices with a national popular discourse that will secure and deepen popular, cross-generational identification with Labour's modernising project. Labour intends to display the 'moving equilibrium' of the hegemony it is trying to create beneath the synthetic and synthesising canopy of the dome.

An equally ambitious civic nationalism is also under construction, informed by Labour's programme of democratic reform. It offers a 'constitutional patriotism' that is both an alternative to, and an incorporation of, the range of ethnic collective imaginaries in the polity.[39] A modernisation of the monarchy is expected to assist the development of a new popular sovereignty. Blair's 'enlightened patriotism' and Hague's 'patriotism without bigotry' are both attempts to address Anglo-British anxieties about the loss of ethnicity and distinction with constitutional projects designed to restructure the two Unions, British and European.

The remedy throws up challenges of its own: can the United Kingdom survive the dynamic of devolution and democratisation which has already resulted in calls for Scottish Independence, a Northern Assembly and an English parliament? [40] This problem is intensified by the troubled ethnic legacies of Anglo-British whiteness. The question arises as to whether there can be a new English nationhood that does not involve a counter-modern white restoration?

KRISTEVAN POLITICS

The psychoanalytic, ethical and political writings of Julia Kristeva provide a very useful way of conceptualising the processes at work, and issues at stake, in the contemporary transactions between national and social identification, public life and subjectivity.

Kristeva is critical of the American left for not paying enough attention to signification, language and the unconscious in politics, a charge that can be applied with equal force in the British context.[41] Her writings on abjection, the foreigner and nationalism illuminate the processes of identification and differentiation at work in the modernisation of Anglo-Britain and they inform many of the essays that comprise this book.[42]

Kristeva's notion of abjection is a particularly useful way of understanding the changing modes of Anglo-British whiteness (although I find her distinction between the abject and the object, and her attempt to confine the term to descriptions of primary processes of identification too restrictive). For Kristeva the abject is:

> something that disgusts you, for example, you see something rotting and you want to vomit – it is an extremely strong feeling that is at once somatic and symbolic, which is above all a revolt against an external menace from which one wants to distance oneself, but of which one has the impression that it may menace us from the inside. The relation to abjection is finally rooted in the combat that every human being carries

on with the mother. For in order to become autonomous, it is necessary that one cut the instinctual dyad of the mother and the child and that one become something other'.[43]

Abjection is a process of differentiation and exclusion which takes place in the imaginary and through which an identity is founded. Through abjection we leave the chora, a condition of undifferentiated wholeness, and enter the symbolic. Later encounters with the abjected material produce anxiety. They remind us of the chora and the strangeness of identity. They are moments when the subject or the moral codes of collectives are reaffirmed or transformed. Abjects can be created during the processes of national identification and distinction, as well as in the formation of the individual subject.[44] The process of identification, in the imaginary and then in the symbolic, is never completed. Abjected or uncoded drives and impulses constantly strive for expression. The oneness of identity is an aspiration, not an actuality.

Anxieties about the creation and loss of boundaries – a reprise of the relationship with the mother – can be triggered by fresh encounters with the abject, either in the form of the others and alterities into which it has been externalised, or in the form of the uncoded drives and impulses that constitute a permanent internal menace to any representation of the self.

The fragility of all identifications is the reason for the constant political and cultural attention which is paid to our national identity, work which the existence of a fixed and historical national essence would render unnecessary. If it were simply Old, Deep and Enduring, Englishness, like an oak table, wouldn't need much more than an occasional polish.

If citizens and collectives could recognise their own strangeness and division and acknowledge the demonic and desirable abjects that they externalise as the menace of others, they might be able to live with difference. They might, in short, recognise others as the stranger within themselves. 'The Freudian message, to simplify things, consists in saying that the other is in me', Kristeva explains.

It is my unconscious. And instead of searching for a scapegoat in this foreigner, I must try to tame the demons that are in me ... recognising what is not doing well in myself – my death drives, my eroticism, my bizareness, my particularity, my femininity, all these uncoded marginalities that are not recognised by consensus – I would tend less to constitute enemies from these phenomena, which I now project to the exterior, making scapegoats of others.[45]

Kristeva's psychoanalytic politics of national identification does not suggest that abjection can be discontinued, for without abjection there is no possibility of meaning. But it does raise the possibility of the 'disappearance of the notion of the foreigner'.[46] That is what would follow if we were to 'develop a different conception of the nation in which foreigners will find a polyvalent home'.[47] Kristeva suggests that our national identity could be based on 'the togetherness of those foreigners that we all recognise ourselves to be'.[48]

The result would not much resemble the intimate and intensely homogeneous community proclaimed by Blair, which invokes the chora. Instead, it would be a heterogeneous 'paradoxical community' in which 'only strangeness is universal', in which 'recognition of otherness is a right and a duty' and to which a nation state should provide universal rights.[49]

'In the imaginary', Kristeva argues, 'maternal continuity is what guarantees identity'.[50] To this we can add another inflection of the imaginary, as developed by Laclau:

> The imaginary is a horizon ... it is not one among other objects but an absolute limit which structures a field of intelligibility and is thus the condition of possibility for any object.[51]

Anglo-British whiteness is one such collective imaginary defining the field within which we can speak of politics, culture and citizenship. Enduring notions of the Anglo-British nation – motherland, the Royal family, white nationhood, landed pastoral or the workshop of the world – provide the continuities and boundaries required for identification with an English imaginary. Discourses of modernity, democracy and rights have threatened to dissolve those borders and identifications for nearly two centuries, as the encounters related in the chapters that follow make clear.

Moments of instability and vulnerability are the inevitable accompaniment to our ongoing and changing relations with others, as allies, competitors, partners or externalised abjections. We need to learn to accept our own strangeness, our non-congruence with these precipitate Anglo-British national identities, similarly structured to and continuous with our individual subjectivites. If we do not our unavoidable exchanges with the once abjected – including other nations in Europe, black people and the popular citizenry, or the uncoded material and processes brought back into consciousness by contemporary art practices – will result in anxiety, injustice or atrocity, and not in renewal, inclusion or community.

The Anglo-British abject has returned in the form of Scottish and Welsh separatism, Irish republicanism, democracy and popular sovereignties, the simultaneous pooling of sovereignty within Europe, the prominence of black migrants in British cities and cultural industries, the arrival of refugees resulting from the collapse of states and economies in the South and in the East, and in the reflexive debates about Englishness, particularly in the fields of art, fashion and music: all of which engenders scepticism about the very possibility of authenticity and identity. Ours is a volatile moment, not entirely under the sway of reason, driven by the somatic and the symbolic, with no guaranteed outcome. 'You see something rotting and you want to vomit', reminds Kristeva, 'It is an extremely strong feeling.'[52]

Kristeva helps us understand how the competition for jobs and homes, the debates on citizenship, sovereignty and the inner cities, become racialised, gendered, regionalised or xenophobic. Her work suggests the depth of feeling with which Labour has to engage if dangerous exclusions are not to be reaffirmed. It also suggests the high price that will be paid if Labour fails to modernise Anglo-Britain and its imaginary, leaving behind an accumulation of grievances and anxieties in which a reactionary English nationalism might flourish.

Kristeva says that it is possible to have national pride and to exhibit tolerance. She cites the example of the organisation Ne Touche Pas Mon Pot (Don't Touch My Buddy) in France.[53] This example suggests that a new and inclusive national popular is at least feasible. Even if it does not guarantee that states will not engage in coercive assimilationist policies. The question of whether nationalism and new ethnicities can cohabit in Anglo-Britain will be answered over the next decade.

The relation between Kristeva's ethics and the means by which political institutions and agencies might be renewed or recreated is a complex, if pressing, question that will not be dealt with here at any length. But it is possible to suggest what they require of the Anglo-British. Kristeva believes that the delegation of power to political parties 'is no longer the most appropriate or efficient representation'.[54] She favours the development of forms of power that are 'provisional and stabilising', 'dispersed and flexible', and which foster a form of 'desirable dependency'.[55] This would require a modern decentralised pluralism and a non-communitarian politics that is wholly at odds with the residual structures of the Anglo-British imperial state and the discourse of new Labour. Kristeva's ethics are an essential contribution to the political arrangements required by our new global and local cohabitations and our increasingly decentralised, federated and pooled sovereignties. She sets a high standard against which to assess Labour's programme of constitutional reform and national renewal.

If we recognise the degree to which we are strangers to ourselves, non-unitary subjects only partially present in the identifications which enable us to speak, constructing others as a menace or problem, as the result of our self-constituting abjections, we may find a way to live with difference. Britain will not become a country of intimates, familiar because similar, sharing responsibility for its children and sick parents. Paradoxically, if it is to endure, England must first become a nation of strangers.

NOTES

1. Tony Blair, *New Britain: My Vision of a Young Country*, Fourth Estate, London 1996, p71.

2. Here I endorse the important modification which Adrian Hastings, in his *The Construction of Nationhood: Ethnicity, Religion and Nationalism*, Cambridge University Press, Cambridge 1997, suggests must be made to the thesis put forward by Linda Colley in *Britons: Forging the Nation 1707-1837*, Pimlico, London 1992, and in his general critique of theories which link nationalism to the late eighteenth century inauguration of modernity, such as those offered by E.J.Hobsbawm in *Nations and Nationalism Since 1780*, Cambridge University Press, Cambridge 1990; John Breuilly, *Nationalism and the State*, Manchester University Press, Manchester 1993 and Benedict Anderson, *Imagined Communities*, Verso, London 1983.

3. Gayatri Spivak, 'Inscriptions: of Truth to Size' in *Outside the Teaching Machine*, Routledge, London 1993, p211.

4. Key texts in that debate are contained in: Perry Anderson, *English Questions*, Verso, London 1992; Edward Thompson, *The Poverty of Theory*, Merlin, London 1978; Tom Nairn, *The Break Up Of Britain*, Verso, London 1977; *The Enchanted Glass*, Radius, London 1998; Anthony Barnett, *Iron Britannia*, Alison and Busby, London 1982 and *This Time: Our Constitutional Revolution*, Vintage, London 1997.

5. Colley, *op.cit*, 1992.

6. Tom Nairn, *The Enchanted Glass*, Radius, London, 1998.

7. This is not to underestimate the degree of resistance to these identifications. See *British Muslims and Islamophobia*, The Runnymede Trust, London 1997 and Tariq Modood, *Not Easy Being British: Colour, Culture and Citizenship*, Trentham/Runnymede Trust, London 1992.

8. Paul Ricouer, 'Universality and the Power of Difference' in R.Kearney (ed), *States of Mind: Dialogue with Contemporary Thinkers on the European Mind*, Manchester University Press, Manchester 1995, p36.

9. Tony Blair, speech to Welsh Labour Conference, 10 May 1996.

10. As Richard Kearney argues in *Postnationalist Ireland: Politics, Culture, Philosophy*, Routledge, London 1997, p2: 'We cannot expect to transform the political reality of a nation state without a corresponding revision of its political imaginary.'

11. See David Harvey, *The Condition of Postmodernity*, Basil Blackwell, Oxford 1989; Arjun Appadurai, 'Global Ethnoscapes: Notes and Queries for a Transnational Anthropology' in Richard Fox (ed), *Recapturing Anthropology*, Sante Fe School of American research 1991; and Kearney, *op.cit*, 1997.

12. Paul Virilio, *Open Sky*, Verso. London 1997, p47.

13. IK Lecture, Peter Mandelson, 1997.

14. Simon Ford and Anthony Davies, 'Art Capital', *Art Monthly*, no 213 February 1998, pp1-4.

15. See 'England Swings: Great Britain Invades America's Music and Style. Again', a special issue of *Rolling Stone*, 10 November 1983.

16. See Kevin Davey, 'The Impermanence of New Labour' in Mark Perryman (ed), *The Blair Agenda*, Lawrence and Wishart, London 1996, pp76-99.

17. Rt Hon Chris Smith MP, 'Culture and Our Sense of National Identity' in Michael Jacobs (ed), *Creative Futures: Culture, Identity and National Renewal*, Fabian Pamphlet 583, London, December 1997, pp3-9.

18. See Barnett, *op.cit*, 1997.

19. Quoted in Yasmin Alibhai Brown, Black Britain and Labour, for Better or Worse', *Guardian*, 11 February 1997.

20. Barnett, *op.cit*, 1997.

21. Tony Blair, speech in Washington, 6 February 1998.

22. Trevor Jones, *Britain's Ethnic Minorities*, Policies Studies Institute, London 1993.

23. Richard Skellington, *'Race' in Britain Today*, Sage, London 1996, p233.

24. See *Runnymede Trust Bulletin*, no. 280, Runnymede Trust, London 1994; John Solomos and Les Back, *Race, Politics and Social Change*, Routledge, London 1995; David Butler and Dennis Kavanagh, *The British General Election of 1997*, Macmillan, London 1997, pp191-2 and pp199-200.

25. Martin Jacques, 'The Melting Pot That is Born-Again Britannia', in *The Observer*, 28 December 1997, pp14-15.

26. Frantz Fanon, *Studies in a Dying Colonialism*, Penguin, London 1965, p48.

27. Paul Gilroy, New Times, 24 May 1997, p8; Jonathan Rutherford, *Forever England: Reflections on Masculinity and Empire*, Lawrence and Wishart, London 1997.

28. See Barnett, *op.cit*, 1997, p134.

29. David Butler and Dennis Kavanagh, *op.cit*, pp105-8 and p152; and Solomos and Back, *op.cit*, 1995.

30. Lord Tebbit, speech to a Conservatives Against a Federal Europe meeting, Blackpool, 7 October 1997. For abjection, see below, note 42.

31. See Chris Baldick, *The Social Mission of English Criticism 1848-1932*, Clarendon Press, Oxford 1983; Terry Eagleton, *The Function of Criticism*, Verso, London 1996; Gauri Viswanathan, *Masks of Conquest: Literary Study and British Rule in India*, Faber, London 1990.

32. See Patrick Wright, *On Living in an Old Country*, Verso, London 1985; and Robert Hewison, *The Heritage Industry: Britain in a Climate of Decline*, Methuen, London 1987. For the argument that heritage may not be passively consumed but might act as a popular antiphon to modernisation see Raphael Samuel, *Theatres of Memory*, Verso, London 1994.

33. For a survey see Bart Moore Gilbert, *Postcolonial Theory: Contexts, Practices, Politics*, Verso, London 1997.

34. Interview with Stuart Hall, 'Culture and Power' in *Radical Philosophy*, Nov/Dec 1997, p29.

35. Kevin Davey, 'O Tempora', *New Times*, 14 February 1998, p2.

36. Synergy Brand Values Ltd, *Insight 96: a Survey into Social Change*, British Market Research Bureau, London 1996; Mark Leonard, *Britain^{TM}*, Demos, London 1997, p23.

37. Cherry Norton, 'Youth Rallies to English Flag', *Sunday Times*, 21 September 1997, p11.

38. *The British Social Attitudes Survey*, November 1997.

39. Maurizio Viroli, *For Love of Country: An Essay on Patriotism and Nationalism*, Oxford University Press, Oxford 1995; Barnett, *op.cit*, 1997.

40. *Declaration for the North*, The Campaign for a Northern Assembly, November 1997.

41. Catherine Francklin, 'America: A Society on the Move', in Ross Mitchell ⸱ Guberman, *Julia Kristeva: Interviews*, Columbia University Press, New York 1996, p142.

42. Julia Kristeva, *Powers of Horror: An Essay on Abjection*, Columbia University Press, New York 1982; Julia Kristeva, *Strangers to Ourselves*,

Columbia University Press, New York 1991; Julia Kristeva, *Nations Without Nationalism*, Columbia University Press, New York 1993.

43. Quoted in Elaine Hoffman Baruch, 'Feminism and Psychoanalysis' in Ross Mitchell Guberman, *op.cit*, 1996, p118.

44. As Norma Claire Moruzzi argues in 'National Abjects: Julia Kristeva on the Process of Political Self Identification', in Kelly Oliver (ed), *Ethics, Politics and Difference in Julia Kristeva's Writing*, Routledge, London 1993, pp135-149.

45. Suzanne Clark and Kathleen Hulley, 'Cultural Strangeness and the Subject in Crisis' in Ross Mitchell Guberman, *op.cit*, 1996, p41.

46. *Ibid*, p40.

47. Vassiliki Kolocotroni, 'Avant-Garde Practice' in Mitchell Guberman, *op.cit*, p174.

48. Kristeva, *op.cit*, 1991, pp2-3.

49. *Ibid*, p195.

50. Julia Kristeva, *op.cit*, 1993, pp21, 31.

51. Ernesto Laclau, *New Reflections on the Revolution of Our Time*, Verso, London 1990, p64.

52. Kristeva, *op.cit*, 1996, p118.

53. Edith Kurzweil, 'Psychoanalysis and Politics' in Mitchell Guberman, *op.cit*, 1996, p158.

54. Bernard Sichere, 'Interview: The Old Man and the Wolves' in Mitchell Guberman, *op.cit*, 1996, p174.

55. Suzanne Clark and Kathleen Hulley, 'Cultural Strangeness and the Subject in Crisis' in Mitchell Guberman, *op.cit*, 1996, p37.

2

Nancy Cunard:
'a half foreign eye'

The turbulent life of Nancy Cunard reveals how in the inter-war years, in the late middle age of the colonial period, the Anglo-British still expelled from their imaginary, if not their actual nation, all those who jeopardised its reproduction as a white imperial state. These sanctions were applied even if the challenge was incomplete, leaving many Anglo-British principles of racial differentiation intact.

Nancy Cunard was ostracised by her Anglo-British and American peers for promoting aesthetic modernism, for taking a black lover, for taking the side of the republic in the Spanish civil war, for opposing the British appeasement of fascism, for embracing the cause of the free French and for urging a second front during the war. Personal exclusion and abjection were the penalty she paid for trying to contest ruling Anglo-British whiteness in its heartland – the salons and the canons of inter-war High Society. She attempted to redefine the racial constructs deployed in late colonial culture and differentiate herself from the gendered national identifications and roles that it offered her.

Cunard was denounced as a drunk, a promiscuous negrophile, a communist and, finally, a lunatic. In the festschrift assembled by Hugh Ford after her death, even her friends stigmatised Cunard as 'forever in a state of liquor', 'self destructive', 'vulnerable', committed to 'sex all the way, sex sans cesse', 'disturbed and violent', living in 'a state of fury' and subject to 'a ferocity of wants'.[1] These were the ways in which the majority of her peers represented her transgression of the racialised and gendered codes of Anglo-British High Society.

For envisioning an inter-racial modernisation of colonial Britain, Nancy Cunard was culturally disenfranchised and penalised financially. From a new position on the left margin of British cultural life, the semi-detached milieu of British communism, she tried to fashion a postnational collective imaginary that was at once European and anticolonial, strengthening her attachment to the avant-garde in culture and what passed for a vanguard in politics.

As the owner-publisher of the Hours Press, then as the editor and funder of the anthology *Negro*, and later as a self publisher, Cunard helped bring the marginal into the mainstream. She assisted the avant-garde to find a voice – as Beckett's first publisher, and then by publishing black, Spanish republican and French voices at times of crisis. These projects were fired by her dissociation from dominant Anglo-British political and cultural identifications and the forms of knowledge and power on which they were based.

A contemporary reading of Cunard's life and work still serves to make whiteness appear strange, and this in itself is an index of the endurance of the colonial imaginary in Anglo-British culture and politics, despite the changing nature of racism – specifically the shift from a biological to a cultural differentialism. Despite the limited nature of her transgression, in her own time Cunard was rendered black and abject as a means of preserving Anglo-British – and at times, transatlantic – whiteness.

THE PERFECT STRANGER

Nancy Cunard was born in 1896 into an Anglo-American family formed by the then widespread rendezvous between wealthy American women and members of the British aristocracy. In fact the Cunards were nouveau riche, of shipping line fame. Cunard's father was a culturally assimilated baronet and master of hounds, an amateur topiarist who also turned his hand to wrought iron. He married a wealthy heiress from California. Lady Cunard was one of many migrants whose dowries substantially enriched the British establishment, including Lady Ribblesdale, Lady Granard, Lady Curzon and Lady Astor. Nancy Cunard was born in a palimpsest of Anglo-British architectural history, a medieval-cum-Georgian pile in Leicestershire known as Nevill Holt. Tennis and croquet were regular fixtures on its lawns and the yew trees were still fed with bulls' blood.

Cunard's landed habitus was both traditional and cosmopolitan, and she had links, through her mother's family, to the Anglo-Irish, and to Robert Emmet. She studied in the pensions of Paris and Munich and she suspected that she might be the love child of a close friend of Lady Cunard, George Moore, 'Nancy's imaginary, if not actual, father.' After the separation of her parents – an emblematic incident which in itself raises important questions about the compatibility between Anglo-

British tradition and modernity – mother and teenage daughter relocated to London. In the breeder's language characteristic of the English landed gentry, on the eve of her marriage Cunard was described as 'an exquisite specimen of English girlhood', a trope still in circulation when Diana Spencer married Prince Charles seventy years later.[2]

Already empowered by class, culture, and wealth, Nancy Cunard was never involved in the suffragette movement, the constitutional feminism of her day. Taking full advantage of the changing place of women in Edwardian society, she became a prominent pacesetter amongst the Bright Young Things of the late wartime and immediate post-war years, smoking, drinking and flouting convention in their short skirts. Her capacity for alcohol and affairs propelled her into the gossip columns which were fascinated by her transgressions as they tried to establish the boundary between decent and indecent female behaviour. The triumvirate of Nancy Cunard, Iris Tree and Diana Manners flitted between Charlotte Street and Percy Street, the Chelsea Arts balls, the Cafe Royal and, above all, the Eiffel Tower club and restaurant, which she would look back on as 'our carnal-spiritual home'.[3] Richard Aldington characterised the avant-garde milieu in which she moved as one of 'drink, cynicism and unlimited promiscuity'.[4]

Her companion Iris Tree recalled the cosmopolitan heteroglossia of the early modernist culture on which that travelling band of twenty-somethings drew. 'Transition and danger were in the air', she recalled:

> We responded like chameleons to every changing colour, turning from Meredith to Proust to Dostoevsky, slightly tinged by the Yellow Book, an occasional absinthe left by Baudelaire and Wilde, flushed by liberalism, sombered by nihilistic pessimism, challenged by Shaw, inspired by young Rupert Brooke, T. S. Eliot, Yeats, D. H. Lawrence; jolted by Wyndham Lewis's Blast into Cubism and the modern French masters, 'significant form', Epstein's sculpture, Stravinsky's music (booed and cheered), the first Russian ballets and American jazz; nightlong dancing, dawnlong walks...[5]

In the 1920s Nancy Cunard was a modernist icon. She sat for portraits by Kokoschka and Wyndham Lewis. She was photographed by Cecil Beaton and Man Ray, was featured in novels by Hemingway, Arlen, Huxley and Aragon and had works dedicated to her by Tzara and Brancusi.

Although she lived at an aestheticised distance from the major Anglo-British social convulsions of her day, she confides her apprehensions to her diary. 'How hidden and remote one is from the obscure vortex of England's revolutionary troubles, coal strikes etc', she writes. 'So much newspaper talk does it seem to me, and yet – is it always going to be so?'[6]

Her primary cultural identification was aesthetic, and she resolved to become a poet. In 1916 she contributed to *Wheels*, an anthology published by the Sitwells. In the 1920s three volumes of poetry were published: *Outlaws* (1921), *Sublunary* (1923) and *Parallax* (1925).

Whatever his biological status, Moore was certainly one of Nancy Cunard's literary parents. 'From Moore she seems to have imbibed a high Edwardian tone and a conscious diction', Charles Burkhart observes of her poetry.[7] The point is also made by her biographer, Anne Chisholm:

> Cunard, for all her approval of modernism and the avant-garde and her long arguments with George Moore about free verse and the necessity of abandoning poetic conventions, had been too deeply imbued with the Edwardian notion of poetic language and the romantic, old fashioned image of the poet and his calling ever to let it go.[8]

Cunard was neither a distinctive nor a successful poet. As Burkhart rightly points out, repeating a point made by the *New Statesman* at the time of its publication, '*Parallax* is, plainly, warmed-over Waste Land … The Woolfs published her poetry, and one wonders why.'[9]

She cultivated a radically individualist posture that refused Anglo-British conventions: 'I am the perfect stranger/Outcast and outlaw from the rules of life/True to one law alone, a personal logic/That will not blend with anything, nor bow/ Down to general rules.'[10] That her actions and differentiations placed her outside any established national imaginary is recognised by her Armenian lover Michael Arlen: 'She didn't fit in anywhere, to any class, nay, to any nationality', he writes. 'She wasn't that ghastly thing called bohemian, she wasn't any of the ghastly things called "society", "county", upper middle and lower class.'[11] Her trajectory had a momentum that would soon take her beyond the boundaries of acceptable behaviour, into activities that threatened the Anglo-British codes she toyed with. The reflexes and sanctions of late colonial Englishness would eventually force her displacement into new and prescient identifications.

Trailblazing modernism was far from a precondition for entry into London's avant-garde habitus and Cunard soon gained access to a European, transnational network. Home during the 1920s was France, if anywhere. 'I seldom went to England and saw it already with a half foreign eye', she later recollected. 'My home was France; Paris in fact. And in Paris where surrealism had come into being, was a permanent state of avant gardism whose activities and creativeness were for ever stimulating.'[12]

RACIALISED MODERNISM

In Paris, in the early decades of the twentieth century, modernity, European modernism and primitivism co-existed in triangulation. 'The Cubist mask of modernism covers a black Bantu face', as Henry Louis Gates Jnr points out.[13] Aesthetic modernism, while critical of modernity's shortcomings, was simultaneously a colonial formation. If it generated mulatto artefacts that valorised blackness – albeit a black and primitive sublime, a sensuous and hedonistic alterity to Western enlightenment – modernism also reinforced the racial binaries of the colonial imagination, even as it challenged the notion of the unified, masterful white subject.

Twentieth century modernism built on the legacy of Gauginesque primitivism. In her memoir of the Hours Press, Cunard reports that it was Curtis Moffat who 'stimulated my interest in African and Oceanic art around 1921'.[14] Gilman argues that in Paris at that time, black people represented a 'sexual expression untrammelled by the repressive conventions of European society'.[15] Colonial culture was based on the repeated, but never completed, white abjection of the body, and in particular the abjection of the sexual voracity externalised as the menace of the black male. Paris was one place where whiteness could let down its guard and reverse that loss.

However, Cunard's Africanism predates her encounter with black people, and can be linked to other modernist appropriations of non-Western forms of representation. Her house in Reanville – Cunard's home from 1927 until the outbreak of the war, during which it was sacked by villagers and German soldiers – contained an enormous display of African bracelets and idols alongside paintings by de Chirico, Malkine, Picasso and Tanguy.[16] Harold Acton remarks of its interior that 'The furniture, a mixture of solid English and African, had counterparts among her friends'.[17] Burkhart, another visitor, recalls that 'Nancy's personal taste in decoration, not that she could not admire Riesener or Chippendale, was for everything that was ethnic, home-made, indigenous, natural, primitive, uncluttered and functional'.[18] The Hours Press shop she ran in Paris had a similarly bricolaged decor.[19]

Soon after the inauguration of her Africanism, Cunard was initiated into the discourse of the European left by the French surrealists, and in particular by Louis Aragon, her lover from 1926-8.[20] French surrealism was programmatic and political and, as such, was clearly distinct from its deradicalised offshore station in England, whose membership tolerated abstractionists and signally failed to embark on anything resembling the French dialogue with its colonised Other.[21] The charismatic founder and leader of international surrealism, André Breton, disapproved of Cunard. Her socialite profile – and her praise of Dada and surrealism in Vogue magazine – accelerated the commercialisation of the movement, threatening its purity and revolutionary objectives.

At one point Cunard tried to imagine Lewis Carroll's response to Aragon's translation of The Hunting of the Snark, which they printed together on her letterpress: 'I think he would have been astonished at the way these mid-Victorian characters could suddenly be seen as men without nation ... But then, it might be said, do not all those who cruise the seas develop a sort of supra-national identity.'[22]

In the 1920s and the 1930s Cunard operated in a postnational space. She journeyed incessantly in a deterritorialised, expatriate zone frequented by individuals whose sexuality transgressed Anglo-British codes. Her closest friends were figures like Norman Douglas, who fled England in 1917 after a scandal involving a young boy, and homosexuals like Brian Howard and John Banting who also found that it was necessary to leave England in order to pursue an openly homosexual lifestyle.

The early twentieth century phase of globalisation – of tourism and travel, of literary markets and the deterritorialised habitus of an ejected Anglo-British elite – began to delocalise English identifications. It was a moment of transfiguration, often experienced as emancipatory by women and homosexual men. For Cunard, this was irrevocably the case after a visit to a black jazz performance in Venice in 1928. But, as we shall see, the right to supranationality was not extended to black people. Instead, Cunard's evolving white imaginary simply reversed the flows of slavery and modernity, prescribing for black people an

Afrocentric identity based on a notion of 'blood nationality' which disavowed their participation in a modern and diasporic Black Atlantic.[23]

THE WHITE AFRICAN

In Nancy Cunard we have an almost unique example of Anglo-British female subjectivity transfigured through an exploration, personal and political, of its abjected black Other. This is what underlies her memory of the impact of the lover who helped make her a stranger to herself: 'Henry made me'.[24]

Henry Crowder, a black American from Georgia with a half American-Indian mother, played piano for Eddie South and his Alabamians. Cunard's epiphany and conversion took place in 1928.

> My cousin Edward Cunard and I had gone to sup and dance in the Hotel Luna and here we met some people so different to all I had ever known that they seemed to me as strange as beings from another planet. They were Afro-Americans, coloured musicians, and they played in that 'out of this world' manner, which, in ordinary English, would have to be translated, I suppose, by 'ineffable.' Such Jazz and such Swing and such improvisations! And all new to me in style.[25]

The exotic music of the black other was figured as a bodily movement: 'Swing'. Crowder opened up a space for reidentification and for the expression of drives and impulses that could not be figured in the gendered and racialised collective imaginary of England. Having said that, in many ways Cunard treated Crowder as an artefact, and tried both to collect and to edit him. In her English imaginary, his source was sculptural: 'My feelings for things African had begun years ago with sculpture, and something of these anonymous old statues had now, it seemed, materialised in the personality of a man partly of that race.'[26]

Her Africanism, an inverted colonialism, provided an imaginary template that the transatlantic Crowder could not match. Harold Acton overheard Cunard telling Henry to 'be more African, be more African'. "But I ain't African. I'm American" he replied.'[27] An indifference to Africa was a failing Cunard regularly bemoaned in black Americans. In 1931 she regretted the way in which 'their civic nationality is confused with their blood nationality'.[28] She repeats the amodern lament in *Negro*.[29] Cunard wrote a poem for Crowder about an angry black American leaving the United States for Africa, even though both of them disagreed with the strategy of return advocated by Marcus Garvey.[30] Crowder became the vehicle for Cunard's disavowal of the consequences of the imperial relation to Africa. For the cover of *Henry-Music*, an Hours Press edition of Crowder's works, Cunard persuaded Man Ray to photomontage an image of the black pianist in which his shoulders are both framed and burdened by her white arms and African ivories.[31]

Crowder soon found that Cunard's wanderlust and attempted exit from the English imaginary meant that he was expected to be an opening in her identificatory process, not a patriarchal closure. 'She has no bridle to her desire', he complained in his autobiography. 'She goes from one to the other with evident pleasure'.[32] He described himself as 'a pawn upon her chessboard of life. I realised I was no longer the King' and confessed that he subsequently became 'detached and coolly calculating'.[33]

Cunard began to read the American journal *Crisis*, produced by the National Association for the Advancement of Colored People, after Crowder had brought it to her attention late in 1928. She became aware of segregation, lynch culture and, in particular, the case of the Scottsboro boys (in which a number of young unemployed black Americans riding freight cars had been charged with rape and sentenced to death by white law enforcers). The case prefigured, at much greater cost to those involved, the transgression of whiteness with which Cunard and Crowder were also to be charged.

Inter-racial relationships were easier in the multiracial demi monde of Montmartre in Paris than they were in England, later prompting Cunard to make the exaggerated claim that racism in France was 'non-existent'.[34] Their spatial and affective distance from the Anglo-British imaginary is nicely caught in Cunard's memory of the two of them 'laughing at the strange hierarchy of English titles as they have to be written for the post' when mailing books from the Hours Press to subscribers in England. [35]

Cunard's first visit to London with Crowder as her companion, late in 1929, was uncontroversial. But a crisis broke when a return trip was planned in 1930. Cunard's mother, by now not only a fully assimilated American, but a leading hostess to the Anglo-British political elite, had belatedly been informed of the relationship. Her social distinction had been compromised when her daughter was triply abjected in a notorious question asked by her social rival, Margot Asquith: 'What is it now', she asked, 'drink, drugs or niggers?'

According to Cunard, she then received a warning letter from Thomas Beecham, her mother's lover, who pointed out that 'while friendships between races were viewed with tolerance upon the continent, by some, it was ... a very different pair of shoes in England.'[36]

Not only did Nancy Cunard breach Anglo-British colonial propriety by cohabiting with a black social inferior during her second stay in London, she also organised a screening of the controversial surrealist film, *L'Age D'Or*, which attacked religion, conventional sexual morality and the state. Cunard had obtained one of the few copies which had not been impounded by the French police after the riots which had followed its first public screening in Paris a few months before. Cunard's second London visit, valorising blackness and aesthetic modernism, was thus doubly, if not quadruplly, transgressive of the established modes of reproduction of Anglo-British whiteness.

Her mother imposed financial sanctions, reducing Cunard's allowance, and may also have used her influence to have the couple's hotel visited by the police. For Cunard these defensive reactions of the Anglo-British elite, designed to protect their racialised national identity, and enforce her ascribed responsibility as a woman, for its unsullied reproduction, made the personal and the political synonymous many decades before the slogan was coined.

Cunard had long been a differentiating self, transgressive of the Anglo-British imaginary by avant-garde preference. But her relationship with Crowder was a defining moment. 'Hitherto', argues Chisholm:

> For all her erratic behaviour, she had remained someone whose conduct and interests were containable within the loose boundaries of upper-class bohemia. Through Crowder she became something else: a woman who chose, deliberately, to cross the boundaries of convention, class and race in pursuit of a cause.[37]

Cunard's first response to Anglo-British racism was an article for *Crisis*, 'Does Anyone Know Any Negroes?', which addressed a number of her mother's disdainful comments about black people.[38] It was quickly followed with *Black Man, White Ladyship*, Cunard's counterblast against Britain's closed imperial culture – figured as Lady

Cunard's salon – and the most powerful representation of the struggle to disengage from the Anglo-British white imaginary to appear in the first half of the twentieth century.

Cunard threatened her mother with black violation, confronting white Englishness, and assimilated transatlantic whiteness, with the return of its abject. 'As yet', she writes, 'only the hefty shadow of the negro falls across the white assembly of High Society and spreads itself, it would seem quite particularly and agonisingly, over you'.[39]

Later she repositioned herself in the African sublime by telling the story of a childhood dream in which 'I'm one of them, though still white'.[40] Bhabha has shown that mimicry is a strategy of the colonised. Cunard's example reminds us that it is also an identificatory strategy of the anticolonial white. In place of the self contrasting other, Cunard was attempting to construct an other-resembling self.

Stuart Hall has written that in the process of identification the subject 'has to go through the eye of the needle of the other before it can construct itself'.[41] In the late 1920s, Cunard attempted to pass through the eye for a second time, abjecting Anglo-British whiteness but also, in part, the opposing civic notion of bloodless nationality.

Edwardian colonial representations of Africa, part of her late imperial education at Nevill Holt, had a strong impact on her imaginary as a child. Cunard later claimed that an identification rather than a distinction had taken place. Whatever the timing of this renegotiation of whiteness, by the early 1930s Cunard was caught in the eye of the colonialist needle, struggling to invert a former abjection, revalorising blackness and dislocating her identification from the white Anglo-British collective imaginary.

> [At] about six years old … my thoughts began to be drawn towards Africa, and particularly towards the Sahara. Surely I was being taught as much about El Dorado and the North Pole? But there it was: the Desert. The sand, the dunes, the huge spaces, mirages, heat and parchedness – I seemed able to visualise all of this. Of such were filled several dreams, culminating in the great nightmare in which I wandered, repeatedly, the whole of one agonising night, escaping through a series of tents somewhere in the Sahara. Later came extraordinary dreams about black Africa – 'The Dark Continent' – with Africans dancing and drumming around me, and I one of them, though still white, knowing, mysteriously enough, how to dance in their own manner. Everything was full of movement in these dreams; it was that which enabled me to escape in the

end, going further, even further! And all of it was a mixture of appre-
hension that sometimes turned into joy, and even rapture.[42]

Clearly, the affective binaries of colonialism, designed to disavow
but unable to erase what Kristeva enumerates as 'my death drives, my
eroticism, my bizarreness, my particularity, my femininity, all these
uncoded marginalities that are not recognised by consensus', were able
to point beyond and to a degree unravel the colonial identifications
offered to the young Cunard.[43] This process of reidentification makes
Shrijver's theoretically innocent aside on Cunard's 'desire always to be
where she was not', prescient.[44]

In *Black Man, White Ladyship* Cunard ridicules the Anglo-British
salon culture presided over by her mother, as a charade of representation without depth or authenticity, a reflection on the dominant
languages of nationhood that will recur in the essays that follow. 'Is it
an amusing atmosphere?', she asked. 'It is a stultifying hypocrisy. Yet,
away from it, it has no importance; it is, yes it is, unreal. There is no
contact, the memory of it are so many lantern slides. They move and
shift together in a crazy blur of dix-huitieme, gold plate and boiserie,
topped with the great capital C, conversation, rounded off with snobbery and gossip.'[45] The dominant codes of Anglo-Britishness had
become strange and inauthentic.

The culture of the London salon did not provide a climate in which
aesthetic modernism could be sustained. 'A Braque, a Masson, a
Picasso drawing have gone their way', Cunard reveals. Nor could
homosexuality be disclosed at the English dining table.[46] In *Black Man,
White Ladyship*, Cunard clearly signals that the search for an alternative, counter-hegemonic authenticity was underway.

If, as Kristeva argues, identity is guaranteed by maternal continuity,
it is no wonder that Cunard's traumatic rupture of the English imaginary followed the discovery of a maternal racism opposed to her
desire.[47] However, Cunard's transgression and partial self differentiation from white Anglo-Britishness also involved a denial and splitting
off – indeed an abjection – of a number of unacceptable if residual,
racialised feelings, which appear to have been transferred to the mother,
rendering her a persecuting figure.

In this new articulation, the binaries of the colonial imagination
were reversed and imperial culture was itself rendered savage: 'I believe
that no fallacy about the negroes is too gross for the Anglo-Saxon to
fall into', Cunard wrote. 'You are told they are coarse, lascivious, lazy,

ignorant, undisciplined, unthrifty, undependable, drunkards, jealous, envious, violent, that their lips, noses and hair are ugly, that they have physical odour – in the name of earth itself what people, individually, can disclaim any of these? The knave and the fool will out, the dirty will stink.'[48] She announced that Anglo-British modernity would require the social inclusion of the black man.

> The days of rastus and Sambo are long gone and will not return. The English prejudice gets a hard knock by the revelation that the pore ole down-trodden canticle-singing nigger daddy who used to be let out to clown for the whites has turned into the very much up-to-date, well educated, keen, determined man of action.[49]

Finally, modernity would require an acknowledgement that the regimes of knowledge and power constructed by the white Anglo-British were both contingent and contestable: 'There are many truths. How come, white man, is the rest of the world to be re-formed in your dreary and decadent image?'[50] The woman who was secretly disturbed by the unrest of 1919 now confidently predicted the political downfall of the Anglo-British. 'Bolshevism is going on too', she asserted. 'England is breaking up'.[51]

The racialised Anglo-British identifications of the aristocratric and literary elite reasserted themselves in response to her challenge. As Chisholm argues, 'she was in danger of being written off as someone whose bohemian eccentricity had turned into dangerous, distasteful unacceptability'.[52] The friends to whom Cunard sent the privately printed pamphlet were shocked, not so much by its revelations about English racism, but by her symbolic matricide and challenge to power. In the dominant Anglo-British imaginary, respect for one's mother and motherland took precedence over the dissemination of personal and democratic rights to colonised Others. It is perhaps no accident that the most positive response in the small archive of commentary comes from the Chilean Pablo Neruda.[53] Cunard had exited both the habitus and the imaginary of Englishness. 'I need no patrie, no motherland' became the main vector of her subsequent itinerary. [54]

The dismissal of Cunard was a gendered reflex. Even her 'imaginary father', George Moore, abandoned his wayward daughter. Richard Aldington, a former lover, figured her as an 'erotic boa constrictor' and had her slashed across the face with a bottle in a short

story entitled 'Now Lies She There' published in 1932.[55] Cunard
herself had become an English abject which had to be suppressed in
order to maintain and reproduce properly gendered and racialised
Anglo-British subjects.

Dyer's recent study of whiteness helps to explain the nature of
Cunard's crime against the nation. 'Inter-racial heterosexuality threatens the power of whiteness because it breaks the legitimation of whiteness with reference to the white body. For all the appeal to spirit ... if
white bodies are no longer indubitably white bodies, if they can no
longer guarantee their own reproduction as white, then the 'natural'
basis of their own dominion is no longer credible ... If races are concep-
tualised as pure (with concomitant qualities of character, including the
capacity to hold sway over other races), then miscegenation threatens
that purity.'[56]

In a society where any woman marrying a non-British national lost
her British citizenship, white women held a central responsibility for
white reproduction, even if only at the level of the symbolic. Cunard's
hysterectomy in 1920 had, early on, disqualified her from a physically
reproductive role. The harsh sentence for her offence against the colonial imperative also took into account a number of additional threats to
the Anglo-British imaginary and national reproduction which were
present in the late imperial moment. Cunard was, or would soon be,
associated with them all: aesthetic modernism, Americanisation,
changes in family structure, the democratic challenge of Labour and
the anticolonial struggle. Nationalism within the Union was perhaps
the only movement she was not involved in.

In England, race and nation were articulated in a way that de-
emphasised the fact that whiteness and cultural identity were important preconditions of citizenship (irrespective of the fact that all imperial subjects were legally British). While Cunard recognised that citizenship was racialised, she later appeared bewildered at the strength of
the black cultural identification with the English motherland which she
encountered on her visit to colonial Jamaica.

Cunard's representation of the colonised black woman articulates an
essential and aestheticised black physicality with blood nationality:
'The black women come out of their houses laughing. "Take us to
England with you" (in a rich sing-song), "we want to go a-way from
here" (scanning it unforgettably). To England, "mother-country" of so
many plundered black peoples, to the brutality of the colour bar and all
the talk about the "not wanting the damned niggers"? They know

nothing about these things. "Oh we would like to see England so much." These are the loyalest subjects of Great Britain. I pass on, wondering how much longer the roguery, insolence and domination of the whites must last.'[57] Cunard considers the appeal that Anglo-British cultural identity holds for black Jamaican women to be a diminution of their essentially African identity.[58] Her symbolic erasure of colonial modernity meant that she was unable to engage with the utopic, pluralist and on occasion deracialising impulse that had already made the Atlantic a terrain of modernity and migration, a space in which new identities could and would be created.[59]

There was much that was not exemplary about Cunard's form of white flight from racialised Anglo-Britishness. According to Dyer, whiteness involves a notion of embodiment, a sense that it is an incarnation of something – spirit, initiative and enterprise – that is not the body. As a result it tends to reduce non-white people to their bodies.[60] White binaries that attributed powers of instinct and improvisation to blackness were deployed in Cunard's constructions of blackness, for example in her account of Crowder's 'innate musicianship'.[61] For Cunard, Africans have 'the best body'. They produce the best 'music and unparalleled rhythm and some of the finest sculpture in the world.' They also have 'priority of descent'.[62] Affirmations of Anglo-British cultural superiority also persist, however, in her attempts to recode black American vernacular – for example, the word 'spunk' – as Old English. 'Might it be Shakespearean?' she wonders, when a musician friend of Crowder's uses the word.[63] An ideology of blackness as presence and authenticity emerges when she writes about the realness of Harlem. 'Notice how many of the whites are unreal in America', she notes. 'They are dim. But the Negro is very real; he is there'.[64] The themes converges when she emphasises the 'rhythmic undersurges' and 'nature-rite' of a 'collective life' on visiting a black evangelical church.[65]

These assertions of the 'fresh and uninhibited view of life' of Afro-Americans are a clear case of difference represented as authenticity in a simple reversal of Anglo- British binaries. At this point, some readers may find themselves recalling Raymond Williams' account of 'negative identification'. Williams argued that one set of struggles could be confused with another.[66] Today we are less likely to regard such a translation as a mistake. Given the dissolution of traditional class identities, the dynamic that arises from 'envy in the ofay' could well be an essential step in assembling what post-Marxists call the chain of equivalences necessary to generalise and link diverse identities in a contemporary struggle for democracy. Cunard, more than any other in her time, went on to assemble a counter-hegemonic multiracial partnership that tried to construct such a chain, and in doing so, demonstrated that Anglo-British whiteness would have to be transformed if Anglo-British modernisation was to take place.[67]

Cunard's fast moving process of reidentification carried her into a transatlantic antiracist formation. In the 1930s, the Communist movement appeared to be the main antiracist and anticolonial voice in Britain and the United States. International Labour Defense (ILD) had mobilised an international campaign in defence of the Scottsboro boys and the CPUSA was even standing a black candidate – James W. Ford – for vice president in the 1932 election.

FROM WHITE TO RED

Nomadic, rejected by and rejecting the motherland, Cunard went on to produce a form of travel writing that broke fundamentally with the conventions of the most common female genre of Empire. Over the next three years she displaced her anger and found new points of identification in a project designed to give a voice to the black subaltern, an anthology of 'the struggles and achievements, the persecutions and the revolts against them, of the negro peoples'.[68] Michelet, a lover from this period, describes the formlessness of the enterprise that eventually became *Negro*. It was not a catalogue of exotica, nor a colonialist taxonomy of the other, nor the work of a detached academic eye; *Negro* was 'a work of passion, and impassioned.'[69] In *Negro* a new form of knowledge was being crafted, in association with a wide range of black partners and interlocutors as well as white. During its compilation, Nancy Cunard was an identification in rapid process, aroused rather than stalled by her extended re-engagement with an Anglo-British abject. *Negro* was both a painful and pleasurable breaking and remaking of the self. It was just as Michelet understood, a passion.

Kristeva talks of jouissance as a form of satisfaction through which an excess of signification expresses unconscious drives that up to that point have produced conscious suffering. The very bulk of *Negro* is an instance of jouissance and transformation. Cunard herself recalls 'the indignation, the fury, the disgust, the contempt, the longing to fight' that went into its discursive excess, the unprecedented 855 oversize pages filled with writing and images provided by 150 contributors, black and white, its eight pounds in weight embodying the scale of her transgression of Englishness.[70]

Negro was an extremely important counter-hegemonic showcase of black creativity, intended to repeat, for a transatlantic readership, what Alaine Locke's curtain raiser on the Harlem Renaissance, *The New Negro*, had done for blacks in the United States in 1925.[71] It was a grand riposte to Anglo-British whiteness, to American racism, and to the lack of attention given to ancient Africa in the 1931 exhibition of colonial art in the capital of Cunard's adopted homeland, France.

Today, the range and diversity of *Negro* is still as impressive as ever. Essays on the jazz of Duke Ellington, Louis Armstrong, Cab Calloway and Bojangles sit alongside articles on creole, beguines and tribal songs, and poems by Langston Hughes, Nicolas Guillen and Cunard herself. There is a surrealist manifesto, a series of studies of Africa, an account of white attitudes to the 'dark continent', and photographs of Cunard's own bracelet collection. Two young nationalists based in London, who would later take leading roles in successful anticolonial struggles, Ben Azikiwe and Jomo Kenyatta, contributed articles. So did Anthony Butts, who contributed a piece on the colour bar in the capital.

Cunard's enabling of black voices was simultaneously an engagement with the international communist movement, which provided many of her contacts with contributors, and also served to rearticulate the terms of Cunard's opposition to Anglo- Britishness as figured by her relationship with mother.

'In such close combat', argues Kristeva, 'the symbolic light that a third party, eventually the father, can contribute helps the future subject, the more so if it happens to be endowed with a robust supply of drive energy, in pursuing a reluctant struggle against what, having been the mother, will turn into an abject. Repelling, rejecting; repelling itself, rejecting itself. Ab-jecting.'[72]

The third party was in part, the Communist International. Although Cunard's aristocratic and cosmopolitan individualism and the disciplines of democratic centralism were not easily compatible discourses, becoming 'red' was a way of consolidating her new position as 'non-white'. Internationalism, anticolonialism and a shared antipathy to English codes of class were three points of connection for her new identification. However, despite the years of fellow travelling, intimate relationships and solidarity work which were about to commence, Cunard was never fully able to enter Stalinist discourse, even during the years of the Popular Front. Her liberal, avant-garde and Africanist formation prevented her full assimilation. As John Banting, a British surrealist and friend who briefly joined the Communist Party in 1940, said, 'any totalitarianism would be abhorrent to her'.[73]

There are moments in *Negro*, however, where Cunard's endorsement of the Comintern seems unqualified. If the communist imaginary provided an alternative vision, its networks also provided partners for the struggle against white supremacy. 'There are certain sections of the negro bourgeoisie which hold that justice will come to them from some eventual liberality in the white man', argues Cunard. 'But the more vital of the negro race have realised that it is communism alone which throws down the barriers of race as finally as it wipes out class'.[74] *Negro* consequently published, but simultaneously denounced, the work of Du Bois and the NAACP.[75] 'The communist world order is the solution of the race problem for the negro ... Today in Russia alone is the Negro a free man, a hundred percent equal.'[76] A slightly more instrumental articulation of Cunard's counter-supremacist project with that of the Comintern appears in her report of a discussion she had with a revivalist preacher in Harlem. She told him that black freedom would come 'only by organised and militant struggle for their full rights side by side with communism'.[77]

In 1932 Cunard went to Harlem, then in the twilight of its renaissance, to solicit material for *Negro*. She was heavily dependent on contacts that had been sourced by George Padmore, who from 1931-3 was the editor of *Negro Worker* (a Comintern sponsored monthly publication produced for RILU's International Trade Union Committee of Negro Workers, of which he was also secretary). Cunard was hounded by British and American tabloids during this trip, and she tried to turn her high profile to the advantage of the ILD campaign on behalf of the Scottsboro boys.[78] Cunard was taunted by *Empire News* which, mocking the terms of her challenge to Anglo-British whiteness, 'gave her less than twelve months in which to change the colour of her opinions'.[79] She was later able to fund the publication of *Negro* with the proceeds of libel actions against the British newspapers who claimed that inter-racial sex was one of the major motives for her trip.[80] *Negro* contains a summary of the hate letters sent to her in America, by whites outraged at her imagined intimacy with the black abject. Cunard was degenerate and depraved, they wrote. Her number was up.[81]

In 1933 she returned to London with a finished manuscript and illustrations, desperately seeking a publisher. She had met Edgell

Rickword, an editor at Wishart and Co, through the Scottsboro campaign. Both were admirers of the Communist Party and Rickword too had been a broker for modernism in England, as the editor of the *Calendar of Modern Letters* from 1925-7, shortly before Cunard established the Hours Press. Wishart agreed to publish *Negro* in the extraordinary form that she wished, provided it was at Cunard's own expense. Cunard and Rickword then worked together on the book. Soon after its publication in 1934, Rickword joined the Communist Party,[82] which at this time was working with sailors and colonial students in London, in a half-hearted attempt to maintain a shrinking League Against Imperialism.[83]

Cunard was made honorary secretary of the British Scottsboro Defence Committee and helped to organise film screenings, galas, inter-racial dances, and demonstrations. This led to her first clash with the CPGB as she was not willing to hand the cash she had raised to the Party and insisted on forwarding it directly to the ILD in the United States. Her flat became a regular venue for meetings organised by black communists like Padmore and Chris Jones. Her sympathies widened as she engaged with a British working-class alterity, the left habitus in which she now moved multiplying the causes of her antipathy to the Anglo-British establishment, reconfiguring her identification once again. When *Negro* was finally published in February 1934, hunger marchers were converging on London. The inscription in the presentation copy she sent to Michelet enthuses that 'revolutions are breaking out in the days of its production.'[84]

By then Cunard had been described in *Negro Worker* as 'a staunch friend and champion of the Negro masses'. The profile accompanied a historical poem by Cunard which addressed an assertion by Lincoln in 1862 that the security of the Union was more important than the issue of abolition. Leninism was described as a sign of the reawakening of the freedom struggle, and in the poem's closing lines Cunard vocalised a black American embrace of a counter-segregationist and counter colonial white female body, figuring her own relationship with the editor, George Padmore: 'My love, my friend, my comrade – black on red'.[85]

Cunard first met Padmore in Paris in 1932, when he was a senior figure in the international communist movement who often commissioned writers who subsequently appeared in *Negro*. 'It was Padmore who, even before we met, put me in touch with many coloured writers and personalities', Cunard acknowledged to his biographer.[86] Padmore contributed to *Negro* himself, and he was in London when it was completed, having been deported by Hitler from Germany. By this time, however, the Comintern was beginning to mute its support for anticolonial struggle. It abolished the International Trades Union Congress of Negro Workers, of which Padmore was secretary, in order to improve the prospects of a united front with the democracies of the West against Hitler.[87] Padmore opposed the strategy, resigned and was then ritually expelled in June 1934. He made his way to a shocked Nancy Cunard, still in many ways a novice in the ways of the Comintern, at her Reanville cottage. It was here that the two radical Africanists worked together on Padmore's *How Britain Rules Africa*, a defiantly anticolonial, and anti Stalinist text.[88]

Cunard questioned Padmore's dismissal on a trip to Moscow in 1935, during which officials raised the possibility of a Russian translation of *Negro* as well as exhibitions and further publications. But anticolonialism was still sliding down the Comintern's agenda, Padmore was regarded as a problem and Cunard was a loose cannon: nothing came of the appeal or the publishing projects.

Padmore's experiences revealed that the dominant forms of Anglo-Britishness were not the only obstacle to multiracial democracy. The discourses of left politics were also unable to accommodate the transformations of identity that had commenced in and around this modern, Africanist and transnational relationship between Cunard and Padmore.

Negro was an Afrocentric collection, based on notions of an essential black identity. Cunard's affirmation of black cultural achievement, linked to a vision of emancipation, is surprisingly close to what Senghor was later to develop as the discourse of negritude. Cunard's Africanism shared many of the weaknesses of the later movement: eliding the differences between black cultures, emphasising separate development from the coloniser rather than a two-way relationship of alterity and identification, and positing an alternative black history and black modernity. To Padmore and Cunard, the global politics of the mid 1930s must have made even more remote the possibility that the Anglo-British imaginary might one day accommodate and acknowledge blackness, rather than thrive on its abjection.

NERVES STRUNG LIKE A CATAPULT

In the late 1930s Cunard's political identifications were at the same time black, transnational and congruous with the priorities of the

Comintern. As a reporter for the Associated Negro Press she covered the crisis in Abyssinia (from Geneva) and then the defence of the republic during the Spanish civil war.

The news stories she filed from Spain were heroic simplifications of the struggle and contained no criticism of the government or any trace of the political conflicts that raged on the republican side. In 1937 she published *Poets of the World Defend the Spanish People*, a series of leaflets she printed herself on her old Hours Press machine. She then assembled the best-selling collection *Authors Take Sides on the Spanish Civil War*.[89] Cunard's poem 'To Eat Today' appeared in 1938. In it she talks of 'Europe's nerve strung like catapult, the cataclysm roaring and swelling' as the pace of rearmament quickened.[90]

After a holiday in Tunisia, during which Cunard, as tourist, confirmed some of her preconceptions of the Ancient splendour of Africa (and again encountered the colonial abject – a Bedouin girl scavenging on a rubbish tip, who found and ate 'a long, slime covered, snake-like object – a liquefying bean pod'), she returned to Spain and wrote a number of powerful reports for the *Manchester Guardian* on a new displacement of Anglo-British anxiety, the exodus and plight of hundreds of thousands of defeated Spanish republicans.[91]

During the Spanish civil war, and then in her crusade on behalf of occupied France, Cunard always inverted the priorities of her mother's salon, which comfortably accommodated the pro-Nazi agendas of the Prince of Wales and Mosley. John Lehman confirms that 'Emerald's salon had an unqualified right wing bias'.[92]

Cunard's formal definition of patriotism was Leninist in inspiration: 'To me it means fighting the common enemy in any way, in any country.'[93] But, like Orwell, an attitude of 'My Country Right Or Wrong' seems to be her initial response to the Second World War, even if that country was quickly transmuted, once again, to France. At first Cunard was herself a refugee, fleeing to Chile with Spanish republicans to escape the occupation. She returned to London in August 1941, shortly after the invasion of the Soviet Union had ended the dilemmas of the CPGB, previously torn between international obligations and Anglo-British imperatives.[94] Cunard doubted the ability of Anglo-British whiteness to prosecute a popular war against the European advocates of racial purity. 'This is my war too', she states, 'in so far as it is (if only partly) against Fascism. That word seems out of favour here. Despite the great bombings, people do not seem to me to be very much aroused.' Like much of the left, she was also influenced by

Churchillian national-popular discourse: 'one is impressed by the fortitude of the English'.[95] Characteristically, however, her contribution to the war effort reflected the twin priorities of rescuing French culture and territory from fascism, and maintaining the case for Anglo-British decolonisation. Later she would describe her postwar return to France as a 'return from exile'.[96]

'France has made hate "her only lover"', Cunard wrote in 1941.[97] Another wartime poem condemned Vichy and praised the Maquis, a national movement which she saw in traditionally gendered terms and as continuous with Spanish republicanism. The France of the Resistance was figured as masculine, and the proposed exchange of labourers for French prisoners in Germany as an emasculation. 'They want a France unmanned.'[98] Her anthology *Poems for France* assembled an alliance of unusual breadth, combining contributions from Lord Vantissart, the Anglo-British libertarians Herbert Read and Alex Comfort and a substantial number of communists.

Unapologetically anticolonialist, in the same period Cunard also co-wrote *The White Man's Duty* with George Padmore, then well advanced on his journey to pan-African socialist nationalism. 'Are the white people to be the sole beneficiaries (of the war)?' they asked. 'The logical feeling exists among coloured peoples: Now Britain is in trouble she needs us but when it is over we shall be as before.'[99]

Anglo-Britain at war was augmented by a segregated US soldiery and anxious about colonial unrest. The national imaginary, like its racist landlords and hotel managers, still refused to accommodate black people. Cunard and Padmore called for legislation against the colour bar and the introduction of self government in the colonies on the basis of the democratic commitments contained in the Atlantic Charter. 'Race prejudice (of Jew, Negro or any people) belongs to Nazi-Fascism and not to Democracy', they argued, re-deploying national popular themes against Anglo-British racialisation.[100] Cunard's earlier biologistic celebrations of abjected blackness had been partly recoded by a new democratic discourse of citizenship.

RETURN OF THE ABJECT
For the last two decades of her life Cunard was haunted by images of fascism. By 1960, writes her biographer, 'Anyone who tried to calm or restrain her became a fascist spy, especially if they were in uniform'.[101] Was this a displacement of unacceptable white Anglo-British impulses, an acknowledgement of her abjected bond to mother and motherland,

externalised as a menace? Was it simply the understandable consequence of the war's devastating impact on her political confidence,
utopic longings and former relationships of trust? Or could it have
been simply a symptom of her alcoholism?

Cunard's imaginary was under siege. The Reanville home she had
abandoned during the occupation, a hybrid space, had been attacked
and looted, first by local French villagers, and then by the German
army. Her collection of paintings, ivories and books, a library in which
new forms of knowledge and identification were being created, was
dispersed, stolen and destroyed.

A series of anxious events followed: she threw away her passport in
Switzerland, she diatribed against an American foreign policy which
allowed Germany to re-arm, she criticised 'cellophane' American
culture, fully sharing the fear of Americanisation prevalent on the
European left in those years. She also proposed a toast to Anthony
Thorne which reaffirmed her longstanding sense of the inauthenticity
of Anglo-British modernisation: 'NEVER ENGLAND FOR ME
(Please God).'[102]

The only affirmation, and her main locale for authenticity, was Spain
– then still under fascist tutelage. In 1949 she published *Poems for
Spain*. A decade later she wrote a hybrid, multilingual sonnet in five
languages dedicated to the International Brigade which had fought to
defend the republic.[103] It is a significant and neglected highpoint of
European modernism, its multivocality focussing the problem and
reaffirming the promise of transnational identification.

> Adesso e altra sosta, ma Dove su dante?
> If the fire burn low, it is the same, I see;
> Por mudo que vas tiras por adelante,
> Et tout ce qui fut avant peut renaitre ici.
> Noch gibt es einigen Moorsoldaten die
> Are ready to spring to their appointed place.
> E quanti altri, vicini et lontani...
> Se no se dice, consabido es.
> So mischt man Sprachen mit Hoffnung wohin man geht,
> I trenni misti vanno molto lontano;
> May our sons and moons coincide in the rising spate,
> Pero quien me dira la fecha de este ano?
> Courage persiste si le couer conserve ses as...
> Y cuando te toca el turno, ah! Cuanto cosecharas!

The difficulties involved in reading this postwar Wasteland are an index of the strangeness that characterises any contemporary poly-valent community, national or regional. Cunard's reflexive attempt to dismantle Anglo-British distinction and difference in her own process of identification and cultural politics was evident in a note she wrote in 1956, two years before, when she was considering an autobiography:

> When of SELF writing: Re the three main things.
>
> 1. Equality of races.
> 2. Of sexes.
> 3. Of classes.
>
> I am in accord with all countries, and all individuals who feel, and act, as I do on this score.[104]

The effort to overcome distinction and create community from strangeness could be sustained for a sonnet, but the book was never written. Nor did she complete another about African ivories on which she was reported to be working in 1955.[105] Her two major postwar publications were both memorials and partly autobiographical.[106]

Alcoholism and breakdown were to narrow Cunard's habitus. She was certified as insane, in England in 1960, after an arrest for solicit-ing. A complex and unfinished book-length poem on which she was working in 1964, *The Visions*, linked the poetry of pre-medieval English bards to the tribulations of twentieth century Spain in a paired abjection of European modernity. Cunard's uncoded longings, individual and political, were once again seeking jouissance through literary excess. The work struck the author herself as 'very strange'.[107] Any satisfaction was brief. Soon after, Nan Green reported, her letters became 'unintelligible'.[108] One month after writing that she was 'uplifted by the thought of living in England again', she was dead.[109]

MADDENED OR MAD?

There is a choice to be made in any evaluation of Cunard's life and work. We can regard her as a mixed up, wealthy drunk, exploited by a black lover and an unscrupulous political party, seduced by grand causes but confined to the margins of Anglo-British public culture. That is the received account.

Or we can see Cunard as a startling straw in the winds of global change that were to blow more intensely in the postwar years. A straw broken in her own time by the reproductive imperatives of the colonial Anglo-British and the structured and fragile game of chance that is identification. A pioneer of an English modernity that has yet to arrive and therefore, as Burkhart suspects, 'maddened, but not mad.'[110]

The verdict will probably depend on whether you think that a transformation of white Englishness was or remains a matter of urgency.

NOTES

1. See Charles Burkhart, *Herman and Nancy and Ivy: Three Lives in Art*, Victor Gollancz, London 1977, pp 59, 63, 64; Raymond Mortimer, 'Nancy Cunard' in Hugh Ford (ed), *Nancy Cunard: Brave Poet, Indomitable Rebel 1896-1965*, Chilton Book Company, Philadelphia 1968, p49; Leonard Woolf, 'Nancy Cunard', *ibid*, p58; Mary Hutchinson, 'Nancy: An Impression', *ibid*, p98; Solita Solano, 'Nancy Cunard: Brave Poet, Indomitable Rebel', *ibid*, p77.

2. Anne Chisholm, *Nancy Cunard*, Alfred A Knopf, New York 1979, p35.

3. Nancy Cunard, 'To the Eiffel Tower Restaurant' in *Sublunary*, Hodder and Stoughton, London 1923, pp93-5.

4. In a letter to Bridget Patmore, quoted in Chisholm, *op.cit*, 1979, p131.

5. Iris Tree in Ford (ed), *op.cit*, 1968, p19.

6. Quoted in Chisholm, *op.cit*, 1979, p49.

7. Burkhart, *op.cit*, 1977, p60.

8. Chisholm, *op. cit.*, 1979, p87.

9. Burkhart, *op. cit.*, 1977, p62.

10. Nancy Cunard, 'In Answer to a reproof' in Cunard, *Outlaws*, Elkin Mathews, London 1921.

11. Michael Arlen, *The Green Hat*, Collins, London 1924.

12. Nancy Cunard, *Grand Man: Memories of Norman Douglas*, Secker and Warburg, London 1954, p71.

13. Henry Louis Gates JR, 'Harlem on Our Minds' in *Rhapsodies in Black: Art of the Harlem Renaissance*, The Hayward Gallery, London 1997, p163.

14. Nancy Cunard, *These Were The Hours: Memoirs of My Hours Press, Reanville and Paris 1928-31*, Southern Illinois University Press, Carbondale and Edwardsville 1969, p80.

15. Sander L. Gilman, *Difference and Pathology: Stereotypes of Sexuality, Race and Madness*, Cornell University Press, 1985, p120.

16. Georges Saduol, quoted in Chisholm, *op.cit*, 1979, pp108-9.

17. Harold Acton in Ford (ed), *op.cit*, 1968, p73.

18. Burkhart, *op.cit*, 1977, p15.
19. Chisholm, *op.cit*, 1979, p147.
20. *Ibid*, pp102-115.
21. Michael Richardson (ed), *Refusal of the Shadow: Surrealism and the Caribbean*, Verso, London 1996.
22. Cunard, *op.cit*, 1969, p48.
23. See Paul Gilroy, *The Black Atlantic: Modernity and Double Consciousness*, Verso, London 1993.
24. Chisholm, *op.cit*, 1979, p229.
25. Cunard, *op.cit*, 1954, p83.
26. *Ibid*, p86.
27. Chisholm, *op.cit*, 1979, p134.
28. Nancy Cunard, *Black Man, White Ladyship: An Anniversary*, privately printed, 1931, p10.
29. Nancy Cunard, 'Jamaica – the Negro Island' in Hugh Ford (ed), *Negro: An Anthology. Collected and Edited by Nancy Cunard*, Frederick Ungar Publishing Limited, New York 1970, p49. Due to the extreme scarcity of Nancy Cunard, *Negro*, Wishart and Company, London 1934, all references will be to this modern abridged edition.
30. Cunard, *op.cit*, 1969, p149.
31. Henry Crowder, *Henry-Music*, Hours Press, Paris 1930.
32. Henry Crowder and Hugo Speck, *As Wonderful As All That?*, Wild Tree Press, California 1987, p185.
33. Chisholm, *op.cit*, p125.
34. Cunard, *op.cit*, 1931, p9.
35. Quoted in Ford (ed), *op.cit*, 1968, p47.
36. Cunard, *op.cit*, 1931, p1.
37. Chisholm, 1979, *op.cit*, p118.
38. Nancy Cunard, 'Does Anyone Know Any Negroes?' in *Crisis*, National Association for the Advancement of Coloured Peoples, September 1931.
39. Cunard, *op.cit*, 1931, p2.
40. Cunard, *op.cit*, 1954, p140.
41. Stuart Hall, 'The Local and the Global' in Anthony D King (ed), *Culture, Globalisation and the World System*, Macmillan, London 1991, p21.
42. Cunard, *op.cit*, 1954, p140.
43. In Suzanne Clark and Kathleen Hulley, 'Cultural Strangeness and the Subject in Crisis' Ross Mitchell Guberman (ed), *Julia Kristeva: Interviews*, Columbia University Press, 1996, p41.
44. In Burkhart, *op.cit*, 1977, p108.
45. Cunard, *op.cit*, 1931, p6.

46. *Ibid*, pp4-5.
47. Quoted in Elaine Hoffman Baruch, 'Feminism and Psychoanalysis' in Ross Mitchell Guberman (ed), *op.cit*, p118.
48. Cunard, *op.cit*, 1931, p9.
49. *Ibid*, pp9-10.
50. *Ibid*, p11.
51. *Ibid*, p3.
52. Chisholm, *op.cit*, 1979, p188.
53. *Ibid*, p235.
54. Daphne Fielding, *Emerald and Nancy: Lady Cunard and her Daughter*, Eyre and Spottiswoode, London 1968, p132.
55. In Richard Aldington, *Soft Answers*, Heinemann, London 1932.
56. Richard Dyer, *White*, Routledge, London 1997, p25.
57. Ford (ed), *op.cit*, 1970, p284.
58. *Ibid*, pp272-284.
59. Gilroy, *op.cit*, 1993.
60. Dyer, *op.cit*, p14
61. Cunard, *op.cit*, 1969, p149.
62. Cunard, *op.cit*, 1931, p11.
63. Ford (ed), *op.cit*, 1968, p45.
64. Ford (ed), *op.cit*, 1970, p49.
65. *Ibid*, pp50-1.
66. Raymond Williams, *Culture and Society: 1780-1950*, Chatto and Windus, London 1958.
67. Ford (ed), *op.cit*, 1970, p49.
68. Cunard, 'Foreword' in Ford (ed), *op.cit*, 1970, pxxxi.
69. Raymond Michelet, 'Nancy Cunard' in Ford (ed), *op.cit*, 1968, pp127-132.
70. Chisholm, *op.cit*, 1979, p191.
71. Alain Locke, *New Negro*, Macmillan, London 1992.
72. Julia Kristeva, *Powers of Horror: An Essay on Abjection*, Columbia University Press, New York 1982, p13.
73. Ford (ed), *op.cit*, 1968, pp127-132.
74. Cunard, in Ford (ed), *op.cit*, 1970, pxxxi.
75. Quoted in Chisholm, *op.cit*, 1979, p215.
76. Cunard, in Ford (ed), *op.cit*, 1970, pxxxi.
77. Nancy Cunard, 'Harlem Reviewed' in Ford (ed), *op.cit*, 1970, p52.
78. See her account 'Scottsboro – and Other Scottsboros' in *ibid*, pp155-174, and her poem 'Southern Sheriff', *ibid*, pp265-6.
79. Quoted in Chisholm, *op.cit*, 1979, p209.
80. *Ibid*, p210.

81. Ford (ed), *op.cit*, 1970, pp120-24.

82. Charles Hobday, *Edgell Rickword: A Poet at War*, Carcanet, Manchester 1989.

83. Stephen Howe, *Anticolonialism in British Politics: The Left and the End of Empire, 1918-1964*, Clarendon Press, Oxford 1993, particularly pp53-77.

84. Chisholm, *op.cit*, 1979, pp209, 213.

85. Nancy Cunard, 'Lincoln's Grinding Verbiage', *The Negro Worker*, vol 4, No. 8-9, August-September 1933, p32.

86. Letter quoted in James R. Hooker, *Black Revolutionary: George Padmore's Path from Communism to Pan-Africanism*, Pall Mall Press, London 1967, p28.

87. Howe, *op.cit*, particularly p107.

88. George Padmore, *How Britain Rules Africa*, Wishart, London 1936.

89. Nancy Cunard (ed), *Authors Take Sides on the Spanish Civil War*, Left Review, London 1937.

90. *New Statesman and Nation*, 1 October 1938.

91. *Manchester Guardian*, February 1938, passim; extracts appear in Ford, (ed), *op.cit*, 1968, pp191-7.

92. Quoted in Chisholm, *op.cit*, 1979, p269.

93. Cunard, *op.cit*, 1954, p169.

94. See the account in Kevin Morgan, *Against Fascism and War: Ruptures and Continuities in British Communist Politics 1935-41*, Manchester University Press, Manchester 1989.

95. Cunard, *op.cit*, 1954, p189.

96. Nancy Cunard, 'Letter from Paris' in *Horizon* XI, June 1945.

97. Nancy Cunard, 'And Hate's Resistance' in Nancy Cunard, *Poems for France*, La France Libre, London 1944, pp56-7.

98. Nancy Cunard, *Releve into Maquis*, The Grasshopper Press, Derby 1944.

99. Nancy Cunard and George Padmore, *The White Man's Duty*, W.H. Allen and Co. 1943, p6.

100. *Ibid.*

101. Chisholm, *op.cit*, 1979, p311.

102. See Ford (ed), *op.cit*, 1968, p305; also Irene Rathbone in *ibid*, p247; and Charles Burkhart in *ibid*, p327, p296.

103. Reproduced with her own notes in *ibid*, pp172-3.

104. Chisholm, *op.cit*, 1979, p307.

105. *Ibid*, p303.

106. Cunard, *op.cit*, 1954, and *GM: Memories of George Moore*, Rupert Hart-Davis, 1956.

107. Letter to Nan Green dated 6 March 1964, in Ford (ed), *op.cit*, 1968, p175.

108. *Ibid*, p176.
109. Letter to W.J. Strachan, 17 February 1965, quoted in *ibid*, p285.
110. *Ibid*, p331.

3

J.B. Priestley:
premature postscripts
to Churchill

In the 1990s the name of J.B. Priestley is often taken in vain. He is frequently used to summon the spectre of a Little England, intemperate of modernity.[1] This is something from which each and every one of his biographers have failed to protect him. The opening sentence of the most recent account of his life, by Judith Cook, highlights the fact that Priestley often looked back on the Edwardian period as a golden age, casting him once again as a backward looking rather than a modernising spirit.[2]

Neither Cooper's hagiography, Brome's compendium nor Collins' memoir address the complex cultural politics developed by Priestley. All fail to explain adequately the trajectory of his politics and his changing representations of the nation.[3] As we shall see, these evolved from his early celebration of an authentic national community, into a popular democratic crusade for a modern, decentralised and transnational reconfiguration of the Anglo-British imaginary and its political arrangements. When this failed, he once more affirmed the traditional cultural and political pre-eminence of the English, now qualified by a nagging sense of inauthenticity and dislocation and a good measure of idiosyncrasy. The context for Priestley's changing cultural and political identification was the unfulfilled modernisation of Anglo-Britain: 'If we are half ruined', he reflected in his last volume of autobiography, 'we have done it ourselves, without any sinister plotting abroad.'[4]

Some commentators on Priestley have recognised the trajectory of his work, but disavowed its significance. John Atkins's characterisation of Priestley's wartime writing as 'essentially propaganda' is typical of this error. In an old and failing trope designed to maintain the distinction between the fields of literature and politics, Atkins suggests that

Priestley's 'deep involvement in political matters damaged his work as a creative writer'.[5]

The fact is that for half a century much of Priestley's writing – as a journalist, a dramatist, a novelist, critic and autobiographer – addressed the nature of Anglo-British community. In his search for a model of national renewal that could motivate and reward the civilian army of the Second World War, and in his representations of race in the late 1930s, Priestley roamed well beyond what would become the postwar English consensus. Now that settlement is over, his texts must be rescued and reconsidered, not excised. The challenges they identify, and the proposals for Anglo-British modernisation they contain, are much closer to our own concerns than the received accounts of Priestley would lead us to expect.

Today Priestley is often, wrongly, passed over as a little Englander diffident towards modernity and modernism, a middlebrow provincial of little relevance to our times. In fact he articulates an important, new and feasible but overruled vision of Anglo-British modernisation – but this new cultural and political settlement for the nation was disregarded by the Attlee government in the years immediately after the Second World War. Exiled to the margins, he voiced hesitations about the postwar Keynesian welfare state that prefigured the ecological, democratic and regionalist critiques which have now emerged. Priestley's self-confessed postwar oscillation between 'general grumpiness and downright anger' is a valuable index of the limits of the 1945 settlement.[6]

A controversialist, Priestley actively solicited the charge of Little Englander, which has hidden the heterogeneity of his work from view.[7] Actually the little England that he celebrated in the 1930s, whatever he said later, was neither Eurosceptic, resistant to globalisation, nor designed to exclude or segregate the colonised others of the Anglo-British. It was certainly not compatible with the defensive, racialised social identity that Little England is known as today. At his best, Priestley's populist engagements with aspects of modernity was articulated to a cultural and political programme requiring a complementary modernisation of Anglo-British identifications and institutions. His descriptions of a pre-bourgeois democratic state, and the cultural assimilation of manufacturing to landed traditions, prefigure the critique later developed by the new left in the early 1960s.[8]

Criticisms like those which Orwell made of *Angel Pavement* – 'his writing does not touch the level at which memorable fiction begins'-

and Leavis's comment that 'life isn't long enough to permit of one's giving much time to Fielding or any to Mr Priestley'- are an additional reason why Priestley's significant contribution to the shaping of national-popular identifications has been seriously underestimated.[9] Virginia Woolf's famous characterisation of Priestley as a middlebrow 'tradesman of letters' deploys an elite aesthetic code to devalue the literary practice – based on his opposition to the modernist shift away from the general reader – which enabled Priestley to shape a democratically inflected Englishness in the mainstream-reading public.[10]

Priestley developed a reflexive sense of the whiteness of the Anglo-British and the colonial structure of their imagination. This did not invariably inform the settlement he makes with his imaginary general reader. In *Faraway*, an early work by Priestley, the distinction of white Anglo-Britishness from abjected blackness is explored in a picaresque, humanitarian, but largely uncritical manner. Later, in the 1930s, an understanding of modernity as postcolonial and racially hybrid began to emerge in his writing.[11]

During the Second World War Priestley provided a radical and populist counter-narrative to the official war mission. In Angus Calder's estimate, he became 'a rival to Churchill as a master of morale'.[12] In the highly popular radio talks he gave as postscripts to the Sunday news during the Battle of Britain, Priestly directly addressed one in every three people in the nation. He disseminated one of the core national-popular images of the war, the myth that Dunkirk was a 'sudden democratic improvisation'.[13] More controversially, he spoke of community as more important than property. A dissenter who urged the constitutional modernisation of the imperial state, he was involved in breaches of the wartime electoral truce by the 1941 committee and Richard Acland's Commonwealth Party. In 1945 he campaigned for Labour, but stood as an independent.

During the war, Priestley was a popular and populist advocate of electoral reform, new forms of citizenship and modernisation of the monarchy, a full half century before they became the accepted business of any government or opposition. His unwelcome attacks on the unresponsive structures of the Anglo-British state and the irresponsible profiteering of the nation's businessmen and financiers at the expense of community; his preference for civic and associational forms of organisation; his valorisation of regional and transnational bodies and methods of decision-making; his belief that only non-hierarchical, non-regimented forms of work were desirable and fulfilling; and his critique of the trade union constriction of Labour politics, all suggest that a new reading of his work is long overdue. In this essay I can provide no more than a few signposts to indicate where the revaluation might start.

In the years that followed the war, Priestley was critical of state socialism, public taxation and the education system.[14] The alternative he celebrates is self reliance – a value which seemed to have been transferred from the working to the middle class. In so doing he drew upon himself the wrath of an unforgiving left. But to dwell on these later incidents, without locating their source in the defeat of his modernising vision by the transatlantic imperatives of the Cold War and Labourism, is unhelpful. The White House and the Labour government extended the lease of the pre-modern, centralised British state at the precise moment in which Priestley believed, with some justification, that a popular and democratic modernisation was possible.

Priestley's inherent hostility to an over reliance on the state – an enduring trace of his formation by Edwardian liberalism and a socialist culture structured by syndicalism, guild and ethical socialism – fuelled his rage at unresponsive, unrepresentative Anglo-British government. The state was aristocratic, not democratic. The state had let the people down. Given what we know now – as the global market adapts to the rubble left by Stalinism and the corporatist state, as new Labour struggles with welfare dependency and belatedly initiates decentralisation, desperate to return trust to politics, newly licensed by a resonant ethical socialism – the marginalisation of Priestley appears tragic, short sighted and even downright irresponsible.

EDWARDIAN BRADFORD'S GLOBAL IDENTITY

The international habitus of educated Edwardian Bradford, and white collar wool trade employees like Priestley, was not conducive to the construction of an abjected German Other, the enemy Hun whose projection was crucial to mass participation in Britain's war effort and which led the young working men of the Bradford Pals Battalion to their deaths at the Somme. As Cook comments:

> It must have been a particularly confusing situation for Bradford people, who had been dealing amicably with Germany and Germans for years in the course of their work, suddenly to be told how dastardly, evil and vicious they were.[15]

J.B. Priestley had an unusually heterogeneous notion of the nation and a porous sense of its people and borders. This was the effect of the fiercely democratic culture of 'regional self sufficiency, not defying London but genuinely indifferent to it' that characterised the Bradford hub of the international wool trade.[16] Priestley later described Edwardian Bradford as 'extreme Yorkshire provincialism mixed and leavened with German-Jewish liberalism in exile and other exotic elements'.[17] Fibre samples and sales representatives arrived from every corner of the globe. In that cityscape, Priestley recalled, 'a Londoner was a stranger sight than a German'.[18]

The regionalised circuits and rich global habitus of Bradford make it necessary to reconsider the nature of the link between the suffering of war and Priestley's motivations as a writer – a practice defined by Braine, and reaffirmed by Cook, as an attempt to forget.[19]

Instead, I suggest that the difficulties of articulating the discourses of Bradford to the dominant wartime representations of Anglo-British national identity, in particular his perception of the inauthenticity of the distinctions used to abject the enemy and legitimate the carnage, placed Priestley, who 'was not hot with patriotic feeling', outside the national imaginary, and made him a stranger to himself.[20] For Priestley, alerted to the artificiality of most representations of national community, writing became a search for a new Anglo-British authentication.

The gulf that existed between Bradford and Britannia is evident in Priestley's later abjection of the exponents of that militarised national identity.

> I have had playmates, I have had companions, but all, all are gone. They were killed by greed and muddle and monstrous cross-purposes, by old men gobbling and roaring in clubs, by diplomats working underground like monocled moles, by journalists wanting a good story, by hysterical women waving flags, by grumbling debenture-holders, by strong silent beribboned asses, by fear or apathy or down-right lack of imagination.[21]

It is not just shells, but signs, that trouble the young man from Bradford when he writes home from the front: 'I suppose I am a man now, and am certainly going through an ordeal. Perhaps it would be as well if everybody went through some test of manhood'.[22] Bombarded by artillery and the national symbolic, his ordeal was one of identification as well as survival.

The solidarities, flat and responsive hierarchies and gendered identifications of the trenches did not persist into the peace:

> It is not war that is right, for it is impossible to defend such stupid long range butchery ... It is peace that is wrong, the civilian life to which they returned, a condition of things in which they found their manhood stunted, their generous impulses baffled, their double instinct for leadership and loyalty completely checked. Men are much better than ordinary life allows them to be.[23]

Demobilisation demanded a new process of identification, gendered and national, by all who had served.

GOOD COMPANIONS ARE NOT GOOD COMRADES

Priestley graduated from the front to Cambridge University and then decided to risk a career in literature in London. The publication of his best selling breakthrough novel, *The Good Companions*, coincided with the beginning of the Great Depression.

In *The Good Companions*, a range of impoverished Britons become travelling players and songwriters by acting on their long repressed impulse to break with established settlements and identifications, leaving stultifying families and unrewarding workplaces, in order to sing and buy gaudy clothes.[24] The narrative valorises these popular and utopic impulses in an accessible, if modified, vernacular at the very opening of the Great Depression. Priestley's little Englanders thrive on change, not settlement: 'Chance and Change are preparing an ambush. Only a little way before him there dangles invitingly the end of a thread.'[25] The Anglo-British people were granted the right to authentication and to happiness and the characters in Priestley's novels often achieved this as the result of bold and disruptive action. It is no surprise then, that *The Good Companions* has never been out of print.

The *Times Literary Supplement*, indifferent or oblivious to the stresses and longings of the culture in which the *The Good Companions* would be received, observed that the narrative 'belongs to the old and spacious tradition of the English humorous novel where the complications, the adventures, the encounters and the vicissitudes of external life are considered good enough matter to hold the interest without prying into the still more complicated deeps of the soul'.[26]

The Good Companions succeeded in connecting the fields of literature, politics and popular culture, a task at which the left had consistently failed. The novel offered a cultural and political imaginary which went well beyond the administrative confines of the Labour Party's aspirations and the limited socialist realist figurations of class interests constructed by Marxist discourse. Priestley's evocation of the pleasures of autonomous labour – long hours and non-demarcated complex tasks – could only antagonise the Labour, communist and trade union movements.[27] Although Oakroyd's escape from the mill to a form of non-regimented labour as a set builder – beyond the regulation of the state and the labour movement – clashed with orthodox socialist discourse, it has much in common with the contemporary views of, say, Robin Murray, on the new forms of work the left should attempt to create.[28]

To my mind, *The Good Companions* and the polemical reportage of Priestley's *English Journey* are the two interwar texts that directly address the national-popular identifications of the English reader in a potentially transformative way. Both were widely read and accessible critiques of the state of the nation, fuelled by the wish for better lives for ordinary people, on their own terms. The upbeat closure of *The Good Companions* both parallels the fortunes of a friend of Priestley's and explains the disconnection between modernism and the national-popular: 'It had all turned out as events in the more respected contemporary novels are not allowed to turn out, for the best.'[29]

This theme is also seen in *English Journey*, where Priestley vented his anger at the appalling conditions in which the low paid, the unemployed and the elderly lived and worked, at the instrumental labour and pollution that characterised the industrial environment, and at an emerging media and consumer culture that he associated with inauthenticity. He re-articulates the discourses of Romantic anti-industrialism with ethical socialism and liberalism, delivering his rebuke with the sharp tongue of a left-wing moralist who passionately believes in personal independence and in the local as the major arena for politics. This construction of politics and form of address placed him outside the dominant discourses of the left, which were increasingly attributed to by Stalinist and Fabian formulations of techniques for the management of the masses and the machinery of the state. Although there was a convergence of opinion on the threat posed by fascism, Priestley can be distinguished from his socialist peers by his superior ability to intervene in the popular culture.

The Good Companions invokes a set of essential Anglo-British continuities, but these are plebian rather than patrician.[30] The authentication of the experience and tradition of the popular classes persists in

Priestley's wartime representations of the nation, for example in his broadcast tribute to the Home Guard: 'I felt a powerful and rewarding sense of community; and with it too a feeling of deep continuity. There we were, ploughman and parson, shepherd and clerk, turning out at night, as our forefathers had often done before us, to keep watch and ward over the sleeping English hills and fields and homesteads.'[31] As we shall see, in Priestley's evolving national imaginary the time had arrived for that timeless and authentic community to assert itself against property and privilege in order to prevent degeneration.

BRITAIN'S GRAMSCI?

In many ways, Priestley echoes the concerns of Gramsci. He shares the belief that an opportunity for democratic modernisation had been lost after the First World War: 'We exchanged a New England for victory parades and promises meant to be broken.'[32] He pays close attention to the lives, languages and aspirations of ordinary people in their regions and fabulates an inclusive national-popular in his fiction, his drama and his journalistic representations of the political agency of socialism. The programme of national democratic reform, based on non-Labourist, and anti-statist aspirations, that Priestley articulates in the domains of politics and popular culture in the 1930s and 1940s could be viewed as the Anglo-British counterpart to the Gramscian rewriting of the meaning of modern socialism which expanded the notion of hegemony. The expansion of the British state from 1906-1951 was a 'passive revolution' from above, lacking a popular and democratic component, which Priestley resisted and was never reconciled to. However, unlike his jailed Italian contemporary, it was far less easy for Priestley to articulate his attempt to construct a national-popular discourse to socialism – or communism. As we shall see, he was also ambivalent about the American production systems that Gramsci welcomed into Europe as a means of dislocating older cultural and political settlements.

During a fascist meeting in Bristol in 1934 protestors sang the *International* to drown out the speaker. Priestley distinguishes the democratic and heterogeneous people from the homogeneities of the class struggle as defined by orthodox Marxism. 'I heard something about "the rising of the masses" … And why is it always "the masses"? Who cares about masses? I wouldn't raise a finger for "the masses". Men, women and children – but not masses.'[33]

'Because they are my own people,' he says of the English, 'naturally I prefer them to all others.'[34] But there is an instability in Priestley's representation of the popular democratic community. He is, at times, ambivalent about the unlettered mass. Eulogies are sometimes converted into their disdainful opposite, for example when he describes the physical ugliness of people attending a Birmingham whist drive or the 'vision of dark sub-humanity, like those creatures in Wells' Time Machine' in the crowd at a Tyneside boxing match.[35] In his critique of the impact of Hollywood in the English suburbs and on the popular culture, the former Lance Corporal is quite capable of abjecting aspects of popular modernity, particularly when violence, or representations of violence, were the context.

The legacy of Bradford's Gramsci resides in his example rather than a codified theoretical discourse. Priestley's roots in the non-conformist and ethical traditions of British socialism made a reconciliation of his concerns with any systematic social theory, let alone Comintern-sponsored Marxism, difficult. In *Rain Over Godshill* he objects to the 'false materialism' of Marxism and happily confesses that he didn't understand its dialectic, before praising English socialism from Owen to Morris as an alternative tradition.[36] However, during the 1930s his antipathy to the discourses of Marxism, sociology and the British state, particularly in relation to their limited purchase on the process of identification, propelled him towards the esoteric theories of time developed by Dunne, and Ouspensky, and Jungian psychology. In his later years this trajectory led him into the Gurdjieffian occult. The Anglo-British search for a theoretical alternative to economism, which was Gramsci's enduring achievement, took Priestley into strange waters indeed.

A DEMOCRATIC ENGLISH REGIONALISM

For Priestley, the dominant culture and politics of Anglo-Britain operated as a brake on the most desirable aspects of modernity, namely democracy, urban improvement and equality of opportunity. However they offered no resistance to what he feared to be the worst consequences: a war-prone nationalism, commercialisation and cultural homogeneity. Priestley was therefore engaged in a debate over the form that Anglo-British modernity should take, not an insular resistance to modernisation in the name of Little England.

The nation mapped by Priestley's *English Journey* was in a sorry state. If Britain's economic development had been distorted by the needs of finance and the city, its political development had been stunted by Westminster. Local economies had been overridden and local political cultures were undernourished, leaving a crude nationalism as the residue. The Labour Party's ability to rise above this was constrained, Priestley felt, by a narrow-minded trade unionism. Aspects of Priestley's critique, and many of the solutions he goes on to offer, anticipated by half a century many of the themes of the centre-left and the constitutional reform lobby of today.[37] Banks, freeloaders, financiers and big businesses were responsible for England's plight. 'The shoddy, greedy, profit-grabbing, joint-stock-company industrial system' was 'the real villain'.[38]

In the early 1930s Priestley believed that Anglo-British modernity should be driven by manufacturing and not rentier capitalism, and that industry should become socially responsible and develop new and more satisfying forms of work. 'There is England the producer of goods. And there is England the lender of money. From the standpoint of the happiness of the people, the first seems to me the more important.'[39] However, the nation was organised according to a different set of priorities. 'The City is much too near Westminster; they can hear each other talking.'[40]

As a result, Priestley is critical of the forms that industrial modernity had taken, drawing on traditional pastoral evocations of Englishness. In his most famous formulation, industrialism itself is represented as abjecting a defining component of the English imaginary, the countryside. Nineteenth century industrialism, Priestley argues, 'had found a green and pleasant land and had left a wilderness of dirty bricks. It had blackened fields, poisoned rivers, ravaged the earth and sown filth and ugliness with a lavish hand.'[41]

Contrasting its work processes with autonomous forms of craft labour – in the figure of a Cotswold stone mason – Priestley criticised the factory system even where it operated at its most benign, under the paternalist supervision of the Wills and Cadbury families.[42] But he had no illusion that the core institution of Fordism would disappear in his time.

Re-affirming his own dissent from dominant representations of Anglo-Britishness, and prefiguring the historical critique that would later be offered by the new Left, Priestley describes how manufacturing capital cloaked itself with the cultural authority of the gentry in order to speak on behalf of the nation: 'The man who was notorious in some North-country industrial city for paying poor wages and driving hard bargains suddenly vanishes, and then up pops another good old English gentleman in Hampshire or Hereford, to sit under the Union Jack (as if he owned it) on Tory platforms and to put in his plea for 'our good old English ways'.[43] For Priestley, the codes of

Englishness that resulted were the product of a vanishing, signs without referents, and inauthentic representations of the national community.

Priestley offers regionalism as a countervailing force to the hollow nationalism fostered by the undemocratic state. *English Journey* is an impassioned manifesto for decentralisation. His tongue in his cheek, Priestley even calls for Home Rule for East Anglia![44] In Priestley's formulation, as in the contemporary discourse of new Labour, democratisation and decentralisation are presented as an enhancement of the sovereignty of the House of Commons, rather than its supersession. 'Under a democratic system', argues Priestley in a passage that still has striking relevance more than sixty years later,

> politics should be local, so that you can keep an eye on them. Indeed, in a large modern state you need a very elaborately constructed pyramid of representational government, with parochial councils for the base and a national assembly at the apex, in order that the democratic system can work properly ... Centralisation is one of the deadliest enemies of the system. For this reason alone there is much to be said in favour of regional government in England. But I also suggest that such government would bring a new dignity to provincial life, just as it would increase the importance of the various new provincial capital cities, where the deputies or senators would meet.[45]

Priestley was a lifelong advocate of the positive contribution that regionalism, nested within federal and global structures, could make to the revival of Anglo-British community and democracy. 'The real flowers belong to regionalism', he insisted during the Wilson government, some thirty years later.[46]

> We are still backing the wrong ism. Almost all our money goes on the middle one, nationalism, the rotten meat between the two healthy slices of bread. We need regionalism to give us roots and that very depth of feeling which nationalism unjustly and greedily claims for itself. We need internationalism to save the world and to broaden and heighten our civilisation.[47]

FROM COLONIAL TROPES TO RACIAL HYBRIDITY AND BACK AGAIN

Racialised identifications as well as transitions in the empire are acknowledged to be active shapers of English life during Priestley's middle period. He began to articulate dramatic changes in both in his many constructions of the future of England.

Faraway is one of the least read and appreciated of Priestley's novels. Brome says it is not 'of major consequence in Priestley's ouevre'.[48] The author himself characterises the book as unsatisfactory and a disappointment.[49] This is a pity because *Faraway* is in fact an important exploration of the interwar articulation of racialised Anglo-British national identifications, culture, territory and masculinity. Written in the very same months that Nancy Cunard was privately circulating *Black Man, White Ladyship*, Priestley's account of the crisis of Anglo-British whiteness was prompted by his first trip, in 1931, to America and the South Pacific.

The book tells the tale of a Suffolk maltster, William Dursley, one of three intended beneficiaries of a map bequeathed by Dursley's uncle, a retired Pacific trader who had cohabited with a series of black colonial women. The map provides the location of a valuable pitchblende deposit he discovered on a distant South Pacific island, *Faraway*.

The name given to this modern treasure island suggests a place without definite location. However *Faraway* is a much visited spot in the colonial imaginary, not so much an elsewhere as a not-Britain. The narrative embarks on a voyage into the 'phantasmagoria' of the colonial periphery, and manoeuvres Dursley through a series of encounters with representative figures of the Anglo-British colonial imagination: Americans, black alterities and 'exotic' women.[50] It charts the dissolution – and eventual recovery – of a white English identification confronted with difference.

At first glance, *Faraway* is a narrative romp through the exoticising tropes of Anglo-British colonial discourse. South American rivals for the mineral wealth pass through Suffolk 'like a combined carnival, tornado and plague'.[51] In California, Dursley is waited upon by black Americans who 'seemed to have retained some secret of a rich luscious life that their masters had lost'.[52] But the odyssey of *Faraway* introduces the reader to real complications, for on leaving England 'reality broke down for William. He walked through an invisible crack into another world ... he said goodbye to sense'.[53]

The first Polynesians mentioned in the book are diverse, but animal. 'There were one or two men, like shining brown bulls, and there were one or two syphilitic-looking scoundrels; there were one or two young girls, like lovely shy animals.'[54] However, as Dursley departs from the United States for the imagined South Pacific of unregulated sexuality, a place that his experienced naval colleague has pronounced unfit for decent white women to visit, Priestley supplements the panorama with a figure from the colonial abject, a disturbing and unclassifiable externalisation of white Anglo-Britain's anxiety and internally menacing desire for the other. As Dursley enters a liminal space, beyond Anglo-American regulation, he sees a Polynesian woman dying from a venereal disease, the victim of a carnality that is figured as cannibalistic: 'a terrible figure ... possibly a half caste, who might have been only middle aged or might have been elderly, but who seemed to stare up ... out of the very grave, for her face was eaten away to a death's head'.[55] After this encounter with 'the in between, the ambiguous, the composite' of Kristeva's abject, a colonialist epiphany, it is perhaps no surprise that what Dursley initially discovers in Polynesia is neither fullness nor authentication, but vacancy, melancholy and death.[56]

A sexual transgression on a Tahitian beach collapses white distinction. 'He was happily drowning in the mixed odour of the tiare, frangipani, coconut oil, and in warm flesh.'[57] Dursley recovers from his erotic engulfment by the abject ('dark shafts of weakness and nausea' ... 'It was like being dead and knowing that you are dead') under the supervision of a marooned widow from Suffolk, a displaced but nurturing Britannia whom he eventually marries and returns with to southern England, her rightful abode. But his racialised national identification is now extremely fragile. Dursley is still vulnerable to a longing for escape, adventure, American modernity and the Tropics, much to the displeasure of the book's reviewer in the *Times Literary Supplement*.[58]

Restored to his Suffolk home, Dursley is summoned back from the involuntary jouissance prompted by his South Pacific photographs, to an ongoing game of chess. Briefly, his wife and best friend are transfigured into 'a pair of lumpish warders'. The incident reprises Priestley's wartime encounter with the artificiality of representation. 'He stared stupidly at the pieces. He knew they were in some significant array, but for the moment he was too bewildered, baffled, annoyed with the world and himself to discover exactly what it was.'[59]

Although the narrative fails to escape the colonial imaginary, Priestley did establish the contingency and inadequacy of the codes of Anglo-British whiteness. In *Faraway*, England becomes a stranger to itself and the menace of Americanisation and blackness recedes.

The novel also questions the administrative as well as the imaginary boundaries of Anglo-Britain. On their arrival at *Faraway*, the three partners argue about how to dispose of the pitchblende, a booty they would, in fact, never own. To the highest bidder? To England? Or, as Dursley urges, to an international trust? For Dursley the sale became an issue of transnational principle: 'Every time you ignore national boundaries,' he argues, 'you bring the possibility of a sane, happy, peaceful world a bit nearer.'[60]

The porosity of national boundaries in an era of global trade – clearly visible, as we have seen, in Edwardian Bradford – is celebrated during Priestley's visit to a dockside area of Liverpool on his *English Journey*. 'Port Said and Bombay, Zanzibar and Hong Kong had called here. The babies told the tale plainly enough. They were of all shades, and Asia and Africa came peeping out of their eyes.'[61] The local school-yard, a 'miniature League of Nations assembly gone mad', was a humorous domestic figure for his transnational aspirations. Priestley taunted Anglo-British whiteness with its fear of extinction, 'a glimpse of the world of 2433, by which time the various root races, now all members of a great world state, may have largely inter-married and interbred.'[62]

For Priestley, who praised the physical beauty of mixed race children, miscegenation was not degeneration.[63] In *English Journey* he registers that a deracialising hybridisation, beyond the existing structures of identification, was already underway. White Americans are also 'a race new to the world', the result of 'unimaginable adventures in pioneering and gold-rushing, lust and love, of the strangest encounters of odds and ends of humanity from the older peoples.'[64]

This hybridisation is a positive aspect of Americanisation, comparable perhaps to the 'admirable leavening' that central Europe had once brought to Bradford.

For Priestley, differences in skin colour were not an essential precondition for the process of abjection and distinction formative of national identity.[65] In the structuring of his imaginary, the Black Atlantic appears to be less significant than the Irish Channel.

'The relation to abjection is finally rooted in the combat that every human being carries on with the mother', Kristeva writes. 'For in order to become autonomous, it is necessary that one cut the instinctual dyad of the mother and the child and that one becomes something other.'[66] Priestley's representation of the Irish – significantly the most likely ethnicity of the mother he never knew – reveals the distinction from Irishness to be the primary abjection on which his Englishness is based. 'If we do have an Irish Republic as our neighbour ... and it is found possible to return her exiled citizens, what a grand clearance there will be in all the Western ports, from the Clyde to Cardiff, what a fine exit of ignorance and dirt and drunkenness and disease.'[67]

After the watershed of Labour's postwar failure to modernise Anglo-Britain, Priestley appears to retreat from the pleasurable fissures in the boundaries of whiteness which he had discovered in *Faraway* and at the Liverpool dockside. They are sealed with the primitivising tropes of blackness, and the exoticising and on occasion intemperate, representations of migrants to Britain, that mar his civic egalitarianism and later formulations of Anglo-British distinction.[68] This may be an effect of the 're-racialisation' that Bill Schwarz suggests the English underwent in the late 1950s and 1960s.[69] But I would also suggest that they are abjections which result from Priestley's increasing anxiety about Anglo-British modernity, externalised as the threat of Americanisation.

AMERICANISATION: EXTERNAL OR INTERNAL MENACE?

Priestley is ambivalent about modernisation. Certainly he is a militant advocate of many of its possibilities: an inclusive public sphere, civic pride and democracy. But he externalises, as Americanisation, much of the rest, including suburbanisation, popular fashion, the ready availability of cheap consumer goods, widespread car ownership, the burgeoning film industry and the growth in advertising.

Generally speaking, this is not a racialised doubling. However, on at least one occasion when an American export was enthusiastically taken up in place of what Priestley believed to be an authentically Anglo-British popular culture, it was figured as black. 'The Blackpool that sang about Charlie Brown and the girls with their curly curls was the Mecca of a vulgar but alert and virile democracy. I am not so sure about the new Blackpool of the weary negroid ditties.'[70] Black modernity unsettled Priestley's Anglo-British populism between the wars precisely where it would be most acceptable later in the century, in the field of popular music.

Although he frequently found much to admire on his visits to the United States, Priestley was concerned about the cultural homogenisation which he feared that modernity and international trade – in this phase, after all, dominated by American producers – threatened to deliver. If modernisation as democracy would increase the authenticity of identifications, modernisation in the form of American commodities and advertising techniques would reduce it. His ambivalence results in a doubling of the new culture of suburban England. On the one hand, the outer fringes of Southampton 'differ in a few minor details from a few thousand such roads in the United States, where the same tooth-pastes and soaps and gramophone records are being sold, the very same films are being shown.' On the other, this new England is 'as near to a classless society as we have got yet'.[71]

The postwar checklist of Priestley's Anglo-British anxieties about modernisation and America, and about the relocation of an ambiguous boundary between what could be represented as the unnecessary repli-cation of American culture and the thrust of indigenous development, is famously caught in his mid-1950s characterisation of Admass. Admass was a 'whole system of increasing productivity, plus inflation, plus a rising standard of material living, plus high pressure advertising and salesmanship, plus cultural democracy and the creation of the mass mind, the mass man.'[72]

Of course this cultural and economic modernisation was being selectively assisted by an unmodernised state. Priestley feared that Anglo-Britain would receive only the negative fruit of modernisation, the standardised work routines, leisure and commodities that lent themselves to England's 'iron autocracy', or 'America without equal-ity'.[73] The degree to which these features became embedded in Britain's economy and culture provided an ongoing reminder of Labour's fail-ure in 1945, Priestley's political explanation for the absence of a distinc-tively Anglo-British modernity.

To understand the depth of his postwar dissatisfaction, and take the full measure of his argument, we must therefore audit what he said was wrong, and what he urged was possible, in the 1940s.

WARTIME MODERNISER

Far from resisting modernity, during the war Priestley actually promoted a modernising democratic and socialist agenda through his association with the 1941 Committee and Common Wealth. Given the electoral truce, and his broadcasting and publishing profile, Priestley's was the most important contemporary challenge to the Churchillian imaginary and bipartisan formulation of the national-popular that Barnett identifies as a major restraint on the postwar modernisation of Britain.[74]

As the clouds of war had gathered over the depression, Priestley had located their twin cause in a constitution which empowered the wrong people and misrepresented the nation and its interests:

We are not a democracy, but a plutocracy roughly disguised as an aristocracy. All our real government is done by the Right People. Not only in Parliament ... but in all the various positions of authority, in the Civil Services, Finance, the Church, the fighting services, and so on ... Our election methods are out of date, and so are all in favour of politicians who are also out of date. To begin with, the Parliamentary seats are not equitably divided among the population ... because we have not proportional representation, millions of progressive electors never put a member into the House ... Parliament has a quite disproportionate number of members who have substantial private incomes and cannot help having a private income point of view.[75]

Once war had been declared, Priestley felt that politics was more, not less, relevant to the nation. As the leading spokesperson for the 1941 Committee and the Author's National Committee, Priestley proposed that a modernising, and decentralising programme of parliamentary and social reform should commence as soon as hostilities ceased. His proposals included a greater devolution of parliamentary powers to regional councils, a proportional electoral system, the annual election of one fifth of the members of Parliament, the use of opinion polls to guide decision making, the replacement of the House of Lords with a senate, the retention of the monarchy albeit shorn of its 'feudal flummery' and the introduction of a guaranteed minimum standard of living.[76] He argued that the state 'must not swallow all other associations' that make up Britain's democratic life. With only one exception, the constitutional agenda Priestley was urging in 1941 is precisely that which new Labour considers overdue and urgent today. It bore little resemblance to what was being incubated for 1945.

The differences on economic management were even wider. Taking his prewar socialist critique of rentier and manufacturing capital to the limit, Priestley believed it was necessary to 'destroy' capitalism, 'an unworkable and decaying system' and replace it with a new system of production based on common ownership.[77] His work in the Ministry of Information had made Priestley too aware of 'the mandarin's contempt for the general public' for him to endorse wide-ranging nationalisation under the control of government.[78] Although essential utilities should be taken over by the state, most production should remain in private hands.[79] While Priestley was outlining his radical programme of reform, Labour was developing blueprints for a state-directed welfare capitalism which became the basis of a postwar settlement that endured for the next thirty years.

In *Let the People Sing*, a book that Priestley started to read on air on the day war was declared, a character says of a British aristocrat that 'he is a democrat in the evening and a Nazi in the morning'.[80] Priestley's attitude to the Right People who ran the country became even harsher as invasion threatened, and the disparity between his proposals and the government's war aims became apparent.

Priestley's dislocation from the ruling culture, and his related suspicion that it was capable of an accommodation with fascism in order to reproduce itself, is the subject of his wartime thriller *Black-Out in Gretley*.[81] In an extended and updated reprise of his abjection of the voices that misled England during the First World War, Priestley generates a set of English characters with lifestyles that predispose them to collaboration. A spycatcher's suspect list includes people with shameful secrets, immoral pasts and, more importantly, anyone whose forms of cultural distinction are based on the notion that ordinary people are inferior. The genre of spy and counter spy writing was highly suited to Priestley's antipathy to simulations of community and national identity. The spycatcher's target is anyone whose language or behaviour seems inauthentic or imperious. As Priestley operates a construction of fascism that is able to contain most authoritarian traits and much that normally passed for Anglo-British leadership and tradition, the book teems with potential Quislings: an adulteress, a homosexual, a colonel, a justice of the peace, a doctor, a comedian, a trapeze artist. As the man from counter-espionage warns, 'don't forget that when we catch him, he may be singing Rule Britannia at the top of his voice and be smothered in Union Jacks'.[82] In *Black Out in Gretley* Priestley seeks to compromise the official language of the war effort by demonstrating it is related to power rather than to community.

A similar differentiation of the nation occurs in Priestley's 1943 political comedy *They Came to a City*, a wartime *News From Nowhere* in which the English socialist utopia is urban and tantalisingly off stage.[83] A group of individuals reflecting the gradations of the Anglo-British class system find themselves in the vicinity of an unknown city surrounded by a high wall. They spend a carnivalesque day in the future during which English hierarchies and a number of discursive binaries are reversed. A businessman reports that he is regarded as mentally ill, a knight reveals that he is perceived as a savage. Distinctions are erased. An aristocratic ex-colonial cannot adjust to the loss of deference. A middle-class suburban wife fears new freedoms. For some, the day is an emancipation. A young educated woman embraces a new independence and decides to stay in the utopic community, as does an elderly working-class woman and a bank clerk. Two more, a young working-class woman and a widely travelled ship's engineer also endorse the values of the new society. However, they decide to return to England in order to encourage the rest of the Anglo-British nation to change the way they live.

During the war Priestley further developed his prescient view that the new forms of travel and communication which had emerged in the twentieth century would transform national identifications and forms of government:

> This world of rapid aerial transport – and of almost instantaneous communication – is clearly shrinking fast, and is really quite different from the world of yesterday. This world of air travel cannot help but be an international world. The airman moves too fast for national boundaries, and his work urgently demands that the nations cooperate with him and with each other ... A narrow national spirit, pretending that there is something sacred and magical about a frontier, with its old fashioned paraphernalia of customs sheds and passport examinations, is clearly out of place in such a world.[84]

Although Priestley became an advocate of transnational government, involving new forms of citizenship and sovereignty, he combined his support for these modernisations with a defence of cultural particularities that was more commonly associated with the discourses of ethnic nationalism.

As a counterweight to the 'world monotony' which he expected globalisation would inaugurate, Priestley urges a 'cultural regionalism' in which ethnic differences – foods, habits, music, art – would be actively cultivated.[85] While nationalism had to be discouraged and avoided in political and social affairs, it should be actively encouraged in the field of culture: 'We must stick to our own hats and puddings and jokes and songs.'[86]

Priestley clearly underestimated the degree to which these forms of culture and representation were linked to power and the reproduction of Anglo-British whiteness. If Priestley successfully counterposed the authentic communal pleasures of everyday life to the preoccupations of the Anglo-British elite, he nevertheless failed to identify the way in which popular cultures are racialised fields of power and representation in which processes of identification, abjection and alterity, operate.

The ethnocentrism of Priestley's English imaginary reduces the purchase of his civic egalitarianism, thus privileging Anglo-British whiteness. A similar process is enacted in the wider national culture where white cultural capital had more impact on the distribution of opportunities than the citizenship rights given to black migrants. Whether we are talking of Priestley's 'Cultural regionalism' or England's cultural nationalism, black people were always going to foot the bill in any resistance offered to Americanisation.

WAITING FOR NEWS FROM HOME

Politically marginalised and institutionally homeless in the period of postwar reconstruction, Priestley's associational, non-statist socialist politics – and a longstanding irritation over the level of his income tax payments – meant that there was a great deal he found objectionable in the Keynesian welfare settlement. One of the earliest figures to identify the failings of postwar state socialism, Priestley inadvertently prepared many of the themes of the authoritarian populist discourse which would assist Margaret Thatcher to office.

In a private letter, Priestley describes the first year of the Attlee government as 'unimaginative' and 'dreary', a 'revolution without bloodshed' that had failed to lift people's spirits.[87] Three years later the postwar reissue of *English Journey* is prefaced with a prescient warning about the political dynamic of the postwar settlement. The Anglo-British were 'hastily fastening ourselves into a system that lacks flexibility, does not encourage initiative or a general sense of responsibility, and fails to create enthusiasm and release energy.'[88]

By the late 1940s Priestley was criticising the National Health Service as undemocratic (its creation had involved the abolition of local and accountable structures), and denying the significance of Anglo-British and Cold War political binaries, insisting on the similarities of the Labour government and the Conservative Party, the United States and the USSR. 'All the powers are moving away from democracy as fast as they can go,' he insisted in a response to Michael Foot's denunciation of his views in *Tribune*.[89]

In the late 1950s he anticipated the argument that the welfare state generated a culture of dependency. 'I cannot help wondering if some of the results of the Welfare State do not show the re-entry of Eros in an inferior form, creating a dim passivity.'[90] Priestley's assertion that the major parties were converging is repeated right through to the late 1960s.[91] In 1967 the anti-statist wartime advocate of world citizenship counsels against joining the common market.[92]

By then Priestley was irrevocably dissociated from all the dominant Anglo-British national identifications. 'It's a terrible thing ... to know you're at home and yet to feel you're waiting for news from home.'[93] His Englishness was not only disembedded from the life of the nation but divided, a stranger to itself. His antipathy to top-down planning, and the state, found few points of articulation in the present, and could only be justified through the remembered emphases of Bradford's ethical socialism and regional political culture, the 'gleam of real gold in the wreck' of Edwardianism.[94] Hence Priestley's widely remarked look over the shoulder. If Priestley in the 1960s and 1970s looks back fondly to Edwardianism, it is in order to avert his eyes from Labour's negligible impact on the Anglo-British state and failure to modernise the English imaginary.

Notes

1. See Geoff Mulgan's citation of Priestley, for example, in David Marquand and Anthony Seldon (eds), *The Ideas That Shaped Postwar Britain*, Fontana Press, London 1996, p212.
2. Judith Cook, *Priestley*, Bloomsbury, London 1997, p3.
3. Susan Cooper, *J.B. Priestley: Portrait of an Author*, Heinemann, London 1970; Vincent Brome, *J.B. Priestley*, Hamish Hamilton, London 1988; Diana Collins, *Time and the Priestleys: The Story of a Friendship*, Alan Sutton Publishing, Stroud 1994.
4. J.B. Priestley, *Instead of the Trees*, Stein and Day, New York 1977, pp81-82.
5. John Atkins, *J.B. Priestley: The Last of the Sages*, John Calder, London 1981, pp95-6.
6. Priestley, *op.cit*, 1977, p35.
7. J.B. Priestley, *English Journey*, Heinemann, London 1934, p415.
8. Key texts in that debate are contained in: Perry Anderson, *English Questions*, Verso, London 1992; Edward Thompson, *The Poverty of Theory*, Merlin, London 1978; Tom Nairn, *The Break Up Of Britain*, Verso, London 1977; *The Enchanted Glass*, Radius, London 1998; Anthony Barnett, *Iron Britannia*, Alison and Busby, London 1982 and *This Time: Our Constitutional Revolution*, Vintage, London 1997.
9. In the *Adelphi*, October 1930, quoted in Vincent Brome, *op.cit*, 1988, p128; also F.R. Leavis, *The Great Tradition*, Chatto and Windus, London 1948. Entry for 8 September 1930.

10. Virginia Woolf, *Diaries*, vol 3, Hogarth Press, London 1980. For Priestley on the general reader, see *The Moments and Other Pieces*, Heinemann, London, p208.

11. The breakthrough has been acknowledged by one black British filmmaker. John Akomfrah's *'A Touch of the Tarbrush'* was broadcast on BBC2, 11 November 1991.

12. Angus Calder, *The People's War: Britain 1959-45*, Granada, London 1971, p125.

13. J.B. Priestley, *Postscripts*, Heinemann, London 1940, pp1-4; J.B. Priestley, *Home From Dunkirk: A Photographic Record in Aid of the British Red Cross and St John*, John Murray, London 1940. See the contrary assessment by Henry Pelling in *Britain and the Second World War*, Fontana, London 1970, pp252-253: 'The operation was a triumph of skill and training on the part of the Navy, the RAF, and regular soldiers.'

14. For example in Priestley, *op.cit*, 1977, pp33-35.

15. Cook, *op.cit*, 1997, p32.

16. J.B. Priestley, *Margin Released: Reminiscences and Reflections*, Heinemann, London 1962, p28. See Priestley's account of his workplace and its trade with European and more 'romantic' locations, *ibid*, pp14-15.

17. *Ibid*, p63.

18. Priestley, *op.cit*, 1934, p160.

19. John Braine, *J.B. Priestley*, Weidenfeld and Nicolson, London 1978.

20. Priestley, *op.cit*, 1962, p78.

21. Priestley, *ibid*, 1934, p166.

22. Quoted in Cook, *op.cit*, p41.

23. Priestley, *op.cit*, 1934, p169.

24. J.B. Priestley, *The Good Companions*, Heinemann, London 1929, p299.

25. *Ibid*, p5.

26. *Times Literary Supplement*, 1 August 1929.

27. Priestley, *op.cit*, 1929, p33 and pp333-4. For the threat of a trade union punch on the nose see *English Journey*, p233.

28. Mike Cooley, *Architect or Bee? The Human Price of Technology*, Chatto and Windus, London 1987; Robin Murray, 'Rethinking Social Ownership', *New Left Review* 164, 1987.

29. Priestley, *op.cit*, 1934, p193.

30. Priestley, *op.cit*, 1929, pp1-5.

31. Priestley, *op.cit*, 1940, p12.

32. Priestley, *op.cit*, 1962, p204.

33. Priestley, *op.cit*, 1934, p29.

34. J.B. Priestley, *Rain Upon Godshill: Further Chapters of Autobiography*,

Heinemann, London 1939, p212.

35. Priestley, *op.cit*, 1934, p294.

36. Priestley, *op.cit*, 1939, pp259-260.

37. For example, those of Will Hutton, in *The State We're In*, Jonathan Cape, London 1995 or Anthony Barnett, *op.cit*, 1997.

38. Priestley, *op.cit*, 1934, p64.

39. Priestley, *op.cit*, 1939, p243.

40. *Ibid*, p251.

41. Priestley, *op.cit*, 1934, p400.

42. *Ibid*, pp53-4, and p34 and pp92-98.

43. J.B. Priestley, *Out of the People*, Collins/Heinemann, London 1941, p25.

44. Priestley, *op.cit*, 1934, p383.

45. *Ibid*, p381.

46. Priestley, *op.cit*, 1962, pp35-37.

47. *Ibid*, p40.

48. Brome, *op.cit*, p134.

49. Priestley, *op.cit*, 1939, p187.

50. J.B. Priestley, *Faraway* (1932), Mandarin, London 1996 edition, p19.

51. *Ibid*, p34.

52. *Ibid*, p130.

53. *Ibid*, p123.

54. *Ibid*, p168.

55. *Ibid*.

56. Julia Kristeva, *Powers of Horror: An Essay on Ajection*, Colombia University Press, New York 1982, p4; Priestley, *op.cit*, 1966, p348. For a fuller exploration of western representations of the South Pacific and their articulation with discourses of sexuality and cultural extinction see Rod Edmond, *Representing the South Pacific: Colonial Discourse from Cook to Gaugin*, Cambridge University Press, Cambridge 1997.

57. Priestley, *op.cit*, 1996, p361.

58. *Times Literary Supplement*, 30 June 1932.

59. Priestley, *op.cit*, 1996, p520.

60. *Ibid*, p424.

61. Priestley, *op.cit*, 1934, p239.

62. *Ibid*, p242.

63. *Ibid*, p243.

64. *Ibid*, pp134-135.

65. Anne McClintock, *Imperial Leather: Race, Gender and Sexuality in the Colonial Context*, Routledge, London 1995, pp52-3.

66. Quoted in Elaine Hoffman Baruch, 'Feminism and Psychoanalysis' in

Ross Mitchell Guberman (ed), *Julia Kristeva: Interviews*, Columbia University Press, New York 1996, p118.

67. Priestley, *op.cit*, 1934, p248.

68. Priestley, *op.cit*, 1962, p174; J.B. Priestley, *Sir Michael and Sir George: A Tale of COSMA, DISCUS and the New Elizabethans*, Heinemann, London 1964, pp148-50; J.B. Priestley, *Found, Lost, Found or The English Way of Life*, Heinemann, London 1976, pp25-6.

69. Bill Schwarz, '"The Only White Man in There". The Re-Racialisation of England 1956-68' in James Donald and Stephanie Donald (eds), *Identity, Authority and Democracy*, University of Sussex, Brighton 1995.

70. Priestley, *op.cit*, 1934, p268.

71. *Ibid*, p22, p403.

72. J.B. Priestley and Jacquetta Hawkes, *Journey Down a Rainbow*, Heineman/Cresset, London 1955.

73. Priestley, *op.cit*, 1966, p215.

74. Barnett, *op.cit*, 1982, pp46-62.

75. Priestley, *op.cit*, 1939, p227.

76. Priestley, *op.cit*, 1941, p122.

77. J.B. Priestley, *Here Are Your Answers*, Common Wealth Popular Library no1.

78. J.B. Priestley, letter to Edward Davison October 1939, quoted in Judith Cook, *op.cit*, p178.

79. Priestley, *op.cit*, 1941, p119.

80. J.B. Priestley, *Let the People Sing*, Heinemann, 1939, p68.

81. J.B. Priestley, *Blackout in Gretley: A Story of and for Wartime*, Heinemann, London 1942.

82. *Ibid*, p82.

83. J.B. Priestley, 'They Came to a City' in *Four Plays*, Heinemann, London 1944.

84. J.B. Priestley, *The New Citizen*, Council for Education in World Citizenship, London 1944, p2.

85. *Ibid*, pp4-5.

86. *Ibid*, p5.

87. J.B. Priestley, letter to Edward Davison 1946, quoted in Cook, *op.cit*, p208.

88. J.B. Priestley, 'Preface' to *English Journey*, Heinemann, London 1949 edition, pvii.

89. See 'J.B. Priestley Replies to his Critics' in *The Sunday Pictorial*, 6 February 1949, written in response to Michael Foot's 'The Futility of Mr Priestley' in *Tribune*, 16 January, 1949.

90. J.B. Priestley, *Thoughts in the Wilderness*, Heinemann, London 1957, p38.

91. *Ibid*, p217 and J.B. Priestley, *The Image Men*, Heinemann, London 1968.
92. J.B. Priestley, *Essays of Five Decades*, Heinemann, London 1968, p307.
93. Priestley, *op.cit*, 1976, p3.
94. J.B. Priestley, *The Edwardians*, Heinemann, London 1970, p289.

4

Pete Townshend: 'talking 'bout regeneration'

In September 1996 a balding and slightly deaf celebrity stuck his head out of a window in Mayfair and unveiled a blue plaque to mark a former home of rock guitarist, Jimi Hendrix. The Handel Society was outraged, claiming that the new plaque devalued their memorial to the German master of oratorio and opera on the building next door. A brief row about musical standards ensued. How fitting that it was Pete Townshend, the craftsman of the hybrid genre of rock opera which had helped erode the distinction between Anglo-British high and low culture in the 1960s, who had revived concerns about the disappearance of distinction from the musical canon.

Townshend has had an enormous influence on Anglo-British music and the national imaginary, even if this is rarely acknowledged in political debate and the accelerating music cycle.[1] When a British musician calls his band The Who, puts on a jacket made from the national flag, drapes his amplifier with the Union Jack and then smashes his guitar into it – Townshend's nightly habit in the mid-1960s – it is clear that an ambivalence towards the dominant languages of Anglo-British identification is being expressed. At the moment of Powellism – not so much the street movement, as the wider national imaginary which concurred in his defence of British parliamentary institutions and white nationhood – Townshend's rock strove for masculine Anglo-British authenticity and abjected the culture of the post-war settlement. His work detonated and then sublimated a crisis of white Anglo-British masculinity.

An angry, intelligent outsider to the nation's cultural and political institutions, Townshend's celebrity status has had the paradoxical effect of disenfranchising him from debates on the nature and future of the nation. He is best known as the power chord guitarist and songwriter for The Who, one of Britain's most successful rock bands, disbanded in 1982 but reformed regularly ever since. In the 1960s Townshend's music retuned the Anglo-British ear, alerting the English body to the excitements of Europe, the United States, young Mods and the aspirations of the counter-culture.

The young Townshend moved from a family of entertainers into the Art School left of the early 1960s. His early membership of the Young Communist League and CND – he played banjo in a trad jazz band on Aldermaston marches – was suppressed by Who managers in order to keep the door open to the Cold War markets of the USA.[2]

After The Who's successful entry into the new market for popular music, Townshend became one of the New Left's most prominent contacts in the global music industry and the growing countercultural niche it addressed. He also became a follower of the Sufi religious leader, Meher Baba. Today Townshend is an associate of the Prince's Trust and 'totally hooked' on music theatre, where he challenges the way in which Andrew Lloyd Weber appropriated rock for that genre.[3] He only smashes guitars for charity.[4]

The importance of Townshend to debates about English national identity and masculinity in the 1960s and 1970s has been overlooked because of the intelligentsia's abjection of rock excess, an attitude licensed by a Western Marxist critique of mass culture, which placed the mandarins of the left shoulder to shoulder with establishment defenders of distinction. Townshend played an important part in the temporary disorganisation of this old nexus of Anglo-British cultural and political power.

The imaginary nation of the young Townshend was an urban work-ing-class youth culture ambivalent about the dominant modes of Anglo-British whiteness. It was the world of the white negro of the Mod imaginary. In Shepherds Bush where The Who secured their earli-est following, that counter identification was demographically even more specific: it was the youth of the London Irish community.

Later the ethnic nation would be figured in the generic White City of urban West London. On the album of that name, *White City* is a space of masculine self assertion and excess, an internal enclave where sex, drugs and crime menace the English settlement, and where the territoriality of white Anglo-Britishness threatens to take on uglier, fascist forms. *White City* is also the place where these threats are over-come, and new forms of community are established.

At a third stage in Townshend's development, Anglo-Britishness is the ethos of the regeneration agencies, moral and economic, which address the recession and the partial modernisation of the imperial state.

For three and a half decades Townshend's musical output, writing and reflections, have helped narrate the ambivalences and dilemmas of a subordinate masculine nation. His songs engage with white youth cultures in England and processes of male identification, from the years immediately following Suez and the liberalisation of world trade – when time was called on Britain's colonial imaginary – through the subsequent period of economic growth, political liberalism and Anglo-British cultural contraflow, to the extended struggle over the appropriate forms of modernisation required of the nation at the end of the century.

Throughout this period, Townshend's reflections on the emergence of global cultural markets have been public, critical and reflexive. Townshend is increasingly acknowledged as 'rock's premier theorist and moralist', one of 'rock's most literate and pensive talents' and a 'generational voice' with auteur status.[5] Townshend's commentary draws attention to the changing articulation between the rock industry – which distinguished itself from pop markets by claiming a greater integrity, virtuosity and a closer relationship to its audience – and popular ethnicities.

Rock in the 1960s, and the contemporary mimicry that is Britpop, is often characterised as the expression of a regressive nostalgia for a white working-class ethnicity.[6] The cultural critic Alan Bloom simply asserts that rock reduces life to 'a nonstop commercial pre-packaged masturbatory fantasy'. Rock is therefore held responsible for the dumbing of youth.[7]

Can rock be held accountable for this? I think not. Anglo-British rock, particularly as manifest in Townshend's work, was a field of representation in which there was significant conflict and critique. Townshend's songs and performances dramatised and explored processes of male identification for a range of music publics, and were active in the reconfiguration of social and national identities. As a result Townshend's output makes new sense in the current period of crisis for Anglo-British white masculinities.

Music, particularly at the innovative margin where The Who originated in the 1960s, is a field in which rhythm, tone and performance exceed the capacities of available languages and give expression to the uncoded bodily drives that Kristeva calls the semiotic. If Townshend's lyrics and extensive exchanges with interviewers attempted to formulate the problems of masculinity and Englishness in received language, his musical performances were cathartic and sublimatory solutions to the flux and trauma of signification, gendering and national identification. As such, Townshend's musical performances provided an alternative technology of the self.

If we are to take the full measure of England's evolving hegemony and Townshend's challenge to it, we must attend not just to what he says, but to what he does, to his mode of performance, his hybridisation of genres and his use of technology

IRISH MOD FOR WHITE NEGROES

Early managers were quick to realise the potential of marketing The Who to the Mod subculture. Far from being the spontaneous expression of a generational zeitgeist, the association between The Who (initially in the guise of The High Numbers) and London Mods was a conscious articulation by cultural entrepreneurs working alongside an intelligent and empathetic young writer-performer.[8]

'Early songs like 'I Can't Explain', 'Anyway, Anyhow, Anywhere' and 'My Generation', recalls Townshend, 'were overtly aimed at trying to reflect street level frustration'.[9] For the Who weren't Mods, at least to start with, and many Mods didn't rate The Who.[10] The sharp marketing strategy was also a deliberate act of cultural geography. The association with Mod, emphasised by designer graphics and the slogan 'Maximum R&B', distinguished The Who's music, and the London audience which danced to it, not only from other bands in the capital – the Kinks, the Rolling Stones – but from the northern Merseybeat boom.

Mods have a peculiar and distinctive importance in the history of the nation. A British youth culture, created by employed and newly-affluent working-class kids, sought out both European and American commodities and spaces. By doing so they improvised a popular transnational habitus, from American burger and coffee bars, soul music and rhythm and blues; Italian fashion styles and scooters; and French clubs, films and haircuts.[11] After work and at the weekends they vacated, wherever possible, the residual spaces of Imperial and Churchillian Britain, where the colonial imagination still held sway – the family home, the workplace and the works club, the church and the church youth club, multi-generational dance halls – and sought a new relationship with modernity. When they returned in the early hours, uneasy compromises between the old and the new Anglo-Britain were hammered out in conflicts with their parents. Seen in this light – as an Anglo-British acceleration of modernity against specific local obstacles – it is less surprising that Mods were not much copied elsewhere, nor replicated in the USA.

Mod was also one of the youth subcultures on which British Cultural Studies, in its own adolescence, cut its teeth.[12] Dick Hebdige describes the compensatory gangster imaginary created by clerks and unskilled service industry staff in London's West End, young men who took the neatness demanded by their parents and employers to hyperbolic extremes, informed by cinematic images of the New York mafia, the occasional encounter with the Afro-Caribbean Rude Boys recently arrived in the capital, and the club-scene rendezvous between cosmopolitan Chelsea and the affluent East End.

Mod, for The Who, was even more hybrid than the generic account provided by Hebdige suggests. Shepherd's Bush, and the Goldhawk Road Club where The Who first performed, were heavily Irish in composition.[13] 'I was something like the artist in residence for the expatriate Irish community in Shepherd's Bush', Townshend later recalled. 'I partly based *Quadrophenia* on one of them, a boy called Irish jack.'[14]

In an encounter full of paradoxical hybridity, Irishness both fuelled and jeopardised The Who's Anglo-Britishness. Their use of jackets made from the flag of the Union elicited a bomb threat from the IRA during a tour of the Republic of Ireland in 1966. A Dublin tailor knocked up tricolour-based replacements. By this time the four musicians were involved in a familiar youth marketing dialectic. 'What the Mods taught us in the band was how to lead by following.'[15] As a result Townshend stole young London Irish thunder for Anglo-British rock.

Townshend's early reflections on Mod pre-empted many of Hebdige's more scholarly conclusions:

> It was an army, a powerful aggressive army of teenagers with transport. They were the lowest, they were England's lowest common denominators. Not only were they young, they were also lower-class young. They had to submit to the middle-class way of dressing and way of speaking and way of acting in order to get the very jobs which kept them alive. They had to do everything in terms of what actually existed around them. That made their way of getting something across that much more latently effective, the fact that they were hip and yet still, as far as Grandad was concerned, exactly the same'.[16]

Townshend, alerted to the discourses of European modernism by
Ealing Art School, and the cultural distinction of Covent Garden by
his manager Kit Lambert, had few illusions about his following: 'You
have to resign yourself to the fact that a large part of the audience is
sort of thick', the twenty-one year old star told a television interviewer
at the time.[17] Nevertheless Townshend preferred Mod's assertive,
action-oriented culture of rejection to what he later saw as the passivity of hippy culture.[18] A friend, Nick Cohn, was even less starry-eyed:
'The archetypal Mod was male, sixteen years old, rode a scooter, swal-
lowed pep pills by the hundred, thought of women as a completely
inferior race, was obsessed by cool and dug it. He was also one
hundred per cent hung up on himself, on his clothes and hair and
image; in every way, he was a miserable, narcissistic little runt.'[19] Mod
was the social identity adopted by a large swathe of a generation of
young men whose expectations of Modernity exceeded their British
prospects.

After the first panic, Anglo-Britain had adjusted to rock and roll.
The domestic music industry Anglicised the formula, muting its eroticism and hedonism with Tommy Steele and Cliff Richard. The Beatles
became modern family entertainment. Townshend and The Who were
far less compromising in their appropriation of R&B on behalf of a
urban masculine nation. Mod was a narcissistic and assertive drinamyl
culture and Townshend's Britbeat vocalised its dissatisfactions with the
wealthy, with women and with power. As he said of 'Anyway,
Anyhow, Anywhere' at the time, it was 'Anti-middle age, anti-boss
class and anti-young married'.[20]

Townshend's most recent explication of The Who's 1965 hit 'My
Generation' reveals it to be the product of a personal encounter with
the unfettered power of the monarchy, the very embodiment of Anglo-
Britain's premodern national identity. Townshend owned a large and
conspicuous American car, which he parked in Belgravia. The Queen
Mother, frequently chauffeured down the same street, had the car
removed, as it offended the royal eye.[21] 'My Generation' was
Townshend's reaction to that unresponsive fusion of age and power,
the 'old' which he would rather die than become.

The stutter in 'My Generation' – usually explained as accidental, or
mimetic of the speech of drinamyl users – also enacts the difficulties
involved in naming the diverse and heterogeneous subject of an Anglo-
British Modernity that was in every sense 'blocked'. The song drama-
tises an ambivalence about the positions of enunciation and identifica-

tion offered to the young Mod – and the counter hegemonic Anglo-British musician Townshend – which is more explicit in 'I Can't Explain'. Through Mod and, as we shall see, late modernism, Townshend tried and failed to articulate a new British identification. The enterprise established a durable imaginary, but simultaneously made him a stranger to himself.

In these early Townshend songs, signification and male identification were in rapid flux. 'I'm a Boy' explores anxieties about separation, castration and gender misidentification: 'I'm a boy, I'm a boy, but my ma won't admit it. I'm a boy, I'm a boy, but if I say I am I get it.' 'Substitute' raises the spectre of miscegenation and the relentless erosion of Anglo-British whiteness – 'I look all white but my dad was black' – as well as evoking the uncanny and melancholic effect of the ceaseless circulation of commodities and signs that, like Townshend's wrecked and replaced guitars, were interchangeable: 'me for him, my coke for gin, you for my mum'.[22]

In the early 1960s, Mod offered Townshend the tantalising prospect of stability and closure, in short an authenticity and identity that might overcome difference and provide an enduring, gendered national imaginary. It was an Anglo-British imaginary that retained, but rearticulated, traces of the white colonial binaries that once defined the nation.

> I know what it's like to be a Mod among two million Mods. It's like being the only white man at the Apollo. Someone comes up and touches you, and suddenly you become black. It's like that incredible feeling of being part of something much bigger than race – it was impetus ... Everybody looked the same, acted the same, and wanted to be the same. It was the first move I have ever seen in the history of youth towards unity: unity of thought, unity of drive, and unity of motive. It was the closest to pure patriotism I've ever felt.[23]

Like Cool Britannia today, Mod sought to accommodate the Black Atlantic into its aspiring Anglo-British Modernity. The Who's first manager, Pete Meaden, characterised Mods in Maileresque terms: 'neat, sharp and cool, an all-white Soho negro of the night.'[24] Ten years later Hebdige reiterates this as the Mod's desire 'to draw himself closer to the negro whose very metabolism seemed to have grown into, and kept pace with that of the city.'[25]

Simon Frith argues that black music invigorates white popular music in each and every generation because it expresses rather than controls the body. This argument draws on an underlying racial essentialism.[26] Instead, the encounter between Mod, Motown, and rhythm and blues, must be seen in terms of a newly diasporic English whiteness establishing trading relations with a diasporic Black Atlantic, supervised by American multinational corporations, on terms far from equality, in its deadlocked, declining and decolonising homeland.

The music that is now regarded as the pop heritage of Britain actually had to go beyond the boundaries of national territory in order to reach the domestic market. The language of piracy – rootless, irresponsible, motivated by base desires – was used to characterise the threat which this music, and the pleasures produced by dancing to it, posed to the reproduction of a compliant white nationhood.

The spaces in which The Who and other bands of the period were formed, and in which they often performed – the art schools, and the audiences and venues of the college circuit – were indeed structured and resourced by the state. But pirate radio was essential for the dissemination of any music that departed from the programming assumptions and Reithian distinction of the BBC – whose dominance of broadcasting was jealously guarded by the British left – from the Labour front bench through to Tribune and the New Left – with very few reservations.

In this sense the early music of The Who came from both inside and outside Anglo-Britain, from its hybrid transnational clubs and enclaves, but also from a place without the nation. England was doubled and divided, for – and by – those who listened and danced to the sounds broadcast by pirate radio.

For whiteness the outcome could not be predicted, even if the later association of rock and roll with the search for a new white ethnicity is accepted.[27] In the capital, between the flashpoints of Notting Hill in 1958 and the Powellite mobilisations of 1968, colonial binaries and national identifications were in flux for a section of the white working class. So it is important to make the black vocalist Ronnie Jones, who once sang with The Who – when they were the Mod High Numbers – visible once again.[28]

Townshend's complex articulation of the themes established in the moment of Mod created an imaginary, which hosted all of his subsequent hierarchies of meaning. In *Quadrophenia*, a song cycle issued in 1973, Townshend figured the dilemmas of the 1960s and 1970s counterculture, and his position in the global music industry, through the story of a young mod.

In the late 1970s, as Labour's corporatism and renewed promise of modernity foundered once again, Mod aspirations were still available as a counterpoint. Townshend's Eel Pie publishing house issued *Mods!*, a celebration by Richard Barnes.[29] 'There was something about it that was very, very fine', Townshend reflected on Brighton pier, as the film version of *Quadrophenia* was being shot. 'Fine is really the right word for it'.[30]

In many ways, Townshend's subsequent albums are groundings with his brothers, a reminder of their shared historic difference, of the new ethnicity that was briefly established in the mid-1960s. But by the time The Who reconvened to perform Townshend's Mod epic before the monarch in waiting in 1996, that new ethnicity had long been assimilated into the English balancing act, Anglo-British hegemony's tottering, post imperial equilibrium.[31]

AUTODESTRUCTION, RICKENBACKERS AND THE FORGING OF THE NATION

The distinctive contribution of the British art school as a crucible for popular music has been widely acknowledged.[32] Less acknowledged, perhaps, is the fact that popular culture itself was gendered as feminine.[33] Its critiques and alterities – Abstract Expressionism, Pop Art, Autodestructive art – and its later self styled antithesis, rock culture, were therefore available for male identification.

At one stage in Townshend's career, Pop Art and The Who – a group notorious for its masculine rivalries and punch-ups – were synonymous in tabloid representations. But some of the art discourses into which Townshend had been inducted were based on an abjection of commercial imagery and commodification. This created a dissonance to which Townshend continually returns. 'My personal motivation is a hate of every kind of pop music and a hate of everything our group has done,' he said in 1966, offering his guitar-wrecking performances as 'autodestructive music'.[34]

Townshend's obsessive guitar smashing was a newsworthy, aggressive masculinity licensed by avant garde aesthetics. 'At the time I considered it to be art . . . The German movement of autodestructive art. They used to build structures that would collapse. They would paint pictures with acid so they autodestructed. They built buildings that would explode. So I used to go out on stage thinking this was high art.'[35]

Who did Townshend smash his guitar for? His employers and his popularisers, to be sure. 'Smash your guitar, the Daily Mail's here' was a management instruction back in the mid-1960s. The ritual was said to originate with an accident in a low-ceilinged venue. Later, a different story was told: Townshend had first smashed a guitar in rage as a child, when his parents had temporarily parted, a separation he later remembered and recognised as an unconscious source for the narrative of *Tommy*.[36]

The repressed memory suggests that the guitar itself became a transitional object for Townshend. Playing it was a way of identifying with his entertainer parents; destroying it a way of separating from the mother, an oscillation and abjection re-enacted on stage night after night, as he compulsively smashed and replaced his instruments in defiance of all commercial logic, and even, on the occasion he claims to have stolen a replacement, the law.

The shattering of Rickenbackers became an equally compelling spectacle for the audience, guitars disappearing and returning like the promise of Modernity in Wilson's Britain. The ritual trashing of luxury goods draped in Union Jacks in 1960s dance halls was the fulfilment and repression of a masculine, Anglo-British desire for transfiguration, for better, each burst of feedback and splintering an enactment of their ambivalence about the national community into whose service they were being gendered, trained, and disciplined, a spectacular and excessive jouissance satisfying a suffering that could not be borne or named, least of all in the received discourse and practice of politics.[37]

It is no surprise, therefore, that Townshend's dismembered guitars appear to have become sacred relics of the Anglo-British nation of the 1960s, uncanny reminders of the trauma of identification and Modernity which fetch huge sums at auction.[38]

Kristeva argues that bodily movement has a 'psychic inscription'.[39] So what are we to make of Townshend's trademark scissors leaps and frenzied, windmilling, guitar style? He suggests that it was, in part, frustration at his own limited ability.[40] In fact his performances mobilise the somatic and re-enact the traumas of identification, reliving the pain of separation, and the fragility of autonomy, rendering his own body abject, just as art discourses devalorised the music industry in which he was successful, and whiteness devalorised the corporeal. Townshend's leaps, windmilling and violence were a return of the abject:

> It is terribly painful. But I'm used to the fact that there will be pain. I know that I will take my nail off at the beginning of every tour. Still. The string gets under the fingernails and rips it off. It's part of the job. I am

playing ... a windmill, 'wang, wang, wang, blood' and then I think, this is it. I've arrived. It is the place where I should be, like a boxer in the middle of a fight.[41]

Townshend's performances were clearly an occasion for Kristevan jouissance: 'One does not know it, one does not desire it, one joys in it. Violently and painfully.'[42]

His musical pugilism was both the struggle for identification and the Battle of Britain, a refusal to accept the cultural and political obstacles thrown up on the path to Modernity by a nation transfixed by its past. Townshend is aware that rock addresses the void created by separation and loss. 'In rock and roll there's this place, this space between childhood and adulthood where you're acutely aware of being alone for the first time – you're not necessarily lonely, but when you decide to leave home you're alone, and you can never go back.'[43] Here rock and roll serves as a figure for the imaginary, for the dissociation from the mother and the motherland, and from the dominant languages available to the Anglo-British speaking subject.

THE WHO SELL OUT

Pop Art in the USA was the work, during the 1960s, of Oldenburg, Lichtenstein, Warhol, Rosenquist and Wesselmanm. But here in Britain the term encompasses the work of Paolozzi, Hamilton, Henderson and Blake, much of which dates from the 1950s, and in Paolozzi's case from the mid-1940s. Pop Art's gallery simulations of commercial images and commodities undermined many of the cultural distinctions on which the authority of British cultural elites were based. As Lawrence Alloway of the Independent Group, the Anglo-British groupuscule which cleared an intellectual runway for the arrival of American Pop Art argues, 'The abundance of twentieth century communications is an embarrassment to the traditionally educated custodian of culture.'[44] Again, an Anglicisation took place. In Butskellite Britain the enthusiasts of Pop Art – and Americanisation – acknowledged the pleasures of commercial imagery but articulated them to a more egalitarian social discourse and a critique of the art establishment.

The relationship of the young Townshend to Pop Art was clearly rooted in a nascent cultural politics of this kind, an educated and youthful hedonism laced with social anger. This reflexive and critical attitude informed *The Who Sell Out*, an important and overlooked musical contribution to the debate about whether Pop Art – and Pop itself – was art or commodification.[45] *The Who Sell Out* took the Pop Art aesthetic into a new realm, that of mass aural culture and dance.

The links between the tracks on the album parody and plagiarise the advertising output of the British pirate radio and American Top 40 stations who were partly responsible for The Who's success. The companies responsible for the named products – from baked beans to cosmetics – were not amused.[46] WCMA radio in New York realised that *The Who Sell Out* was a joke at their expense and banned it. Simultaneously biting and shaking the hand that had fed them, this early Who album was both a parodic farewell to the pirate radio stations closed by the Labour government's Marine Broadcasting Act and a shot across the bows of the new Radio One.

In many ways, however, the album had missed its moment. As Giuliano points out, it was an 'offbeat petal of pop art out of season in the full bloom of the psychedelic era'.[47] Dissonant aesthetic discourses also co-existed in its production. The mini opera *Rael* – as well as the harmonic complexity of 'I can See for Miles' – was the second instalment in Townshend's ongoing engagement with an older form of cultural power and distinction, the opera.[48] And despite the critical Pop Art framework, many of the songs are introspective studies of adolescent pleasures and repressions, the enduring bedrock of pop.

This co-existence is far from accidental. As Huyssen argues, Pop Art images were neither representational nor fully simulacral. Instead 'they registered a dimension of anxiety, melancholy and loss that has perhaps become more visible with the passing of time'.[49] Townshend's songs from this period were intensified by a Pop Art-enhanced awareness of the absence of origin and authenticity, the impossibility of identity. This note was clearly audible in 'I Can't Reach You' and it pervades 'Melancholia', a song which he withheld for two and a half decades.

The fragility of male Anglo-British identification, and a fruitless search for post Mod authentication, characterises Townshend's work of the next two decades. 'I Can See for Miles', the track on *The Who Sell Out* rated most highly by Townshend, expresses the fear of a woman's sexual duplicity, which is countered with violence, even the threat of oral rape, by a drug enhanced male omnipotence. *The Great American Nudes*, by Pop Artist Tom Wesselman, are icons of depersonalised, commodified, sexuality which fetishise fragments of the female body. These anxieties are paralleled in the young Townshend's representations of women in songs like 'Pictures of Lily' and 'Mary Anne with the Shaky Hands'.

Fears about the nation are never far away from the fraught process of male identification in Anglo-British modernity. Townshend's enigmatic second mini-opera, *Rael*, which closes the album, deals with a jeopardised homeland and threatened authenticity: 'Rael, the home of my religion/To me the centre of the Earth' is under siege. Townshend rises to the defence of his imaginary nation. 'My heritage is threatened/My roots are torn and cornered/And so to do my best I'll homeward sail.'

TRANSATLANTIC ROCK AND NATIONAL IDENTITY

The Who were increasingly travelling in the opposite direction, away from their homeland not towards it, leaving Britain for tours of the American market-place, two or three times a year.[50] For Townshend in the late 1960s and 1970s this placed a strain not only on his family relationships but also on the territorialised English imaginary that characterised his work.

During this period Townshend was very critical of the culture of the Anglo-British elite, deploying that nation's abjections back against itself. 'Europe is a piss place for music, and it's a complete incredible fluke that England ever got it together', he told an American interviewer in 1968.

> England has got all the bad points of Nazi Germany, all the pompous pride of France, all the old fashioned patriotism of the old Order of the Empire. It's got everything that's got nothing to do with music ... And just all of a sudden, bang! wack! zapswock out of nowhere. There it is: the Beatles. Incredible. How did they ever appear then on the poxy little shit-stained island?[51]

Needless to say, this endeared him to the emerging and highly politicised underground culture in the United States. But it is also an index of the degree to which his Englishness, uncodable after the end of Mod, could not be articulated with the dominant national identifications.

Right from the start the biggest rewards for Anglo-British rock music were to be found in the United States, the global engine of trade liberalisation and economic growth. Money was the lure for the British Invasion, the transatlantic term for that mid-1960s process in which America ingested English products to feed its internal processes of distinction and the British music industry successfully adapted to the asymmetry of the shared market-place. It was a good example of the non-homogenising, but interconnecting, nature of globalisation. 'Since 1963 American Pop has never been able to re-establish its old dominance over European music', reports one scrutiniser of Americanisation.[52]

In 1964 The Who signed a contract with a production company owned by Shel Talmy, an American producer based in London, in order to benefit from his knowledge of what might sell in the USA. America was 'the beckoning dream' Townshend told Marsh in 1967, and The Who became part of the second wave of the British Invasion.[53] An immediate success, they picked up the Rock and Roll Group of the Year award from *Rolling Stone* magazine. In 1968 they were photographed for *Life* magazine wrapped in a Union Jack.[54] From that date most of their live performances took place in the United States, and most of their income was derived from American fans.

'The English scene for us, unfortunately, doesn't compare with America', Townshend confessed in 1968. 'The States offers us more money, fans and excitement'.[55] The British sector of the Anglo-American rock market provided cheap product launches and useful product differentiation. 'Make your name here', Townshend later said, 'but don't expect to make anything else'.[56]

'America to me is the workplace', he once reflected. 'I tend to think of Britain as the control room and America as the studio.'[57] The dispersal of Mod and the simultaneous disappearance of Anglo-British iconography from The Who's performances in the United Kingdom in the later 1960s might be taken as evidence of the homogenising force of globalisation and the evanescence of a distinctively British identification. But the Anglo-American music market addresses, and thrives on, local difference. As Townshend said of The Who's endless American tours 'we were successful because we went there to be English'.[58] Globalisation, in its transatlantic phase, fostered the local in the booming British music industry.

The development of The Who's visual identity and music away from Mod codes lends support to Stuart Hall's description of the process of globalisation: 'the homogenisation is never absolutely complete, and it does not work for completeness.'[59] Nevertheless, American audiences still posed a challenge to a band that had been modelled on, and niche marketed to, a uniquely British subculture. This was an additional factor contributing to the emergence of rock opera. As John Diamond was later to put it, 'In the Mod-free States, The Who are Tommy'.[60]

ROCK OPERA: THE ALTERNATIVE TO CULTURAL STUDIES
An emerging transatlantic ideology of Rock affirmed authenticity against the melancholy of commodification and pop culture, the prolif-

eration of representation and the circulation of substitutes – 'me for him, my coke for gin, you for my mum'- of which Townshend had long been aware.[61]

Dave Hill summarises the working distinction between pop and rock – the first based on commerce, the second on authenticity – that characterises the reporting of *Rolling Stone* magazine, its later British clone *Sounds*, and the discourse generated by influential American Rock writers like Jon Landau, Dave Marsh and Robert Christgau.[62] 'Pop implies a very different set of values to rock', Hill argues. 'Pop makes no bones about being mainstream. It accepts and embraces the requirement to be instantly pleasing and to make a pretty picture of itself. Rock on the other hand, has liked to think it was somehow more profound, non-conformist, self-directed and intelligent.'[63] Lawrence Grossberg confirms that 'Rock's special place (with and for youth) was enabled by its articulation to an ideology of authenticity.'[64]

Townshend himself was an important architect of the new discourse: 'I was one of the inventors of the late 1960s and early 1970s rock ideology. I was one of the analysts. I colluded with all of the journalists ... to sit down and invent what rock and roll meant in post-Woodstock terms ... a way to free us.'[65]

A pundit and a performer, Townshend became the leading spokesperson and exponent of what Peter Wicke calls the 'ideology of rock': 'Communication, a myth of quite magical power, was supposed to make people open up from the inside, to make them free and lead them back to their own creativity, and this was supposed to be the road to a real change in society. The common nature of the rock experience and the sensory directness of this music made it the most suitable means for achieving this.'[66]

The aim – a unity of performer and audience, the state of one in all – was an attempt to return to what Kristeva calls the chora, the unity before the separation that occurs on entry into the symbolic order. Rock ideology aspired to create a univocal crowd, a homogeneous community that could figure the alternative nation which Townshend had briefly glimpsed in Mod.

The transgressive genre of rock opera was Townshend's post-Mod bid to reorganise Anglo-British national-popular identifications, to consolidate The Who's position in the new American markets, and to achieve the collective chora celebrated in the emerging ideology of rock.

Townshend has sometimes disavowed the designation 'rock opera', but he did use the term at the time and The Who greatly benefited from its use by others to describe *Tommy*, a seventy-five minute song cycle with an overture and tightly-scored themes.

The emergence of Rock Opera coincided with a rush for orchestration by a clutch of rock bands – including the Nice, Deep Purple and the Moody Blues – eager to be associated with elite rather than popular values. Rock opera was an 'enigmatic paradox', Townshend told Andrew Motion, 'but good thinking for a group who stopped getting hits.'[67] This underestimates the genuine radicalism of the new hybrid genre forged by Townshend and his Covent Garden-going manager-mentor Kit Lambert.[68] 'Rock Opera' imploded distinctions crucial to Anglo-British hegemony. Through Kit Lambert, the eclecticism of a pre-war English music – the controversial hybrid of jazz and Franco-Russian classical music constructed by Lambert's father, Constant, a composer and theorist of the relationship between music and nationalism – transformed British rock in the 1970s.

The music of Constant Lambert was an important Anglo-British transaction with black American Jazz, French modernism and the Ballet Russe. It was a defiant disengagement from the then dominant traditions of German romanticism and English pastoral – the latter associated with Vaughan Williams – to which the English classical ear was accustomed.[69]

Although he was firmly opposed to the vulgarisation of the classical by popular influences or mechanical reproduction, Constant Lambert's transgressions – mediated by his son – paved the way for Townshend's reconfiguration of a popular and highly technological music. Fitzrovian ballet posthumously fathered 1960s rock opera. Constant Lambert's counter-pastoral served also to further insulate Townshend from the rural representations of Anglo-British identity that pervaded folk rock and progressive rock at the time, from Fairport Convention to Pink Floyd.[70]

> My father ... brought me up to distrust musical snobbery of any kind', Kit Lambert recalls. 'The music he was writing when he was nineteen and twenty was full of jazz idioms, which was considered unthinkable by the musical elite. When his music was played at the Albert Hall, people were shocked. They couldn't understand how someone of his talents could hang around with such as Louis Armstrong rather than with the classical musicians and the whole establishment BBC crowd of

Queen's Hall followers. Fortunately the musical frontiers are now beginning to disappear; classical influences are being absorbed by pop and pop by classical. And I really think there is more valid new creative music being made at the pop end.[71]

In 1956 Kit Lambert went to Trinity College, Oxford, in order to study history. Decadent in lifestyle, a drug-taking homosexual and Isis gossip columnist who had no time for the Balliol socialists of the new Left, Lambert helped to dissolve the boundaries between high and popular culture over which his peers were to anguish. He was not constrained by the anxiety that the 'Juke Box Boy' might be a 'hedonistic but passive barbarian', a concern which hampered cultural studies until the late 1970s.[72] His pioneering challenge to the monopolies in the recording industry resulted in the launch of Track, the first record label in Britain that could truly be called independent. The Oxford New Left went on to address the popular, creating new modes of discourse in order to do so, but Lambert – with his poor fourth class degree – helped transform the field of popular culture and initiated a modernisation of the music industry. He deserves to be better remembered, for he too helped fashion a distinctive and influential route 'Out of Apathy'.[73]

With *Tommy*, Townshend and Lambert challenged the distinction claimed by English cultural and political elites, interrupting the reproduction of Anglo-British whiteness far more effectively than Wilson's failing, Labourist, modernisation of the nation.

Today, Townshend looks back on the *Tommy* of 1969 as 'a naive and impudent rock piece', but the album helped open a series of new directions for popular music. The new and hybrid genre of rock opera, in conjunction with psychedelia and jazz fusion, prepared the ground for progressive rock, a term at first reserved for a rock ideology combination of art and politics but later used for 'any form of rock music which foregrounds musical expression as a discrete and sovereign means of communication'.[74]

Unfortunately, both of the major studies of this musical scene neglect The Who's contribution to the convergence of rock, classical techniques and new technologies, focussing instead on southern English bands from a university educated and Anglican culture, like Yes, Genesis, and King Crimson.[75]

A misplaced conflation of Englishness with its dominant pastoral mode explains the omission of The Who from Macan's account. He identifies 'an implicit British nationalism' in progressive rock culture, but he reduces it to 'the obvious debt of progressive rock as a musical style to English folk song, Anglican choral music, and the music of English nationalist composers such as Holst and Vaughan Williams ... the medievalism of the cover art and subject matter and the recurrent references to English folklore.'[76]

Townshend's urban, plebeian and ultimately democratising insistence that 'The Kids Are All Right' cannot be accommodated within the landed values, elite preferences and pastoral imaginary that are mobilised in Macan's construction of progressive rock. Townshend is an early but unacknowledged contributor to the 'Anglicisation of rock discourse' that Stump locates in the 1970s. His relationship to Mod, and then to a dissident English classical tradition, make that unarguable. However, for Townshend, the English pastoralism that came to the fore in progressive rock was an abjection of the urban modernity that had shaped him. The key opposition in his work is not that between town and country – the binary which made progressive regressive – but the city and the sea, a reassertion of the centrality of 1960s Brighton to his imaginary, the remembered scene of jouissance and the Mod sublime, the moment when young men fought on the beaches to rid themselves of Churchill's England.

TOMMY: A STRUGGLE FOR THE NATION'S SOUL

Tommy is many things: a survey of twentieth century Britain and its shortcomings; a complex representation of the process of male identification; a critique of the star system of the Anglo-American music industry; and a codification of the thought of Townshend's Sufi teacher, Meher Baba, who had foresworn speech. As the original rock opera has evolved from a concept album – mediated to interviewers throughout Europe and America by a voluble, self-contradicting Townshend – into the rewrites required for a film and a musical, its narrative, already highly fragmented and ambiguous in its original form, has been made to carry ever more freight.[77]

Tommy is born into an English family dispersed by war. He witnesses his mother's adultery and his father's murder of her lover when he returns many years later. The trauma of these events removes Tommy's powers of sight, speech and hearing, taking the stutter of 'My Generation', the inarticulacy of 'I Can't Explain' and the blocked process of masculine and national identification these figured, to a new level of intensity.

Throughout his childhood and adolescence, Tommy is not a speaking subject, he does not participate in language. He lives in Kristeva's lost chora, feeling only vibration. On Christmas Day he 'doesn't know who Jesus was or what praying is' and his father asks 'how can he be saved? From the eternal grave'. Although his soul appears to be in danger, his asocial subjectivity is in fact being shaped by God, from whom he gets music, excitement, opinions and 'the story'. In a desperate attempt to restore Tommy to the symbolic, his parents approach doctors and a drug dealer, the Acid Queen. They also expose him, unintentionally, to abuse at the hands of other members of the family. He is tortured by Cousin Kevin and sexually assaulted by Uncle Ernie. The Acid Queen, cousin Kevin and Uncle Ernie are the externalised menaces into which abjected drives and impulses had been converted.

Having transcended the constraints of language, his spiritual condition makes him a master of technology and a skilled performer, a 'Pinball Wizard'. This is clearly a utopic self figuration by Townshend. Tommy recovers his sight, speech and hearing when his mother smashes the mirror that sustains his silent, spiritual development, an angry reprise of the earlier separations of mother and son – love for the father and adultery – and also a representation of the violent passage through the imaginary to the symbolic.

As a result of his knowledge of the chora and his re-entry into language, Tommy becomes a Messianic celebrity, a surrogate rock star, sharing his knowledge of the sensory world of vibration – the language of God – in the punning 'I'm a Sensation'. But the representations and deprivations are imposed on his audience and therefore experienced as inauthentic. Like an unruly Mod crowd, the congregation of the evangelical, merchandising church that has been built around Tommy revolts: 'We ain't gonna take it'.

The eight line verse of homage which reappears at the end of the song cycle conflates Godliness and the rock audience into a non-blasphemous union. At live concerts it was the point where the fans joined in. It is the clearest expression of the rock ideology of authenticity, the unity of performer and audience, recreating the chora, aspired to in this period.

> Listening to you I get the music
> Gazing at you I get the heat
> Following you I climb the mountain
> I get excitement at your feet!
> Right behind you I see the millions

On you I see the glory
From you I get opinions
From you I get the story

In all the versions of this rock opera, Tommy is traumatised by the loss of an imaginary and stable familial England. *Tommy* the album dates this loss to the First World War, providing a metaphorical commentary on a century of decline. *Tommy* the musical reschedules the opening of the narrative to the Second World War. But in each and every incarnation, Townshend's rock opera is a powerful confirmation of Bracewell's suggestion that in English discourse, sick children figure a national fall from grace, and a cultural loss of innocence.[78]

Anglo-British culture placed real constraints on the performance of Townshend's narrative of the nation. At Radio One Tony Blackburn refused to play Pinball Wizard on the grounds that it was 'distasteful' and 'sick'. When the rock opera was launched at the Ronnie Scott Club in May 1969, Townshend retaliated by saying 'I think Aunty is the sickest thing in this country'.[79] As late as 1972 the Albert Hall banned a performance of *Tommy* orchestrated by the LSO. However, the album was an immediate and popular success in Britain and in the USA. The Who toured *Tommy* in 1969 and went on to play continental opera houses and the Met in New York the following year. *Tommy* was adopted by a series of opera companies.[80] The old boundaries of opera were inoperative. Townshend's rock opera later became an LSO recording, a Ken Russell movie, a Broadway show which won five Tony awards, and a highly successful touring musical.

Mindful of the rock audience's popular distinction from the classical establishment, *Tommy* was carefully balanced with a reassuring showcase of The Who's rock and class authenticity, *Live at Leeds*. However, Townshend's next project would push rock ideology – and his own mental health – to its limits.

LONG LIVE ROCK – ROCK IS DEAD
The goal of a new enlightened community created through non-linguistic, sensory communication – the chimera of the chora, or univocal community on which rock ideology, leavened with Sufi music theory, was based – prompted Townshend in 1970 to initiate the Lifehouse project. 'We want to hear the music we have dreamed about, see the harmony we have experienced temporarily in rock become permanent'.[81] The Lifehouse project was a milestone in Townshend's

search for a new form of Anglo-British community to replace and to transcend the remembered unity of Mod, which had not been recovered or improved upon.

Lifehouse began as an idea for a film about an over-populated, authoritarian dystopic society of the future consisting of a privileged few, who lived underground and wore experience suits programmed by the government, and subordinated many of poor farmers, individualists and hippies living on the polluted surface. During a six month rock and roll concert, a lost chord, the universal note, is discovered. Its vibrations create community and enlightenment.

The Lifehouse project collapsed – along with its author, who had a nervous breakdown – when Townshend tried to deliver the imaginary project for real at the Young Vic theatre in London.[82] The failure of this attempt to create an Anglo-British rock nation was a turning point for Townshend.

By now, rock music, addressing its expanding markets, and the evanescing counter-culture, which was always weaker in Britain than the United States, had taken a different path. In Townshend's case the divorce was conscious and explicit. Amongst the rubble of the Lifehouse project was the song 'Won't get Fooled Again', Townshend's riposte to the insurrectionary fantasies common on the left flank of Britain's rock generation.

Mick Farren wrote to Townshend suggesting that The Who should become the 'tool of the British revolution'. Townshend bridled at the suggestion and wrote a song which bricolaged power chords with new synthesiser technologies, and characterised revolution as a cycle which introduces new forms of injustice – a 'new boss same as the old boss' – and second, as an illusion from which the individual must protect his family. He called the song 'an anthem for the apolitical', but later admitted that he regretted writing it.[83] Somewhat ironically, the Labour Party asked if it could use 'Won't Get Fooled Again' in a party political broadcast during the 1987 election campaign.

The song appeared on *Who's Next* along with other songs from the Lifehouse project.[84] Townshend then began to write a mini rock opera, *Long Live Rock – Rock is Dead*, which along with out-takes from Lifehouse, was to evolve into *Quadrophenia*.[85] *Quadrophenia* is an audit of the successes and failures of the 1960s, the illusions of its youth cultures, and the failure of political projects to connect with popular aspirations. The original album has an even more fragmented narrative than *Tommy*, but was similarly subjected to greater closure by a subsequent film version and a number of additional songs. *Quadrophenia* merges two youth cultures, Mod and the rock audience, into a fictional simulacra of a movement that did not exist. As Marsh explains, pointing to the ahistorical conflation of mod, manual labour and class politics in the song 'Dirty Jobs', 'Townshend's interpretation of the Mod attitude made it virtually synonymous with all the most positive aspects of the 1960s counter-culture.'[86] *Quadrophenia* revisited the male process of identification and gestured towards a possible settlement between the aspirations of Anglo-British youth cultures and English class society.

Quadrophenia tells the story of a mod, Jimmy, undergoing a breakdown that involves a pluralisation of identities – four, each one based on a member of The Who, hence *Quadrophenia* . When he is separated from his girl, his scooter, his dysfunctional family home and the conflated mod-countercultural nation, Jimmy returns to Brighton, just as the culture of Mod expires.

The song 'The Punk Meets the Godfather' is an important and reflexive lament for Townshend's changing relation to youth cultures and the Anglo-British national imaginary. He is no longer 'the punk with the stutter'. The words 'My Generation' follow this line, electronically reprocessed and unrecognisable to many listeners. Townshend became 'the new president but I grew and I bent'. Through the voice of the rock audience that created but which now confronts him, he is told 'Your axe belongs to a dying nation'. 'The Punk meets the Godfather' is a powerful dialogic swan song for the ideology of rock and the most telling epitaph for the failed counter-cultural aspirations of the 1960s.

'Dirty Jobs' links the significance of that confrontation between star and audience, representative and represented, to the political militancy of the early 1970s, using samples of picket line and demonstration slogans, brass bands and the roar of the British lion. That widespread class anger is also indexed in 'Helpless Dancer'. But Townshend was no longer a rock-ideological populist with New Left leanings. 'Is it in My Head', 'I've Had Enough' and 'Drowned' are Townshend at his introspective best; the lyrics vocalise the anxieties of a popular audience without direction, a people disconnected from any national popular or dominant Anglo-British identification, and introduce a spirituality that is no longer embedded in popular culture – as it was in the days of *Tommy* and *Lighthouse* – but is offered as an alternative to it.

The Mod imaginary still calls to Jimmy and to Townshend, but there is no realistic possibility of its resurrection. Jimmy's encounter with a Bell Boy, 'the guy who used to set the paces', now an unskilled menial, is an index of the degree to which the impetus of Mod and the counter-culture is spent. But there's a secret to be learnt from the Bell Boy's job: selfless service (later celebrated in 'The Ferryman') is not a bad thing. The album ends with Jimmy overcoming a suicidal impulse, and, in 'Love Reign O'er Me', a tentative celebration of personal renewal in the form of love, godliness, family and homeland.

Quadrophenia offered little encouragement to those who would celebrate the insurgency and radical otherness of youth cultures. But it also made few concessions to those that casually dismiss them as easily incorporated effects of the market. In *Quadrophenia* Townshend provided a bleaker but more telling account of the sixties than cultural studies would soon produce, and he had the distinct advantage of addressing the nation directly.[87]

PUNK AND AUTHENTICITY

In the mid-1970s punk briefly renewed Townshend's confidence in the possibility of a rock-generated Anglo-British authenticity. Punk returned rock from its pastoral progressive mode to an urban setting, once again providing British product differentiation in Anglo-American music markets.[88] A critique from above and below, a dismissal, situationist and plebeian, of the music industry that had disseminated the rock operatics of Townshend, it was not so different from the detournement of the market that had been offered in *The Who Sell Out* or the semiotic explosiveness of The Who's performances in the 1960s. Punk reaffirmed the rock ideology of authenticity and its DIY commitment was an extension of the aspiration to unite performer and audience. It's no accident that the Sex Pistols reprised Townshend's angrily melancholic 'Substitute' from their first gig to their final album. Reciprocating, The Who themselves covered 'Pretty Vacant'.[89]

'I'm sure I invented it and yet it's left me behind', said Townshend, who had knelt at the feet of two Sex Pistols, asking them to save him. 'I prayed for it, and yet it's too late for me to truly participate. I feel like an engineer.'[90] Not all punks shared the respect accorded The Who by The Sex Pistols. The romance finally ended when the young journalists Julie Burchill and Tony Parsons turned their keyboards on the late Keith Moon, The Who's drummer, saying he was no great loss. This triggered Townshend's outraged and searing counterblast 'Jools and Jim'.[91]

By the late 1970s Townshend had developed a reflexive, if rather self important, critique of rock's place in the reproduction of the national culture. 'I'm not only part of the establishment', he said, 'I am the establishment. I am this country. People come to me to get money for their charities ... to do this or that.'[92] A growing sense, evident from *Quadrophenia* onwards, that the populist affirmation that 'The Kids Are Alright' was no longer adequate as a strategy in the drug-ridden recession of the 1970s and 1980s led to Townshend's formation of the Double O charity, his participation in Rock Against Racism, and a benefit concert for the People's March for Jobs.

Townshend spoke out against the recrudescence, in skinhead fascism, of the racialised Anglo-British insularity which Mod had once challenged with partial success.[93] In the song 'Uniforms' he addresses the negative features of regimented homogeneous, exclusive youth cultures.[94] Later he lent his support to Red Wedge – the Labour Party's attempt to engage with young people – and a campaign against heroin that the Conservative Party attempted to harness.

After his fraught relationship with punk, and the break-up of The Who, Townshend tracked the fragmentation of pop and rock culture into the diverse and increasingly decentred range of music scenes that characterise the field today. He took part in the New Romantics' exploration of gender and their ambiguous play with the trappings of Anglo-Britain's endangered elite culture.[95] He also welcomed rap as a return of the abrasiveness for which The Who remained the archetype.[96]

In the mid-1980s Townshend returned to an examination of the relationship between rock, masculinity, territory, race and nationality, both in his music and in a series of short stories written during his recovery from drug addiction.

STRANGER IN A WHITE CITY

White City was both a song cycle and a film in which Townshend performed. For the cover of the album he is photographed wearing a medal in front of the tiered council flats of Shepherd's Bush, as if he were the returned serviceman and father in *Tommy*. White City is a figure for contemporary multi-racial Britain, a critical metonym which suggests the Anglo-British might be operating a system of urban apartheid. White City is also the remembered scene of white male battles over territory and for identification, a place where 'blood was an addiction'. Give Blood has become a NHS slogan and the subtext of army recruitment appeals. 'Give love and keep blood between brothers', Townshend advises.

White City is the locale of a lost ethnicity, reprising a series of previous mobilisations to preserve the nation from threat: 'we were the defenders, we were the free'. It has become the locale of a new multiracial community that is being created against the odds. The migrant, African township rhythms of 'Hiding Out' are its soundtrack. But the White City of Thatcher's urban Anglo-Britain constantly threatened to become a non-community of weeping women, prostituted children, callous development, loneliness and Godlessness, of women's sexual duplicity and men 'Crashing by Design'. Twenty years after Mod and Wilson, Townshend finds that a non-racialised Anglo-British modernity is far from completion, and spiritually vacant.

On the album, the site at which a national community might be recreated proves elusive, as Townshend, still drawing on a Mod imaginary, puns about the need to resist, and the need to confront God: 'Try to place the place where we can face the face'. In the film, the local swimming baths offer a fragile starting point, a shared public institution that has survived the rigours of Thatcher's reactionary modernisation of the welfare state, a beach in the inner city.

TRUST IN THE PRINCE

During the 1980s Townshend overcame much of the separation anxiety and rage against the incompletion and inauthenticity of identification that had led to the destruction of so many expensive guitars and amplifiers over the years, and which had also motivated Tommy, and rock ideology, and many of Townshend's reflections on the state of the nation. He finally settled his account with drugs and with rock and roll, accepted the radical strangeness of himself and of others, and thereby reduced the tension between Anglo-British elites and dominant representations of the nation. There would be no more stuttering.

The short stories collected in *Horse's Neck* are prefaced with a poetic eulogy for motherhood that pays tribute to a mother's ability to engender separation and autonomy. 'I adored him first/I rejected him first/What did I do for him?/Only what any mother would have done.' The dreamlike recollections of a child in the dunes above a beach, whose parents come and go on horseback, result in 'a strange feeling of autonomy, but with no sense of isolation', suggesting that Kristeva's stranger within has been recognised and a new relation to formerly abjected others is possible.[97]

Rock, however, was fiercely abjected. 'The evening went from mere asphyxia to total necrophilia, and the supposedly living finally retired to another venue.' Performance no longer engaged the semiotic: 'We were the frayed rubber band inside the enormous balsawood airline of rock and roll. Flying was a forgotten art'.

In 1985 the global transmission of Live Aid, a charity concert to assist Ethiopia, repositioned and revivified rock as a commodity for a new generation and a much expanded market. The Who, having briefly reunited to raise money for the cause, regained a great deal of their old profile. But rock ideology's leading exponent had become its leading detractor. 'It's a toothless form', he was to say.[98] 'The only promise of rock is another power chord.[99]

However, the external menace of rock was the sign of a continuing internal attraction. For it has propelled Townshend into music theatre, where he is now locked in a form of 'perverse vengeance' on Andrew Lloyd Webber, for combining theatre and design with scores that are written as if rock had never happened.[100] 'Rock and roll needed to be brought to Broadway ... I always felt that Tim Rice and Andrew Lloyd Webber, with Jesus Christ Superstar, rode off with part of my inheritance. I wanted to claim it back. Now I've done so.'[101]

Townshend's entry into music theatre has resulted in *The Iron Man*, a musical dramatisation of a book by Ted Hughes for children, *Psychoderelict*, a song cycle about the vulnerability of an ageing rock star which takes the form of a radio play, and the Broadway success of *Tommy*.[102] Music theatre is a form which allows not only a narrative didacticism, something rarely missing from Townshend's work, but also a closure – 'it's necessary to bring a story to a conclusion' – that rock disavows.[103]

Townshend's iconoclasm today derives from his apparent scepticism about ideas and cultural forms which suggest that identities are unstable, all meanings are unfixed and all narratives are open ended. Perhaps it's because he feels he's been there before. And perhaps it is also because some form of national-popular is needed in order to secure political action.

For Townshend the twin failures of Wilsonite modernisation and rock ideology had reinforced each other, attenuating public life and displacing youth from politics.

> Something happened between the Trad age and rock ... In the Trad age there were great people doing great things, funding CND or Amnesty,

and trying to mobilise young people. But then the whole subject of politics and the power of the individual to effect change was buried under this tidal wave of rock. Had the Labour government in the 1960s carried out the things that the younger, more radical supporters had hoped, maybe that would have made a difference. It might have made a difference if people like me felt that by wearing buttons, and going on five Aldermaston marches, we were achieving something. But we achieved nothing, and felt we achieved nothing.[104]

He now dismisses the counter-cultural and insurrectionary aspirations of the 1960s, finally laying to rest the ghost of rock ideology. 'In time it will be regarded as one of the great ridiculous ages, largely because of people's lack of perspective, lack of a sense of reality, and their inability to realise how they could change things through the system already there.'[105]

Looking back on the 1960s he now argues for a more inclusive national-popular identification than rock ideology was capable of engineering:

> It's time to admit that we were kids, that we didn't know what our parents had actually done, what they had done on D-day, the horrors they had faced, and that perhaps the only way to deal with them was a more romantic music ... It all used to be about driving generational wedges between people. But it's not about that anymore.[106]

Life is based on interdependence and it requires an 'uncomfortable selflessness'[107] Townshend's new-found familialism – and an articulation of his spiritual themes with traditional notions of emotionally controlled Englishness – is therefore congruent with the ethos of the regeneration agencies and the ethical socialism and communitarian themes that paved Labour's route to office in the mid-1990s.[108]

The Mod fellow traveller whose anger was aroused three and a half decades ago, when the crown commanded the removal of his symbolic reminder of American Modernity and English backwardness from the streets of Belgravia – 'Why don't you all f-fade away?' he wrote – has developed a new relationship with the monarchy.[109] After working with Prince Charles on a collection of speeches while an editor at Faber in the mid-1980s, Townshend began to assist the annual Rock galas of the Prince's Trust.[110] Thus commenced a move from a modern ethnic nationalism to an identification with the surrogate nationalism of the monarchy. A decade later *Quadrophenia* was the highlight of a Prince's Trust concert in Hyde Park which drew a crowd of 150,000 people during the twilight of the Conservative's 'reactionary modernisation' of Britain and what appeared to be a new crisis of succession. Townshend loaned the cultural assets of Mod, and The Who, to the modernising wing of the monarchy.

Townshend still has a powerful ability to vocalise Anglo-British dissent. His 1993 song 'English Boy' – 'Hold me down and I will bite' – spells out the challenge facing those who seek to strengthen and win new identifications to an inclusive national community.[111] 'There are no tools, no toys for any English boys', he complained. 'Your promises to train me, are just attempts to restrain me.' Anglo-Britishness and whiteness clearly dissociated in this compelling unhegemonised figure which threatens Anglo-Britain with its abject: 'I'm black on the tube line, red on the touch-line'. Ignored by politicians, treated with prejudice, despised as thick and regarded as a thug, the urban English boy has no connection to any national-popular. Look no further for an emblem of social exclusion. 'English Boy' suggests that there is nothing complacent or, indeed, irreversible, about the recent settlement Townshend has reached with an elite which can no longer resist modernisation.

NOTES

1. Townshend's music of the early 1960s is an important if frequently unacknowledged influence on punk and on contemporary Britpop. Reflecting on the early years of The Who, the most authoritative popular music directory points out that 'From these albums it is clear where bands such as Dodgy, Blur, Swervedriver and Oasis get their Cockney rock from. One of the finest groups of our generation have now become one of the most influential.' Colin Larkin (ed), *The Guinness Encyclopaedia of Popular Music*, vol 6, Square One Publishing, 1995, p4467.

2. Chris Welch, *Teenage Wasteland: The Early Who*, Castle Communications, Chessington 1995, p29 and Geoffrey Giuliano, *Behind Blue Eyes: A Life of Pete Townshend*, Hodder and Stoughton, London 1996, p31.

3. Pete Townshend, 'Introduction' to *The Who's Tommy: The Musical*, Pantheon Books, New York 1993, p7.

4. Interview in *Playboy*, February 1994.

5. See Dave Marsh, 'The Who' in A. Decurtis and J. Henke (eds), *The Rolling Stone Illustrated History of Rock'n'Roll*, Plexus, London 1992, p165; Larkin

(ed), *op.cit*, 1995, p4209; and Roy Shuker, *Understanding Popular Music*, Routledge, London 1994, p120.

6. I have also taken this position in O Tempora, *New Times*, August 1997, p2.

7. A. Bloom, *The Closing of the American Mind*, Simon and Schuster, New York 1978.

8. Paul Morley, 'The Unimportance of Being Townshend', *New Musical Express*, 12 March 1983, p29.

9. Pete Townshend interviewed in John Tobler and Stuart Grundy, *The Guitar Greats*, BBC Publications, London 1983, p83.

10. For example artist Malcolm Poynter, interview with the author, December 1996: 'I went down to the Marquee and saw them. I didn't like it at all. I said to myself, this isn't Mod, and cleared off.'

11. Richard Barnes, *Mods!*, Plexus, London 1991, p9.

12. Dick Hebdige, *The Style of the Mods*, Stencilled Occasional Papers, Sub and Popular Culture Series, no.20, University of Birmingham Centre for Contemporary Cultural Studies 1973; 'The Meaning of Mod' in S. Hall and T. Jefferson (eds) *Resistance Through Rituals: Youth Subcultures in Postwar Britain*, Hutchinson, London 1977, pp87-98; 'Object as Image. The Italian Scooter Cycle', *Block* 5, Middlesex Polytechnic, London 1981, pp 44-64.

13. See Giuliano, *op.cit*, 1996, p39.

14. Pete Townshend, quoted by Kevin Jackson, *The Independent*, 13 November 1993, p52.

15. Pete Townshend, quoted in Dave Marsh, *Before I Get Old: The Story of the Who*, Plexus, London 1983, p131.

16. 'Pete Townshend interviewed by Jan Wenner' (1968) in *The Rolling Stone Interviews 1967-80*, St Martin's Press/Rolling Stone Press, New York, p38.

17. During a transmission of *Whole Scene Going*, BBC, 5 January 1966.

18. *The Rolling Stone Interviews 1967-80*, *op.cit*, p39.

19. Cited in Andrew Motion, *The Lamberts: George, Constant and Kit*, Chatto and Windus, London 1986, pp299-300.

20. Townshend quoted in Welch, *op.cit*, 1995, p29.

21. Giuliano, *op.cit*, 1996, p63.

22. Pete Townshend, 'Substitute', on The Who, *A Quick One*, Reaction 593 002, 1966.

23. Giuliano, *op.cit*, 1996, pp51-52.

24. Barnes, *op.cit*, 1991, p14.

25. 'The Meaning of Mod' in Hall and Jefferson (eds), *op.cit*, 1977, p89.

26. See Simon Frith, *Sound Effects: Youth, Leisure and the Politics of Rock'n'Roll*, Constable, London 1983, pp16-21; and the critique in Keith

Negus, *Popular Music in Theory*, Polity Press, Oxford 1996, pp100-122. Geoff Dyer's *White*, Routledge, London 1997, clarifies what is at stake in this binary and how it operates.

27. Paul Gilroy, *The Black Atlantic: Modernity and Double Consciousness*, Verso, London 1993.

28. See the picture taken at the Scene club in 1964 in Barnes, *op.cit*, 1991, p14.

29. Richard Barnes, *Mods!*, Eel Pie Publishing, London 1979.

30. Pete Townshend quoted in 'It's Still a Mod, Mod World', *Melody Maker*, 14 October 1978, pp39-41.

31. See Mark Ellen's report in *Mojo*, August 1996, pp110-111.

32. See John A. Walker, *Cross-Overs: Art into Pop, Pop into Art*, Methuen, London 1987.

33. Andreas Huyssen, 'Mass Culture as Woman: Modernism's Other' in Tanya Modleski (ed), *Studies in Entertainment: Critical Approaches to Mass Culture*, Indiana University Press, 1986.

34. During *Whole Scene Going* transmission, BBC, 5 January 1966.

35. Giuliano, *op.cit*, 1996, p55. See also 'Miles interviews Pete Townshend', *International Times*, 13-26 February 1967, pp5-6. This affiliation was the subject of a reunion discussion between Townshend and Metzger at the Institute of Contemporary Arts in London in June 1998.

36. *Playboy*, February 1994.

37. For the close relationship between jouissance and the abject see Kristeva, *op.cit*, 1982, p9.

38. Townshend's guitars have changed hands for prices in excess of £20,000 at auction.

39. Francoise Collin, 'The Ethics and Practice of Love' in Mitchell Guberman (ed), *Julia Kristeva: Interviews*, Columbia University Press, New York 1996, p66.

40. *The Rolling Stone Interviews 1967-80*, *op.cit*, p35.

41. Interview in *Playboy*, February 1964.

42. Julia Kristeva, *Powers of Horror: An Essay on Abjection*, Columbia University Press, New York 1982, p9.

43. Quoted by Kevin Jackson, *op.cit*, 1993, p52.

44. Lawrence Alloway, 'The Long Front of Culture', *Cambridge Opinion* 17, 1959. The article is excerpted in David Robbins (ed), *The Independent Group: Postwar Britain and the Aesthetics of Plenty*, The MIT Press, Massachussetts 1990, pp165-6. However, for a warning against a too simple linkage between the Independent Group and Pop Art see Anne Massey, *The Independent Group: Modernism and Mass Culture in Britain 1945-59*, Manchester University Press, Manchester 1995.

45. The Who, *The Who Sell Out*, Track 613 002, November 1967.

46. Chris Stamp, 'B.O, Baked Beans, Buns and The Who' in *Rolling Stone*, 14 December 1967, p6.

47. Giuliano, *op.cit*, 1996, p83.

48. The first was 'A Quick One While She's Away' on The Who, *A Quick One*, Reaction 593 002, 1966.

49. Andreas Huyssen, 'Popartretrospective', *Documenta X*, Cantz Verlag, Kassel, 1997, p399.

50. The full itinerary can be followed in Joe McMichael and 'Irish' Jack Lyons, *The Who Concert File*, Omnibus Press, New York 1997.

51. *The Rolling Stone Interviews 1967-80, op.cit*, p43.

52. Michael Watts 'The Call and Response of Popular Music' in C.W.E. Bigsby, *Superculture: American Popular Culture and Europe*, Bowling Green University Popular Press, 1975, pp123-39.

53. Marsh, *op.cit*, 1983, p232.

54. *Life*, 28 June 1968, pp62-3.

55. Marsh, *op.cit*, 1983, p285.

56. *Ibid*, p285.

57. Pete Townshend quoted by Dave Schulps in 'Pete', *Trouser Press*, 27 April 1978, p17.

58. The Who, *The Kids Are Alright*, BMG Video 74321-100873.

59. Stuart Hall, 'The Local and the Global' in Anthony D. King (ed), *Culture, Globalisation and the World System*, Macmillan, London 1991, p28.

60. John Diamond, 'Not a Question of Who But Why?', *The Times*, 8 October 1989.

61. Townshend, 'Substitute', *op.cit*, 1966.

62. Jon Landau, *It's Too Late to Stop Now: A Rock'n'Roll Journal*, Straight Arrow Books, San Francisco 1972; 'Rock has betrayed itself', Dave Marsh concluded in *Springsteen: Born to Run*, Omnibus Press, New York 1981, p6; Robert Christgau, *Christgau's Guide: Rock Albums of the 70s*, Vermillion 1982.

63. Dave Hill, *Designer Boys and Material Girls: Manufacturing the 1980s Pop Dream*, Blandford Press, Dorset 1986, p8.

64. Lawrence Grossberg, *We Gotta Get Out of this Place: Popular Conservatism and Postmodern Culture*, Routledge, New York and London 1992, pp204-5.

65. Tom Hibbert, 'Who the Hell Does Pete Townshend Think He Is?', *Q magazine*, July 1989, p6.

66. Peter Wicke, *Rock Music: Culture, Aesthetics and Sociology*, Cambridge University Press, Cambridge 1990, p110.

67. Motion, *op.cit*, 1986, p336.

68. See Clive Barnes 'Opera: Mefistofele as Strong Theater', *New York Times*, 26 October 1969, p82; and 'First Hit Opera', *BMI*, December 1969, p20.

69. Constant Lambert, *Music Ho! A Study of Music in Decline*, Faber and Faber, 1934.

70. Edward Macan, *Rocking the Classics*, Oxford University Press, Oxford 1997.

71. Kit Lambert quoted in Motion, *op.cit*, 1986, p305.

72. Richard Hoggart, *The Uses of Literacy*, Penguin, London, 1958, p250.

73. The title of the original New Left anthology and the proceedings of a 1989 conference on its achievements. See E.P. Thompson, *Out of Apathy*, New Left Books, London 1960; and The Oxford University Socialist Discussion Group, *Out of Apathy: Voices of the New Left Thirty Years On*, Verso, London 1989 for accounts of New Left aspirations and achievements by those involved.

74. Paul Stump, *The Music's All That Matters: A History of Progressive Rock*, Quartet Books, London 1997, p9.

75. *Ibid*, and Macan, *op.cit*, 1997, pp144-166.

76. Macan, *op.cit*, p154.

77. The Who, *Tommy*, Track 613013/4, May 1969. Ken Russell's film version for Colombia Pictures was released in 1975. Des McAnuff and Pete Townshend's adaptation for stage opened on Broadway in 1993.

78. Michael Bracewell, *England is Mine: Pop Life in Albion from Wilde to Goldie*, Harper Collins, London 1997, p7.

79. Townshend quoted in Welch, *op.cit*, 1995, p64.

80. Ira Robbins, 'Twenty Five Years of Tommy' in *The Who's Tommy: The Musical*, Pantheon Books, New York 1993, p17.

81. Townshend quoted in Barnes, *The Who: Maximum R&B*, Plexus, London 1996, p99.

82. See the account in Marsh, *op.cit*, 1983, pp368-379.

83. Pete Townshend quoted in Robin Denselow, *When the Music's Over: The Story of Political Pop*, Faber and Faber, London 1989, p97.

84. The Who, *Who's Next*, Track 2408 102, July 1971. Songs from the Lifehouse project also appeared on *Quadrophenia*, Track 2657 013, November 1973. The ideas behind the project also inform 'Grid Life' on Pete Townshend, *Psychoderelict*, Atlantic 7 82494-2, 1993.

85. Marsh, *op.cit*, 1983, p396.

86. *Ibid*, p422.

87. S. Hall and T. Jefferson (eds), *Resistance Through Rituals: Youth Subcultures in Postwar Britain*, Hutchinson, London 1977.

88. See the account in Vivienne Westwood: Shadow monarch in this volume, pp125–127.

89. Joe McMichael and 'Irish' Jack Lyons, *op.cit*, p180.

90. Marsh, *op.cit*, 1983, p422. See also Chris Welch 'The Return of You Know Who' *Melody Maker*, 17 September 1977 pp8-10. The nightclub encounter with the Sex Pistols generated the song 'Who Are You' on the album of the same name, Polydor 2490 147 WHOD 5004, August 1978.

91. On Pete Townshend, *Empty Glass*, Atco 1980.

92. Townshend quoted by Dave Schulps, *op.cit*, 1978, p18.

93. 'Pete Townshend interviewed by Greil Marcus (1980)', *op.cit*, p412-3.

94. On Pete Townshend, *All The Best Cowboys Have Chinese Eyes*, Atco SD 38 149, 1982.

95. See the analysis of the New Romantics in Michael Bracewell, *op.cit*, p206.

96. Giuliano, *op.cit*, 1996, p262.

97. Pete Townshend, *Horse's Neck*, Faber and Faber, London 1985, p11.

98. *Playboy*, February 1994.

99. Giuliano, *op.cit*, 1996, p223.

100. Hibbert, *op.cit*, 1997, p7.

101. *Playboy*, February 1994.

102. Pete Townshend, *Psychoderelict*, Atlantic 7 82494-2, 1993; *The Iron Man*, Virgin Records, CDV 2592, 1989.

103. Pete Townshend, 'Introduction', *The Who's Tommy: The Musical*, Pantheon Books, New York 1993, p7.

104. Quoted by Robin Denselow, *op.cit*, 1989, p93.

105. *Ibid*, p95.

106. Robert Koehler, 'New Take on Tommy', *Los Angeles Times*, 8 July 1994.

107. Pete Townshend, 'Townshend Lets Loose', in *The Who's Tommy: The Musical*, Pantheon Books, New York 1993, p94.

108. Paul Morley, 'The Unimportance of Being Townshend', *New Musical Express* 12 March 1983, pp28-30.

109. Hibbert, *op.cit*, 1997, pp5-7.

110. 'Townshend lends the Prince a hand', *Rolling Stone*, 5 August 1982, p22.

111. On Townshend, *Psychoderelict*, *op.cit*, 1993.

5

Vivienne Westwood: the shadow monarch

Once 'the Queen of punk', and seamstress to the Sex Pistols, Vivienne Westwood is now described as 'British fashion's controversial madame', and 'the Queen of British designers'.[1] The tabloids call her a 'whacky fashion queen', often greeting her work with raucous, if anxious laughter.[2] By critics and cheerleaders alike, the language of monarchy is used to describe Westwood. After all she was the fashion designer who in 1997 masqueraded as Elizabeth I in a series of photographs promoting her 'Five Centuries Ago' collection and her company has taken an orb as its logo. The tropes of fashion journalism and Westwood's self-coronation are wholly appropriate. For like no other designer before her, she has taken up the task of redefining the English imaginary.

Westwood has made new English identifications possible by retelling Anglo-Britain's sumptuary past and by revealing how the nation has been constantly recoded, othered, and differentiated by costume. Her work has explored the historical figures of the Anglo-British imaginary, overturning and making strange some of its most cherished assumptions. She makes those who wear her clothes, or simply admire them, strangers to themselves. They can no longer dress for authentication and fixity of identity. Reversing the 'glamour of backwardness' identified as the sign of monarchy and surrogate nationalism by Nairn, Westwood deployed glamour against Thatcher's reactionary modernisation of the nation and the residual and insular identifications of the Anglo-British.[3]

Soon after taking office Prime Minister Tony Blair, undeterred by Westwood's tabloid reputation for eccentricity, invited her to a Downing Street gathering for celebrities. Labour was keen to harvest the political associations and economic benefits of Cool Britannia – in part based on the high standing of British designers in the global fashion industry – and was also concerned to check the designer brain drain, an exodus forced in part by the fact that Britain's textiles manufacturers are in the main geared to low quality mass production.

British fashion matters: design houses from New York to Milan snap up talent nurtured in the nation's multiracial urban culture and art schools. They are headhunted to operate at the highest levels of the industry: John Galliano at Dior (pipping Westwood herself to the post), Alexander McQueen at Givenchy, Stella McCartney at Chloe. The editors of the two leading American fashion magazines – Anna Wintour and Liz Tilberis – are British, and British supermodels like Kate Moss and Naomi Campbell are amongst those most sought after.

The cheerleaders for Cool Britannia made the most of this new ascendancy. And so they should, for British fashion's prominence was based on French failings – among them a hierarchical educational system, a lengthy apprenticeship requirement, and an economic downturn producing low morale – that are remediable and possibly temporary.

The British media's ambivalence about Westwood reflects the very small market for luxury goods that exists in a country whose manufacturing pride still rests on its Fordist past and which abjects high fashion as an expression of French and Italian decadence. Valerie Steele has described how in the late eighteenth century – in the very period to which Linda Colley has dated the creation of Britons as protestant Francophobes – 'the fashion in men's attire changed as more and more people came to perceive sober male dress as being a reflection of patriotism (versus arisocratic cosmopolitanism)'. [4]

The discomfort also derives from the ways in which Westwood's catwalk couture and European workspace destabilises traditionally gendered and territorialised Anglo-British identifications. Further compounding the problem is the fact that the cultural status of women is projected on to fashion, so it repeats, on the level of clothing, the mythic situation of Women in Western civilisation, at once sublime and childlike. The nervousness with which the centre left greets Westwood is the reflex of a gendered and racialised nationalism, and comes from people who have forgotten Gramsci's injunction 'not to be afraid of innovations and audacities'. [5]

Although voted British Designer of the Year in 1990 and in 1991, in the mid 1990s Westwood denounced the 'lack of support' for the fashion industry in the United Kingdom and threatened to leave the country. 'I am always thinking of leaving Britain and maybe I should leave now', she said. 'England is too terribly puritan'.[6]

Westwood has relocated her production process to Italy as a result of the lengthy turnaround times and poor quality of finish that characterise British manufacturers with little experience in meeting the demands of a market in which quality is a key aspect of product differentiation. But only a year after her outburst she was back in the national fold, having decided that the launch of her demi-couture Red Label lines should take place during London Fashion Week, thus ending a ten year absence from London's catwalks.

She is a fashion designer with an interest in philosophy and literature, the history of ideas and the social history of dress. 'If I were to die only having done my fashion career', she has said, 'I wouldn't feel that I'd achieved at all what I would want to do'.[7] Her couture is informed by a cultural politics that has grand designs on the English imaginary.

In the 1970s, as the partner of Malcolm McClaren, Westwood helped to engineer the punk assault on three practices shaping Anglo-British identifications – the pop industry, royalty and high street mass-produced clothing. She has dedicated collections to John Stuart Mill, Oscar Wilde and paganism. Westwood, who insists she has now substituted a philosophy of art for arts' sake for her original punk aesthetic, must not be taken at her word. Her catwalk performances are not just recodings of gender and the erotic, based on new articulations of fabrics, cuts, garments and the body. They are often spectacular forums for ideas about history, liberty and national identity, startling promenades that rummage deep into English imaginaries, re-inventing Anglo-British tradition.

In Westwood's work the discourses of politics and of beauty central to racialised processes of national identification and distinction are confronted. For example, there is the early case of the parachute shirt, a hybrid cotton shirt and harness which bore the slogan: 'Only anarchists are pretty'. This theme also appears in her more recent use of invented multi-tartans, Boucher paintings on corsets, or pin striped bowler hats for women.

Although she has promoted Bertrand Russell's argument that 'Every age has its typical folly, and that of ours is nationalism', Westwood's historical exploration of our gendered national identifications produces an idiosyncratic but incisive cultural nationalism of its own.[8] 'I am English, and I parody the English, with the hope that my clothing will have an international significance'.[9] Her counter-hegemonic use of

Anglo-British historical figures is a translation of imperial codes that, in a process of inequitable imperial alterity, shaped competing national identifications across the globe. As a result Westwood's critical nationalism is peculiarly salient in a transnational market.

Westwood rips clothing from the bound volumes of costume history and the constraints placed on 'vestimentary meaning' by received national codes and ideologies of gender.[10] Her design work dislocates and fetishises garments from the national archive in a unique exploration of gender, territory and historical time. Modern pirates wear full sleeved seventeenth century shirts; the inlaid patterns of an eighteenth century mirror are transferred to a contemporary stretch velvet evening dress; the crinoline and the corset return from the Victorian era; the Queen's teenage wardrobe is revamped. Juliet Ash calls Westwood's method a 'surmontage of dissimilarities (cultural and technical) from which emerges a new form and new idea, whether concerning sexuality, dress, cut, history, painting, music, dance, catwalk performance, philosophy, age, youth, time.'[11] I'd like to add national identity to that extensive and accurate list. Westwood's surmontage interrogates many of the historical narratives that shape the English imaginary, establishing new relationships with traditional and present alterities. Her method enacts, at the level of the garment, the 'chain of democratic equivalences' that Chantal Mouffe describes as a precondition for the pluralism required in our time.[12]

Westwood frequently invokes a romantic and elitist critique of the condition of Britain. Her backward looking glamour was developed in order to counter the priorities of Thatcher's reactionary modernisation of Anglo-Britain by means of the free market and the strong state. 'Clothes should be the badges of culture and civilisation', Westwood insists, invoking a binary that has long constituted the core of British romantic anti-capitalism, from Coleridge and Carlyle to cultural studies.[13] Her pastiche arrived too late to provide any comfort to the old Anglo-British elites whose codes it deployed.

In a more complex reversal than the 13 hour clock that runs backwards on her World's End shop, historical time itself is gathered and pleated by Westwood's creations. 'What I tend to do is use things that already exist in history. At least, the elements exist and the originality lies purely in my interpretation.'[14] The historical narrative of the nation, an important source of our gendered national identifications, alterities and abjects, is dismantled and recreated in Westwood's atelier, just as she once dismantled old garments to discover the secrets of their cut. Whatever her stated intentions, Westwood's work is a pointer to a new way of living in modernity.

FASHION IS MODERNISATION

In 1997 there was an attempt to showcase and canonise post-war British fashion in *The Cutting Edge*, a major exhibition, at the Victoria and Albert Museum.[15] This followed a period of renewed government interest in the future of the fashion and clothing industry, which had been restructuring in a period of extended recession and intensified global competition. A state-led attempt to address the issues of the poor competitiveness, poor quality and low market position of British textiles and clothing manufacturers commenced under the Conservatives. The need for change will become even more pressing as European monetary union approaches.

In post-imperial England, national identity is no longer as salient a factor in the differentiating machine that is fashion as it was in the era of the colonies. The Anglo-British today, at their ease in American denim and sportswear, and at work in mass produced lines, retain few defining garments of their own. Outside the Home Counties, where the ideals of a landed gentry and an increasingly assertive lobby for a residual 'country way of life' retain a strong presence, there is little evidence of an explicitly nationalist form of dress, like the Indian dhoti once advocated by Gandhi, or the sari in Bengal.[16]

If the leisure wear of the gentry is still distinctive, and plays a role in the internal differentiation of the cultural and political elite – for example in the Barbour jacket under Thatcherism – the civilian uniforms of Empire have long gone. Neither are there stigmatised garments like the kilt or the zoot suit once were. The battle over the Sikh turban has been fought and lost by the Anglo-British, and there is no indication at present, despite the increase in Islamophobia, that the French crisis of the hajib will transfer to England.[17] So in the clubs and on the streets, it once again falls to the Union Jack, in multiple translations and ethnic recolourings – from the ripped t-shirt of Prodigy's lead singer to the browns and yellows of the version worn on the cover of the new Asian style magazine, *Second Generation* – to serve as the vehicle for national identifications. The flag of the Union is once again a fashionable icon, nowhere more prominent than in its adoption by Oasis and the Spice Girls, or in the body painted version that a topless model paraded up and down the catwalk as she opened London Fashion Week early in 1998.

Fashion studies forgets the nation

While the role of fashion in modernity is increasingly debated, its relationship to national identity has been neglected. Bourdieu argues that fashion is complicit in the reproduction of an unequal class society, while Baudrillard suggests that as 'the most superficial game and the most profound social form', fashion is the perfect expression of postmodernist culture, the sign at play in realm of simulation.[18] In a similarly contradictory vein, the Krokers suggest that fashion is 'an early warning system' of major cultural transformations, but also a conservative practice providing the appearance of change amidst stasis.[19] Lipovetsky regards fashion – understood as the expression of individual choice and the celebration of the new – as virtually synonymous with democracy and modernity.[20] Whichever characterisation you prefer, and I will not be attempting an arbitration here, it is clear that the field of fashion is increasingly acknowledged as central to social reproduction. What is missing is any sense of its articulation with national identifications.

In a popular introduction to the field, Malcolm Barnard has examined 'the ways in which fashion and clothing have been used to construct class and gender identities and the ways in which they have reproduced those identities.'[21] He appears indifferent to the crucial relationship between these identities, fashion and national identifications. Jennifer Craik rightly points out that 'Codes of dress are technical devices which articulate the relationship between a particular body and its lived milieu, the space occupied by bodies and constituted by bodily actions. In other words, clothes construct a personal habitus'.[22] But Craik's notion of habitus is faulty: it excludes any sense of nation. As they do not acknowledge that identity and habitus are always articulated to a national identification, neither writer is able to properly address the complexity and achievement of Vivienne Westwood.

A pursuit of the exotic is one of the defining components of fashion practice. This is not always based on a primitivising representation of racialised others, nor is it always the case that the other is easily marginalised or incorporated by fashion. Kondo shows how the arrival of Japanese designers like Kawakubo, Yamamoto and Miyake in the European and American marketplace during the 1980s helped to destabilise western notions of gender and race.[23] But national codings and readings of haute couture – a factor which Westwood brings to the fore through her displacements of time and raids on the Anglo-British and

118

European costume archives – remain important in the consolidating of national-popular identifications.

ANGLO-BRITISH FASHION HISTORY IN A THIMBLE

Haute couture, the making of customised and limited edition garments for wealthy individuals, began in mid-nineteenth century France, when a British designer, Charles Worth, started to dress the royalty and aristocracy of Europe and began to supply model garments to stores in France, England and America.[24] Paris has attracted the most prominent Anglo-British designers ever since, from Norman Hartnell, who discovered 'the unforgivable disadvantage of being English in England' during the 1930s, right through to the designer brain drain of today.[25]

Over the same period, from the 1850s onwards, Britain became a major textiles and clothing manufacturer. There is a clear dissociation between these two developments. British design's talent for conception did not elicit a parallel interest in execution from its manufacturers. Britain did become renowned for clothes connoting English aristocratic values and country and sporting life, evident in the international sales of companies like Aquascutum, Barbour and Burberry. But its high fashion designers and its manufacturers branded the nation with their backs to each other, and failed to operate as an integrated outfitter.

'Fashion as we know it is the result of the exchange of ideas between France and England', Westwood has said.[26] Certainly, there has always been a cross-Channel rivalry in fashion, even if the field of differences has now expanded to include the work of designers from Italy, America and Japan.

When Charles Worth died in 1895, the *Times* applauded his achievements: 'The boy from Lincolnshire beat the French in their own acknowledged sphere ... and from Paris extended his undisputed sway all over the civilised and a good deal of the uncivilised world'.[27] This nationalist trope was still in common use during the 1990s renaissance of British fashion. 'All Paris awaits the coming of the plumber's son from Streatham' *The Independent* said of McQueen's impact.[28]

In 1909 when Lady Asquith invited the French designer Poiret – whose trotteur walking skirts had granted a new freedom of mobility to women of the elite – to show his work at 10 Downing Street, British designers and clothiers were outraged.[29] British and American designers did not slip the leash of their Parisian pacesetters until the occupation of France during the Second World War. In Britain, however, war shortages quickly overrode the new autonomy, and a government regulated Utility genre was imposed which restricted the number of pockets, buttons, seams and pleats to be used in garments. This was the period of what Cunnington later called 'dictated costume'.[30]

The post-war Labour government maintained the utility regulations into peacetime. While Britain was still subject to rationing, Christian Dior's luxurious New Look – a refeminising gesture which returned to the pre-war convention of a fetishistically narrow waist with heavily emphasised breasts and curves – was launched in France. The New Look was financed and encouraged by the textiles magnate Marcel Boussac, who toured and marketed the style worldwide.

In Britain, Dior's prodigious use of fabric – a post-Liberation jouissance – was condemned as profligate by Harold Wilson at the Board of Trade and by Sir Stafford Cripps, the exchequer of austerity. But Dior won the admiration of a war weary Anglo-British public, the nation's two princesses and many ready-to-wear manufacturers. Paris had snatched back its position as market leader, and Dior's ascendancy – to which Westwood paid homage in her 1991 Dressing Up collection – was soon complemented by the rise of the houses of St Laurent, Fath, Laroche and Givenchy.[31]

The state had failed the fashion industry, in war and in peace. During the war the Incorporated Society of London Fashion Designers had been set up with the support of the Government and of textiles manufacturers. It was meant to develop and deliver a strategy that would earn hard currency – dollars, to be exact – for the nation as the conflict raged. It had little impact on the industry. In 1946 the Council of Industrial Design (COID), staged an interesting but ineffective 'Britain Can Make It' exhibition at the Victoria and Albert Museum. It showcased Anglo-British high fashion, menswear and accessories and also promoted British manufacturers. But fashion was largely omitted from the displays and exhibitions that accompanied the 1951 Festival of Britain. John Woodham's explanation suggests the reason for the failure of these early initiatives: 'Fashion, in its very essence, was readily associated with a short lifespan and was an activity about which the male modernist of the COID felt distinctly uncomfortable'.[32]

The mid-nineteenth century birth of haute couture had coincided with two developments that reconfigured the field of fashion: the arrival in Britain of the sewing machine, developed in the United States, and the birth of the department store. These two aspects of modernity eventually democratised fashion and transformed the purpose and position of haute couture.

In the late nineteenth century, fashion had been driven by the caprices of a cosmopolitan social elite influenced by the stage. Film dominated developments in the mid-twentieth century. In the years since the 1960s the purchase of haute couture has remained the activity of a cosmopolitan elite, but youth and pop culture have become the new catalysts for stylistic change. There is a fast lane to the top of the trade for a small number of the designers able to articulate new developments in pop culture with new textiles technologies and techniques for the construction of garments.

Today, catwalk shows are a form of promotion and brand differentiation for fashion houses whose main business is the merchandising of more affordable diffusion collections, cheaper ready-to-wear garments and mass-produced accessories. These commodities greatly influence popular notions of Italianness, Frenchness and Britishness. Their codings trouble governments too. As Steele notes, an early 1970s controversy over skirt length – the midi versus the mini – was 'interpreted in the United States in geo-political terms: as French dictatorship versus American freedom'.[33]

Mary Quant was Westwood's most significant predecessor as an Anglo-British female designer. Like the early Westwood, Quant also worked at the interface of fashion and pop culture. She became successful in international markets, helping to define Britishness overseas, and was also subsequently courted by politicians. Quant was awarded an OBE in 1966 for her services to fashion exports. She collected the honour in a mini skirt, the garment for which she became famous. It is absolutely characteristic of the nationally articulated field of fashion that the invention of the mini skirt is the subject of a fierce dispute between Quant and French designer André Courreges.

Swinging London, the figurative precursor of Cool Britannia, signalled the convergence of affluence, cultural liberalism, entrepreneurialism and the prospering pop industry that occurred in the capital city in the 1960s. The fashion of Swinging London was produced by designers like David Sassoon, Marion Foale, Sally Tuffin, Ossie Clarke and Anthony Price, who all studied at RCA in late 1950s and 1960s.

During this period haute couture houses lost their ability to set fashion agendas, and a dispersed, polycentric form of development commenced. The late 1960s have been described as a period in which 'fashion was not in fashion'.[34] After the watershed of 1968 St Laurent concluded, rather prematurely, that 'Recent political events make haute couture a thing of the past'.[35] But the reproduction of Anglo-British elite cultures was interrupted. The upper and middle-class Season, which required dress of distinction, did begin to falter. Youth cultures and dress styles began to proliferate. Their styles defied social gravity and trickled upwards.[36]

Ready-to-wear manufacturers also began to lose their market share to fierce competition from eastern manufacturers. Haute couture, mainstream dress options and street fashion were undergoing a major rearticulation, driven by new and dispersed centres of influence, as Westwood opened her first shop on the Kings Road. By the 1990s, as Valerie Steele says, 'the Empire of Fashion had become Balkanised'. There was no central authority and fashion houses had to track lines of development, and select agents of change, in very unfamiliar spaces.[37]

There is no longer a high society for haute couturiers to dress, nor a substantial elite culture that seeks to distinguish itself with high cost customised clothing. In fact it has been estimated that 'the modern market consists of fewer than 3,000 women worldwide prepared to pay £10,000 for a suit'.[38] Fortunately for Westwood, one of them is Lady McAlpine, the wife of the Tory grandee, who has purchased more than 200 of her garments.

Haute couture is now being led by the high street. It is adjusting to its new role as a high profile branding mechanism for the rest of the activities of the house, positioning a wider range of franchised products in the marketplace, from sunglasses to tights, and contributing to 'multiple fashion systems that compete and interact'.[39] Westwood, a self owned company, was long exempt from this logic. But it too is beginning to diversify into franchised products. Early in 1998 Westwood launched a new high street line with an old name – *Anglomania* – recycling the wide range of styles she has created over the years for the affluent sector of the international youth market.

If the Anglo-British fashion industry is to feel the full benefit of the wind of appreciation that is currently blowing its way an imaginative intervention by the government will be required. As fashion is now dominated by large global brands, a significant investment in design houses, new forms of textile engineering, and new partnerships between design and manufacturing, is required if Anglo-British companies are to operate successfully in the changing market. A strategy based on low quality mass clothing will founder on the rocks of the

Pacific Rim, China and the former eastern bloc, all of which will remain cheap sources of manufacturing. The British Fashion Council is encouraging mainstream retailers to take on designers as consultants and it is trying to overcome the historical gulf between British manufacturers and designers that outsource to Italy. This is a start. But if Cool Britannia is to avoid a serious chill, it will require more than exhortation and a stable macro-economic framework.

THE KINGS ROAD AS THE ENEMY WITHIN

Pop musicians, royals and film stars disseminate Anglo-British fashion. It was by dressing the musicians that were associated with her partner Malcolm McClaren – including the New York Dolls, the Sex Pistols, and Adam and the Ants – that Westwood's work first became widely known. In 1997 the Spice Girls were the most prominent globe trotting ambassadors for Britain in the increasingly blurred fields of pop, fashion and diplomacy, as their visit to South Africa with Prince Charles demonstrated. Westwood has dismissed them as 'animals with no style'.[40] A quick sketch of the trajectory of her career will be needed if the apparent reversal of her attitude to pop culture is to be explained.

Westwood was born in a lower middle-class family in a mill town in Derbyshire during the war. She started working as a seamstress and designer in the early 1970s, making clothes for the shop she opened with her partner Malcolm McClaren on the Kings Road. The shop underwent a number of rapid transformations and name changes and it was to promote a series of counter Anglo-British styles.[41]

At first McClaren and Westwood's shared hostility to a residual hippy culture and emerging Glam rock styles expressed itself in a nostalgic transnational celebration of 1950s American rock and roll. Westwood crafted drainpipe trousers and velvet trimmed drape suits for a Teddy Boy revival. The shop, Let it Rock, was dressed as a 1950s sitting room. Biker inspired t-shirts with studded tyres serving as trim at the armholes were an early example of her willingness to use transgressive materials in her garments.

In 1973 the premises were renamed Too Fast To Live, Too Young To Die. Westwood and McClaren traded in fetish wear and sado-masochistic biker gear. Deracialising their Americanised identification, they recreated Zoot suits. After a prosecution for obscenity, the confrontation-seeking entrepreneurs promoted a range of customised sexual rubber goods. Situationist slogans appeared on the walls and the shop was renamed Sex. Sex's ambition was to abolish the distinction between the public and private. It had a naive confidence in the transience of Anglo-British gendered identifications: 'The whole point of Sex is that we want to inspire other people with the confidence to live out their fantasies and to change ... We really are making a political statement with this shop by attempting to attack the system. I'm also interested in getting people to wear some of our sex gear to the office. "Out of the bedroom and into the streets!" now that would really be revolutionary'.[42]

Sex began to trade in the Anglo-British abject, inverting mainstream identifications. Among the garments on sale were the controversial Cambridge Rapist tee shirt, bearing an image of the rapist's mask, and a 'Which Side of the Bed' t-shirt canonising the good and demonising the bad in British culture. One half of the garment listed hates, the other loves. In this reversal of received values, Betjeman, Vogue, pop stars, the Arts Council, country living and the clothing and antiques trades were abandoned in favour of prostitutes, illicit drinking, anarchism, pornography and black culture.[43]

Bondage trousers – a transformed Americanism, the idea having been taken from the suits worn by US pilots – were displayed alongside masturbation skirts, 'God Save Myra Hindley' tops, bondage shirts with long sleeves that wrapped around the body, as on a straitjacket, and a range of 'Fuck your mother', breast emblazoned and pornographic t-shirts. These garments all figured abjected material or key moments in the process of gendered identification. The commodities for sale in Sex raised issues of language and the unconscious, crucial to politics, but unthinkable within most discourses in the political domain.

Whatever the shops' debt to Reich, its practice was informed by the situationist discourse to which McClaren and graphic designer Jamie Reid had been introduced by King Mob, a London network that had been expelled from the Situationist International.[44]

Westwood and McClaren may have overestimated the capacity of the libido to transform the nation, but they had identified processes central to the maintenance of the English imaginary, and set about creating obstacles to its reproduction and dissemination.

A further revision of the shop occurred in 1976. Seditionaries finally abandoned Americana as a means of countering Anglo-Britishness and replaced it with signs from Nazi Germany, the wartime Other of the Allies. One wall of the shop was a blown up photograph of the remains of Dresden after its wartime bombing and firestorm, an incident widely considered an allied war crime. On the facing wall was Picadilly Circus, upside down. A ragged hole in the ceiling simulated bomb damage. Hanging from the racks were 'Destroy' t-shirts bearing inverted swastikas and the defaced head of the Queen. Safety pins, razor blades and silver phalluses were among the accessories offered by this shop for 'soldiers, prostitutes, dykes and punks'.

The trading space of Seditionaries reversed the Anglo-British certainties of the post-war era. Savage points out that the shop's use of the swastika 'served notice on the threadbare fantasy of Victory'.[45] More importantly, it was an appropriation of the abject, a fraternisation with the external menace, hostility to which helped a failing Anglo-Britain to maintain its artificial unity. The Swastika sublime was a provocative, modernising impulse in a counter-imaginary that also famously transfigured the unifying monarch into a savage, deglamorising and primitivising her with a safety pin through the nose on the cover of The Sex Pistols' single *God save the Queen*. In this song, a hit during the silver jubilee celebrations, Anglo-Britain itself was abjected as a 'fascist regime'; Anglo-Britain feared the swastika, and Anglo-Britain was fascist. England was doubled. No authentic national identification was possible. The future was voided.

PUNK, THATCHERISM AND HAUTE COUTURE

Westwood's graduation from punk to haute couture is not the radical departure that it might at first appear. For both punk and haute couture are practices of distinction from the commercial cultures of modernity. And both are based on a dissociation from dominant national identifications that results in a double consciousness and sense of the artificiality of representation. Fred Vermorel suggests that for McLaren and Westwood, 'punk was rooted in a contempt for the values of "the popular"'. It was, he says, 'an exercise predicated on a distrust and despair of what electrified the hit parade or excited the tabloids. Far from being, as it is so often represented, an attack from below, punk was a snob's revenge from on high.'[46]

The musical project associated with Seditionaries had unexpected effects. John Lydon dismissed their situationist affiliation of his mentors as 'Mind games for the muddled classes'; and in her account of situationism Sadie Plant claimed that punk was 'a detournement of the culture industry' which managed its own recuperation. Jon Savage is perhaps closer to the truth when he observes that McLaren and Westwood 'planned a hype which became a real culture'.[47]

In retrospect punk appears more a child of hegemony than its nemesis, despite the contemporary left's attempts to articulate some of its themes with politics – in movements like Rock against Racism – and its continuing inflection and historicisation of punk's meaning.[48] Thatcher's modernisation also aspired to the destruction of the core institutions and identifications of Anglo-Britain. The Conservatives dismantled public services which had formerly unified the experience of the nation – the NHS, the BBC, and education. Thatcher removed the privileges of the cultural and political elites that had been created by the Keynesian welfare state. Her 'reactionary modernisation' was in fact driven by a surprisingly large number of the 'Hates' listed on McClaren and Westwood's 'Which Side of the Bed' t-shirt.

The figuring of Thatcherites as punks in the satirical puppet show *Spitting Image* was probably not wide of the mark as far as Conservative traditionalists and left conservationists were concerned.[49] It was this unacknowledged congruence that made Westwood's April Fool mimicry of Thatcher on the cover of the *Tatler* so disturbing. Westwood wasn't Thatcher. Thatcher wasn't punk. But their similarities wouldn't go away. Thatcher was punk, and punk Thatcher.[50]

Aesthetically, punk was also not what it seemed. Punk may have appeared to attack notions of originality and genius, but it was dressed to kill by a talented cultural strategist who firmly subscribed to these traditional aesthetic categories. The Kings Road engine of 1970s media-oriented punk and the contemporary catwalks of Paris, London and Milan have a radical, anti-commercial mandarinism in common. As Vermorel says of punk, 'the notion that "anyone can do it" was also the idea that it's all crap anyway; the spectre of the Swindle was there from the start ... Far from being a democratising call, this was a sardonic indictment of popular taste – of what could pass for talent, and therefore a covert vindication of elitism. At the core of punk was the aesthete's hollow laugh.'[51]

This antipathy to popular modernity remains Westwood's position today. She believes that far from being democracies our governments are 'plutocracies, ruled by money' in which 'cultivation of art, intellectual speculation and pure science ... have become devalued'.[52] Her continuing opposition to the direction taken by Anglo-British modernisation is what connects Westwood's punk iconoclasm to her later high romanticism, lending support to Elizabeth Wilson's characterisation of fashion as 'modernist irony'.[53] The Anglo-British failure to check the effects of cultural markets is the link between Westwood's early notion of anarchy as beauty and her contemporary dismissal of the '95% of the people in the world' who are weeds and useful plants rather than orchids.[54]

Westwood's itinerary is not a familiar tale of deradicalisation. As she approached the ever dispersing centre of the fashion industry in the years after punk, her costume transformations did become part of the fashion archive and did contribute to the positioning of Anglo-Britain in transnational fashion markets.[55] But her design work cannot be contained by the English imaginary. Gan describes her resort to the historical archive as 'more theatrical than threatening', but accounts of her work as disengaged or incorporated underestimate the force of her belief that 'the only subversion lies in ideas'; they also underestimate the importance of language, signification and identification, and the degree to which Westwood has succeeded in her aim of 'cultivating doubt'.[56]

Today Westwood usually trawls through philosophy and history, rather than street style, for her design resources. The result is a high cultural nationalism with a marked disdain for the American casual wear that dominates the global youth market. 'I hate that American sportswear look. It is for hyper-active idiots who have no taste.'[57] Sporty Spice romps in the field of commerce, popular modernity and market-led modernisation which Westwood has always sought to reconfigure and detourne. That's why the seamstress of punk rejects the populist and inclusive cultural nationalism disseminated by the Spice Girls.

FABRICATING A POST-IMPERIAL NATIONAL IDENTITY

Westwood has a distinctive approach to history and modernity: 'If anyone is trying to be modern', she says, 'it's a cliche'.[58] As an alternative to the constant celebration of the new, Westwood disrupts linear time, exhuming uncanny fragments of figures and narratives from the national past. But there is a forbidden zone in her archive, the period from the early 1960s to punk. She dismisses the work of designers who reproduce styles taken from the 1960s and 1970s as 'historicism scraping the barrel'.[59] Here Westwood's abjects still operate: the codes and themes of Swinging London are viewed as exclusive, complacent and inauthentic from the vantage point of the northern lower middle class, an internal margin of the nation; the counter-cultural rock nation was devalorised by the art-school milieu to which she gained access through McClaren.

Westwood's raids on fields of discourse usually distinct from fashion, and her resort to disruptive materials and improper historical combinations, are reminiscent of the vestimentary codebreaking pioneered by Schiaparelli during the interwar years. Schiaparelli drew freely on aesthetic modernism. She borrowed surrealist, cubist and primitivist iconography and introduced transgressive materials like tree bark, straw and glass into her garments. She also hybridised clothing genres, for example by producing a tweed evening dress.[60]

Westwood's mimicry of the historicised postures and costumes of the Anglo-British and her articulation of these elements with the adornments of national or gendered Others, reconnect dress and identity with somatic and semiotic drives previously abjected. Westwood is partially conscious of the process at work: 'Art is parody: it uses what went before; it simplifies, but it also sythesises something else with it ...'.[61] Westwood's sumptuary memorialising, and the ease with which she handles gendered and national abjects – that 'something else' – is a reflexive renegotiation of an English imaginary that creates and disseminates, however fleetingly, as fashion, the possibility of new positionalities and identifications.

Westwood's designs are often transformations of canonical artefacts, a transfer of material from the fields of painting or sculpture to that of fashion, like the cashmere and sheepskin reproduction of the clothing in a restaged Holbein painting.[62] Juliet Ash has described the links between Westwood's 1990 Cut 'n Slash collection and Watteau's 1717 painting *Pilgrimage to the Island of Cythera*, and those between her 1989 fig leaf tights and Greek male statuary.[63] The slashed shirts of the 1990 menswear collection were transformations of Tudor hose prompted by a Tissot painting; the 1995 Vive la Cocotte collection reworked pagan themes found in the Venetian paintings of Tiepolo.[64] In each case, historical narratives and gender identifications are interrupted by the rearticulations and recodings in her work.

In her first catwalk collection, Pirate, launched at Olympia in 1981, Westwood responded to the tight breeches and frothy lace adopted by the New Romantic movement which followed punk with bagginess, bad cutting and forms of patching that were historically authentic. Pirate was a leap beyond the coded confines and identifications of punk, its excess fabric, ethnic borrowings and proliferation of colours providing a moment of jouissance and transformation.

Pirate was followed by the Buffalo Girls in the 'Nostalgia of mud' collection, another staged encounter with the abjected animality and formlessness of the neocolonial other. These sheepskin capes, peasant skirts and baggy tops with brassieres worn outside, were offered as a tribute to the women of Peru. Nostalgia of Mud cannot be dismissed as a colonial appropriation and recycling of difference, confirming racial distinctions. This clothing was designed to establish a new relationship with the body and with others, unsettling the reproduction of racialised identifications. The hybridity and scopic pleasures of the fashion photograph, which recorded this restaged rendezvous of the abject with racialised western bodies, disseminated figures of the non-reproduction of Anglo-British whiteness and transatlantic blackness. The scorn and laughter directed at Westwood were an index of the challenge she posed to English imaginaries. A year later the Witches collection further addressed the uncoded drives and anxieties of the English with disruptive material drawn from Haitian voodoo rituals. In the early 1980s Anglo-British whiteness was already unstable and re-negotiating its positionalities. Westwood placed rocking platform shoes on its feet.

1983 was a year of change. Westwood was invited to show in Japan and in Paris. She was the first British designer to be asked to exhibit in the French capital since Mary Quant. This breakthrough was not the result of any cosmopolitanism on Westwood's part. As we have seen, her work is a very specific national engagement of wider transnational interest. Westwood's mobile Anglo-Britishness was simply more interesting than other design work that confirmed the gendered national identifications of the English.

By 1983 Westwood had separated from Malcolm McClaren and began to receive financial backing from Italian investors. The mid 1980s were still financially precarious, but Westwood had stepped out of the Kings Road and into a global trading space. As a result her exploration of Anglo-Britishness transferred to a brightly spotlit international stage.

The transatlantic components of Anglo-Britain's national identifications and alterities were the first to receive her attention. In 1984 her Clint Eastwood show shuffled nineteenth century labouring clothes, made from denim, with Amerindian garments and City of London top hats, producing new Anglo-American hybridities and reintroducing aspects of the historical relationship long suppressed or abjected by ongoing fears of Americanisation.

For the rest of the 1980s Westwood was to revisit an eighteenth century European elegance, redeploying Watteau, Boucher and Fragonard in a retro-Rococo counterpoint to the power dressing and profiteering of the transatlantic neoliberal culture crafted by Reagan and Thatcher. 1984 was also the occasion of the first outing of the mini crini, where the 1960s were mediated through Victoriana. This encounter re-eroticised the crinoline, freeing it from formerly distancing and pacifying associations.

In her October 1987 'Britain Must Go Pagan' collection Westwood established historical connections between a contemporary vogue for slashing jeans, the medieval venting of garments and features of renaissance clothing, embracing the premodern as a means of countering reactionary modernisation and the youth cultures she increasingly regarded as integral to it. 'We are materialistic and barbaric', she announced, before launching her 1988 show, Civilisade, one dedicated to Matthew Arnold.[65] Rococo and harlequin styles jostled with armoured sweat-shirts and saris in changing rooms crowded with counter-English iconography.

In Britain, haute couture has always had a special relationship with the Crown. London dressmakers to the Court, from Worth through Hartnell to Hardy Amies, have benefited from the royal family's bestowal of distinction on their garments, informing the fashion preferences of the nation. The late Diana, Princess of Wales, served as a media clothes horse for a troupe of contemporary British designers including the Emmanuels, Conran, Oldfield, Pollen, Wakely, Sassoon and Walker. Westwood dismissed the rendezvous between royalty and popular modernity enacted by Diana. 'The princess isn't a trend setter ... she's someone ruled by the trends'.[66]

In the mid-1980s Westwood laid claim to the throne, metaphorically usurping the pretenders who had allowed neoliberalism to lay waste to the nation. In 1986-87 Westwood erased the distinction between the two faces of the monarchy, the ceremonial figure and the country-woman, normally distinguished by separate modes of Queenly dress. The crown itself was recreated in Harris Tweed and fake ermine. The effect was a hyperbolic, and hyperreal Anglo-Britishness, which reconnected the monarch with the vested interest of landed wealth, reopening the question of the missing national-popular.

The monarchy enters Westwood's work first as a punk abjection, and then from the mid-1980s as an engulfment by the codes of the crown. This encounter was enabled by what the royal family and Kings Road punk were discovered to have in common: an antipathy to

Thatcherism, the form which Anglo-British modernisation had taken, and an attachment to acommercial values jeopardised by the operations of the market. The safety pin inserted into her nose a decade before was also, as it turned out, a claim on the Queen. But even Westwood's usurpation of royal iconography could not insulate it from the pressures of popular modernity. Her designs are now available at the affluent end of the high street, in many dissemination lines and even as a Swatch watch. Nevertheless, in 1997 – in the troubling, doubling tradition of photographic masquerade that includes Anselm Kiefer's Nazi salutes, Cindy Sherman's impersonations and Mark Wallinger's Self Portrait as Emily Davison – Westwood had herself photographed as Elizabeth I.[67]

The highpoint of Westwood's deconstruction of gendered national identities is her work with tartan, the Victorian fiction in which a national identification subordinate to the Anglo-British has long been wrapped. Tartan is the sign of a fictional Scottishness, the cloth of a noble savage translated and supplanted by the Union and modernity. It is a fabric in which the monarchy has long cross-dressed, in order to maintain a working, hierarchical Union with the other, and from which the kilt – long regarded as feminising abjectwear by the Anglo-British male – is made.[68]

Westwood's hybrid multitartan garments – prominent in her 1993 *Anglomania* show – are a pseudomonarchic appropriation of a cloth once proscribed by the English, to assist a reflexive Anglo-British modernisation. In these garments the Anglo-British margins are gathered into the centre in a startling, Baudrillardian hyperreal. Westwood's tartans, constantly inserted into bustles, jackets, suits and hats, are a permanent reminder in her work of the fabrication of national identities, of their contingency and relation to power.

Far from 'modelling Brigadoon', Westwood's dressing of Black British model Naomi Campbell in these hyperbolic fictions induces a violent shuttling between the received meanings of Anglo-British white nationhood, the new positionalities compelled by its Scottish and black interlocutors and their own provisionality.[69] These outfits are an unstable figuration of national and counter-national identifications, fascinating and troubling to the English imaginary.

Westwood celebrated the fall of the Berlin Wall with her Hoenecker collection, which included male suits with bottomless trousers. 'The fabric around the buttocks represents the Berlin Wall – unduly constricting to personal freedom', she explained. 'Now the buttocks are celebrating their new freedom'.[70] Erotic, abjecting, or both, these suits testified to the continuing encounter between the discourses of politics, gender and beauty in her work. These clothes have radical implications for the Anglo-British male and the reproduction of his line.

'It is not possible for a man to be elegant without a touch of femininity', Westwood later observed. 'I am trying to get away from that broad-shouldered, macho look for men. I knew when I did that 'crini' collection that it would influence menswear, inverting the balance of the broad-shouldered line to the hips. I am really proud of the cut of my men's trousers, with ballooning fullness to the leg, but slim on hips and waist.'[71] This profile reintroduced Anglo-British masculinity to an orientalised and gendered alterity. The campaign was sustained with satin codpieces sampling paintings by Boucher in her 1990 Portrait collection, and the smocks, berets and long collars celebrated in her 1991 tribute to Oscar Wilde. Man, a Westwood line of clothing designed to interrupt the reproduction of traditional nationally identified masculinities, was launched in 1996.

Westwood had long reversed the sumptuary laws of the feminism of the late 1960s and 1970s. In the early 1990s, as Euroscepticism and a new British austerity reprised the themes of the immediate post-war years, Westwood's Dressing Up collection re-enacted the post-Liberation jouissance of Dior in an unfettered celebration of the luxuriance of the New Look and a defiant, politically incorrect replication of its hourglass femininity, an impulse further developed in the romanticism of the later collections, On Liberty, Erotic Zones and Cafe Society.

Gendered national identifications, and the mechanisms that produce and reproduce them, have remained a focus of her critique. In 1991 Westwood hyperbolised the traditional clothing of the Anglo-British countrywoman by attaching panniers to outdoor skirts and placing kitsch Spaniel prints on scarves and corsets. In her 1992 Amour show, members of a nuclear family appeared to make love to each other. Sons and fathers in penis-emblazoned underpants undressed mothers and daughters on the catwalk.

Celebrations of a female eroticism long excluded by the rituals of Anglo-British reproduction have continued to characterise Westwood's work. In 1994 she produced the Prostitute Shoe, a seven inch gold stiletto with a loveheart buckle. That year her collection was called Erotic Zones and dedicated to John Stuart Mill's essay *On*

Liberty. A new libertarian feminism, attentive to the fetish and to pluralism, was beginning to catch up with her.[72]

CAN VIVIENNE BE TAMED?

Westwood's attempt to dislocate gendered, Anglo-British national identifications has been countered by strategies of marginalisation, recuperation and closure, with varying effect, by a range of agents: her market rivals, fashion buyers, journalists and Downing Street are among the most significant. The implication of her work – that there can be no authenticity, national, gendered or racial, only an incessant recoding of who we are – has been part acknowledged and part muted by hegemonising strategies. As a result Westwood's accounts of who the English have been and who they might become have been tailored into fragile but traditional tales of Anglo-British distinction.

Certainly it is true that 'what fashion can always coopt is the outrageous'.[73] After a calculated pause, Zandra Rhodes embraced punk couture in 1979, introducing discrete rips and diamante safety pins into her designs. Westwood's externalised corsetry and brassieres were subsequently adopted by Jean Paul Gaultier, Lagerfeld and Madonna. Her innovative mini-crinolines were copied by Lacroix. Her influence was trickle up as well as trickle down, and some of her once startling re-articulations of garments became familiar clothing tropes.

Westwood has also been partially recuperated by the notions of quality and distinction disseminated by Anglo-British elites and marketing personnel. As we have seen, Westwood herself participates in this discourse. Tim Logan, the fashion merchandise director at Liberty's, describes her work as 'Fantastic theatre but the basis is still her exceptional tailoring and use of the best British textiles'.[74] The journalist Hilary Alexander has trotted out the same trope: 'throughout the peacock parade, she displayed her devotion to the tradition of Savile Row tailoring and British style with ... exquisite cut and finish ...'[75]

British companies in luxury non-couture markets have also been able to take advantage of Westwood's design practice. In the mid 1990s the 1783 collection was a joint initiative with the quality carpet manufacturer Brintons, named after the year in which the company was founded. Westwood's garments – coats, waistcoats and morning gowns, court dresses and hats in eighteenth century styles – were all made from Brinton's Axminster and Wilton carpet.[76]

The press for a long time lampooned Westwood the celebrity. It was an offensive her amodern sensibility expected and welcomed; but she underestimated the success it would have in marginalising her work. 'I believe what Mill argued' she has often said; 'that people with exceptional talent are freaks and that some are eccentric enough to get picked on by the herd.'[77] Westwood has not been demoralised by her detractors. 'It is ... a badge of honour in this conformist age.'[78]

In 1989 Jasper Conran protested that 'She's our greatest designer; she's probably the world's greatest designer and she hasn't even been recognised in her own country. The rest of the world is laughing at us because of it. What's the matter with the British?'[79] John Fairchild, editor of the American fashion trade bible *Women's Wear Daily*, cited Westwood as the best of the six greatest designers of the twentieth century.[80] Praised abroad for her deconstruction of Anglo-British identity, Westwood has been treated as peripheral at home, where her work unsettles configurations of power. Anglo-British political and design elites, imprisoned in an English imaginary, could take neither the joke, nor the full measure of her work.

Westwood finally received the Designer of the Year award for two successive years, first in 1990 and in 1991. This recognition was consolidated by an OBE in 1992. With the success of her ready-to-wear Red Label, a £20 million annual turnover and new plans for merchandising and breaking into the youth market, she was increasingly accepted as a successful businesswoman and an Anglo-British archetype – even if her clothes are best appreciated in Japan. As an asset in the international market place, her counter-hegemonic design work is being assimilated into the national-popular. As a result, Downing Street could not afford not to embrace her.

Does Labour understand the stab at English certainties Westwood continues to make with her needle? As an amodern, shadow monarch she is unlikely to provide safe window dressing for national renewal. But a dialogue, of sorts, has begun. It remains to be seen whether Labour's attempt to modernise the social and economic armature of Anglo-Britain, renewing our national and familial identifications, can co-exist harmoniously with Westwood's catwalk transgressions of the English imaginary. The odds, I believe, are not good.

NOTES

1. 'Will this be Dior's new look?' *The Independent*, 14 August 1997; *The Independent*, 13 August 1997, p1; and Katherine Road, Press Association News report, 3 February 1997.

2. *The Sunday Mirror,* 1 September 1996.

3. Tom Nairn, *The Enchanted Glass*, Radius, London 1998.

4. Valerie Steele, 'The Social Political Significance of Macaroni Fashion', *Costume* 19, pp94-109.

5. Antonio Gramsci, *Selections from Cultural Writings*, Lawrence & Wishart, London 1986, p51.

6. Vivienne Westwood quoted in Alison Veness, 'Flouncing Out in Style', *The Evening Standard*, 17 October 1995.

7. Vivienne Westwood quoted in 'She's so 20th century', *The Times*, 11 September 1993.

8. Lynn Barber, 'How Vivienne Westwood Took The Fun Out Of Frocks', *The Independent on Sunday (Review)*, 18 February 1990.

9. Vivienne Weswtood quoted in *Paris Match*, 12 May 1997.

10. The notion of 'vestimentary meaning' is taken from Roland Barthes, *The Fashion System*, Hill and Wang, New York 1967.

11. Juliet Ash, 'Philosophy on the Catwalk' in Juliet Ash and Elizabeth Wilson (eds), *Chic Thrills*, Pandora, London 1992, p169.

12. Chantal Mouffe, 'Hegemony and New Political Subjects' in Cary Nelson and Lawrence Grossberg (eds), *Marxism and the Interpretation of Culture*, Macmillan, London 1988, p99.

13. Vivienne Westwood quoted in Liz Smith, 'Cutting Edge of British Style', *The Times*, 10 July 1990.

14. Vivienne Westwood quoted in Sally Brampton, 'God Save the Queen, The Fashion Regime', *The Times*, 12 October 1991.

15. See Amy De La Haye (ed), *The Cutting Edge: Fifty Years of British Fashion 1947-1997*, V&A Publications, London 1997.

16. A. Mazrui, 'The Robes of Rebellion' in *Encounter* 34:2, 1970, pp19-30; D. Nag, 'Fashion, Gender and the Bengali Middle Class' in *Public Culture*, 3:2, pp93-112.

17. See *British Muslims and Islamophobia*, The Runnymede Trust, London 1997; and Tariq Modood, *Not Easy Being British: Colour, Culture and Citizenship*, Trentham/Runnymede Trust, London 1992.

18. Pierre Bordieu, *Distinction: A Social Critique of the Judgement of Taste*, Routledge, London, pp378-9; Jean Baudrillard, *Symbolic Exchange and Death*, Sage, London 1993.

19. A. Kroker and M. Kroker (eds), *Body Invaders: Panic Sex in America*, Macmillan, London, 1988, p16 and p45.

20. Gilles Lipovetsky, *The Empire of Fashion: Dressing Modern Democracy*, Princeton University Press, New Jersey 1994.

21. Malcolm Barnard, *Fashion as Communication*, Routledge, London 1996, p5.

22. Jennifer Craik, *The Face of Fashion: Cultural Studies in Fashion*, Routledge, London 1994, p4.

23. Dorinne Kondo, *About Face: Performing Race in Fashion and Theater*, Routledge, London 1997.

24. Edith Saunders, *The Age of Worth*, Longmans, London 1954.

25. Norman Hartnell, *Silver and Gold*, Evans Brothers, 1955, p14.

26. Vivienne Westwoood interviewed in de la Haye (ed), *op.cit*, 1997, p198.

27. Quoted in Elizabeth Ewing, *History of Twentieth Century Fashion*, Batsford, London 1997, pp14-15.

28. Marion Hume, *The Independent* 29 January 1996.

29. Ewing, *op.cit*, 1997, pp66-7.

30. C.W. Cunnington, *Englishwomen's Clothing in the Present Century*, Faber and Faber, London 1951.

31. See the account in Valerie Steele, *Fifty Years of Fashion: New Look to Now*, Yale University Press, New Haven and London 1997, pp12-13.

32. Quoted in Amy de la Haye 'Introduction' in de la Haye (ed), *op.cit*, 1997, p18.

33. Valerie Steele, *op.cit*, 1997, pp83-4.

34. *Ibid*, p79.

35. *Ibid*, p68.

36. Ted Polhemus, *Street Style: From Sidewalk to Catwalk*, Thames and Hudson, London 1994.

37. Steele, *op.cit*, 1997, p146.

38. Rebecca Fowler, 'Are these the Emperor's New Clothes', *The Independent*, 15 July 1996.

39. Craik, *op.cit*, 1994, p13.

40. Press Association News, 1 October 1997.

41. A full and detailed account is provided in Jon Savage, *England's Dreaming*, Faber, London 1991.

42. Vivienne Westwood quoted in 'Buy Sexual', *Forum*, June 1976.

43. Fred Vermorel, *Fashion and Perversity: A Life of Vivienne Westwood*, Bloomsbury, London 1996, p72.

44. A Situationist genealogy for punk is provided by Greil Marcus in *Lipstick Traces: A Secret History of the Twentieth Century*, Harvard University Press, Massachusetts, pp18-33; for a detailed rebuttal see Stuart Home, *Cranked Up Really High*, Codex, London 1995, pp19-30.

45. Savage, *op.cit*, 1991, p241.

46. Vermorel, *op.cit*, 1996, p184.

47. See John Lydon, *Rotten: No Irish, No Blacks, No Dogs*, Hodder and Stoughton, London, 1993, p207; Sadie Plant, *The Most Radical Gesture: The*

Situationist International in a Postmodern Age, Routledge 1992, p145; and Savage, *op.cit*, 1991, p537.

48. David Widgery, *Beating Time*, Chatto and Windus, London 1986.

49. Roger Law, *A Nasty Piece of Work*, Booth-Clibborn, London 1992.

50. *Tatler*, April 1989. Reproduced in Gene Krell, *Vivienne Westwood*, Thames and Hudson, London 1997, p21.

51. Vermorel, *op.cit*, 1996, p184.

52. Vivienne Westwood, *'Why Britain should go Pagan'*.

53. Elizabeth Wilson, *Adorned in Dreams: Fashion and Modernity*, Virago, London 1985, p15.

54. Vivienne Westwood quoted in Brampton, *op.cit.* 1991.

55. Since September 1994 Westwood's punk bondage gear has been regularly auctioned at Christie's. See Peter Watson, 'Bondage, up yours', *The Observer*, 3 September 1995.

56. See Stephen Gan, *Visionaire's Fashion 2000: Designers at the Turn of the Millennium*, Laurence King Publishing, London 1997; Juliet Ash, 'Philosophy on the Catwalk: the Making and Wearing of Vivienne Westwood's Clothes' in Juliet Ash and Elizabeth Wilson (eds), *op.cit*, 1992, p179; Vivienne Westwood quoted in *ibid*, p174.

57. Vivienne Westwood quoted in Liz Smith, 'Cutting Edge of British Style', *The Times*, 10 July 1990.

58. Vivienne Westwood quoted in Steele, *op.cit*, 1997, p152.

59. Vivienne Westwood quoted in Mark Holgate, 'The Prime of Miss Vivienne Westwood', *Vogue Catwalk Report*, spring/summer 1998.

60. Palmer White, *Elsa Schiaparelli: Empress of Paris Fashion*, Rizzoli, New York 1986.

61. Vivienne Westwood quoted in Ash, *op.cit*, 1992, p172.

62. In Westwood's *Man*, spring/summer 1997 collection. See photograph in Gene Krell, *op.cit*, 1997, p71.

63. Ash, *op.cit*, 1992, pp167-185.

64. See photographs in Krell, *op.cit*, 1997, pp62-3.

65. Vivienne Westwood quoted in Liz Smith, 'Civilised Anarchy', *The Times*, 4 October 1988.

66. Diary, 'Westwood Ho!', *The Times*, 6 July 1995.

67. See Krell, *op.cit*, 1997, p73.

68. See the discussion of tartan in David McCrone et al, *Scotland the Brand: The Making of Scottish Heritage*, Edinburgh University Press, Edinburgh 1995, pp50-56.

69. 'Modelling Brigadoon' was the description offered by McCrone et al, *ibid*, p53.

70. Vivienne Westwood, quoted in Bel Littlejohn, 'Hail Vivienne, Queen of all our Hearts', *The Guardian*, 12 January 1996.

71. Vivienne Westwood quoted in Liz Smith, 'Cutting Edge of British Style', *The Times*, 10 July1990.

72. Lorraine Gamman and Merja Makinen, *Female Fetishism: A New Look*, Lawrence and Wishart, London 1994; Valerie Steele, *Fetish: Fashion, Sex and Power*, Oxford University Press, Oxford 1996.

73. E. Fox-Genovese, 'The Empress's New Clothes', *Socialist Review* 17:1, 1987, pp7-30.

74. Quoted in Hilary Alexander, 'Westwood has a Beano with her Dandy Designs', *The Daily Telegraph*, 16 January 1996.

75. *Ibid*.

76. *Carpet and Floorcoverings Review*, 17 February 1995, p36.

77. Vivienne Westwood quoted in Brampton, *op.cit*, 1991.

78. Vivienne Westwood quoted in Roger Tredre, 'Westwood Holds Court Among The Soho Tea Set', *The Independent*, 14 October 1991, p3.

79. Quoted in Brenda Polan, 'Joie de Vivienne', *The Independent*, 7 October 1990.

80. John Fairchild, *Chic Savages*, Simon and Schuster, New York 1989.

6

David Dabydeen: coolie lessons for Cool Britannia

The poetry and novels of David Dabydeen, an Indo-Guyanese migrant to England, can be read to reveal what Anglo-British whiteness looks like from the outside into which it reaches, leaks, and to which it has frequent if anxious openings.

Dabydeen's black counter-discourse is an attempt to decolonialise English language and culture, unmasking and replacing the knowledges that once justified imperial authority. His work tries to prevent the reproduction of white Anglo-British distinction and in so doing it searches for non-racialised routes beyond it. The work of a man who has made blackness visible in the white literary and artistic canon can be read to make whiteness visible too.

'The Negro is not. Any more than the White man,' Fanon once wrote.[1] Insofar as Dabydeen reveals that the black figures constructed by the colonial imagination are not, the identifications of the white Anglo-British, enabled by abjection, and later confirmed by symbolic distinction from that other, lose a boundary and much of their cultural authority. This is, of course, a moment of white self-doubling, of anxiety, reflexivity and opportunity. It could lead to closure or to a recognition of the strangeness of white Englishness and the creation of a new ethnicity and relation to others. A moment like this could be a watershed for the English imaginary, and how these choices are addressed will be the acid test for strategies designed to overcome social exclusion.

Anglo-British whiteness continues to project its anxieties and dissatisfactions with the shortcomings of its own collective identifications into complaints about third world practices, or it deploys residual colonial representations when dealing with Black Britons – what McLintock usefully calls 'European porno-tropics'.[2] It erects barriers to black identification with a new national popular English settlement, rendering a new and inclusive multiracial Anglo-Britishness – Tony Blair's young country – a chimera.

Dabydeen's work makes visible, often by mimicry and burlesque, white Anglo-British assumptions about the marginality, physicality and disorderliness of the colonised. At the same time it makes the contrasting primacy, perfectibility and purity of white Britain's own unitary self-conception visible. As Dyer argues, 'whiteness involves a notion of embodiment, a sense that it is an incarnation of something – spirit, initiative and enterprise – that is not the body. And it reduces non-white people to their bodies.'[3] Dabydeen tries to unfix these polarities and as a recent study argues, he 'complicates the binaristic view of colonisation'.[4] This counter-hegemonic move is a precondition for the establishment of multiracial democracy in a Britain that remains far from postcolonial in its discourse and practice.

What the English think of as creolised and hybrid may well be ethnocentric. There is a complacency about the easy celebration of London's multicultures evoked in the notion of Cool Britannia. Traces of the colonial imaginary are clearly visible in its celebration of a dynamic black physicality in dance, music and bodily adornment. The recreation and leisure of urban youth may be creolised but the dominant culture is still racialised and univocal; its social and economic decision-makers are predominantly white and Anglo-British, its inequalities markedly at the expense of Black Britain.[5]

Dabydeen's work rubs against the grain of administrative notions of the process of social inclusion, and suggests that the price may be higher in terms of the self-understanding of the white Anglo-British than anyone in the political domain is prepared to pay.

Cool Britannia is the mitigating plea of a shrinking, amnesiac Empire that has not understood its own founding process of abjection and differentiation from colonised others and historically-rival European nations. These distinctions still shape its imaginary, even in the notion of Cool Britannia that it offers as evidence of the change to the tribunal of modernity. Without a new reflexivity, and an understanding of the historical externalisation of white shortcomings and anxieties as a threatening blackness, there is no prospect of a new inclusive hegemony. Our celebrations of multiculturalism will be pleasant, premature and reversible. For all its legislative talk and measures for economic inclusion, official Britain has not recognised the full implications of heterogeneity. The English imaginary has not yet adjusted to the fact that its bearers share, as Dabydeen calls it, 'the third largest West Indian island'.[6]

YOU CANNOT BE BRITISH WITHOUT BEING GUYANESE

Dyer points out that white people assume they are 'human not raced'.[7] Dabydeen's work sets out to disabuse Anglo-British whiteness of this self deception, thereby assisting the process by which they might become racialised strangers to themselves.

One technique of distinction adopted by the white Anglo-British in their homelands is the attempt to make blackness invisible, a straight refusal to acknowledge difference. Of the 1970s Dabydeen reports that there was 'a very great pressure among us to become invisible'.[8]

A related procedure is the disavowal of the interracial, deeply asymmetric, partnerships which produced the achievements that the Anglo-British claim as their own. As the nameless black narrator of *Disappearance* says of the southern English sea defences that he, and an Irishman, have helped to construct:

> Future generations would see the wall as something that was always there, a quintessentially English monument: the efforts of Christie and myself would be erased by ignorance or national sentiment. Was it not always thus in England: the drift into a deliberate unconsciousness; any awakening being a jolt of patriotic sentiment?[9]

Dabydeen provides a more inclusive vision of Anglo-British history in his ground-breaking study of the representations of black people in Hogarth's prints. His counter readings are a form of self assertion. 'It was an attempt to show that English art has a dimension of blackness to it ... In other words, and on a personal level, that I belonged to British society'.[10] By 'making the black man visible' in England's canonical art, literature and critical procedures, Dabydeen draws attention to the abjection that had inaugurated Anglo-British whiteness, troubling the custodians of Hogarth and contributing to a wider reflexivity. His simultaneous exploration of the erotics of colonialism – most conspicuously in his poetry – reveals the phobias and losses that constitute whiteness, whose recall constantly threatens it with dissolution.

Notions of the primacy and unitary nature of the white Anglo-British were badly dented by this critique. But in two later novels, *The Intended* and *Counting House*, Dabydeen goes a step further by demonstrating that the peoples of the third world, and Guyana in particular, were the first to experience the strangeness of racial and national identifications, and the consequent hybridisation or hardening of ethnic identitifications that results from globalisation. Development is not linear. The colonised world, particularly in formations based on slavery and indenture, is where this dynamic central to modernity first appeared. It is also where the colonial imaginary that still informs English identifications matured.

The Guyanese migrant is therefore particularly attuned to the fictionality of racial identifications and to the transactions through which the colonial imagination has shaped identities over time. Guyana's inequitable cultural diversity, the result of a history of African slavery in Dutch, then in British-owned plantations, followed by the arrival of indentured labour from India, Portugal and China after emancipation, mutated into ethnic violence in the 1960s. In that period, says Dabydeen, 'differences were ... manufactured into the weaponry of hatred'.[11] Although these violent closures of identity, abjecting signs of difference, were based on long-standing essentialist identifications, nurtured by the different historical trajectories of the Afro- and Indo- Guyanese which have been called a 'uni-ethnic pattern in the composition of voluntary associations', they were also a disavowal of the enduring diversity and heterogeneity of many personal identifications and relationships.[12]

Dabydeen's writings celebrate the mobility and impurity of identification. In his first novel, *The Intended*, he provides an Indo-Guyanese first person narrator with an Afro-Guyanese aunt and a Presbyterian great-grandfather who 'each Friday, to the disgust of Hindu and Muslim alike ... slaughtered a cow and a pig'. Later the boy teams up with three peers from different parts of the Asian diaspora, and an Afro-Caribbean rastafarian, in a South London school. The cacophony of similarity and difference in the Guyanese crucible of identification was a good preparation for the unstable social identity of black in Britain, briefly shaped by English racism and migrant political activism during the 1960s and 1970s. This metropolitan matrix, Dabydeen suggests, produced 'sudden hate and sudden companionship' amongst its black members.[13] White Anglo-British exclusions have forced West Indian diversity and multiculturalism into 'new tribalisations based on hatred'.[14]

Dabydeen's measure of social inclusion is far more comprehensive and sensitised to history than that which informs governmental strategies and much pluralist political theory. He insists that the migrant will only feel a 'sense of belonging' when the British acknowledge how much they depended on the colonised for their material and cultural advance.[15] This requires a deep recognition of interdependence, a making strange of Anglo-Britishness that stretches notions of inclusion and national identity well beyond the civic egalitarian, pragmatic adjustments that modernising ministers are prepared to consider. 'You cannot be Guyanese without being British,' says Dabydeen. 'And you cannot be British without being Guyanese or Caribbean'.[16]

He frequently identifies white women and the literary and artistic canon as the central point of black affinity and challenge to the reproduction of Anglo-British whiteness. In his work, the literary and erotic transcodings and equivalencies established in the bedroom and the library, where the abject and the imaginary are renegotiated, are the pre-condition for multiracial democracy and the pluralisation of English culture. But these encounters are also revealed to be volatile and vulnerable to recolonising forms of desire, reading and revenge.

Dabydeen commenced writing at a very specific moment in the relation between the black community in Britain and Anglo-British hegemonic strategies. For twenty years Thatcherism reasserted an English ethnic absolutism, protecting Anglo-British culture and political institutions from the threat of 'swamping' by the anxiety-inducing forces of blackness. This English nationalist imaginary feared, and policed, a black urban abject which was figured as lawless, externalising white anxieties and the uncoded social impulses from which it had distinguished itself for centuries. Black migrants were constructed by Thatcherism as one of many enemies within, a formulation which actually acknowledged that England had already become a stranger to itself.

Now that the Thatcherite form of modernisation has been abandoned, strategies aspiring to hegemony try to rearticulate difference, as the pledges of social inclusion by Labour and 'patriotism without bigotry' from the Conservatives together indicate, whatever their likely effect. But the colonial imaginary still endures. The 'muted claws of Empire', which fear the prospect of Black Britain spilling beyond the inner city schools and estates, occupations and recreational spheres allocated to it, have not been fully retracted.[17]

ENGLAND'S RELUCTANT MULTICULTURALISM
David Dabydeen was born into the small Indo-Guyanese community of New Amsterdam in colonial Guyana in 1955, two years after Britain had re-imposed direct rule over the country in a Cold War reflex triggered by the electoral victory of the multiracial, state socialist People's Progressive Party (PPP).[18] As a direct result of this intervention, the multiethnic partnership of the PPP – symbolised by the joint leadership of Forbes

Burnham and Cheddi Jagan – and the fragile inter-ethnic peace between Afro-Guyana and Indo-Guyana disintegrated into violence during Dabydeen's childhood, forcing his evacuation to a Berbice village.

In 1969 the teenage Dabydeen was forwarded to his remarried father in South London.[19] Expelled by his step family, a period in care preceded 'three unhappy years' at Cambridge University from 1974-7.[20]

'The city of the colonist', wrote Fanon, 'is a city of whites, of strangers'.[21] We can learn something of the imposing presence of Anglo-British whiteness from the anxieties which this migrant teenager with a literary sensibility experienced as he first walked the wintry, racialised streets of south London. 'The white people were frightening to begin with', he recalls.

> On the second evening I ventured outdoors to view the street and was overtaken by a middle-aged white man wrapped in a winter overcoat whose skin, in the streetlamp light, took on a ghostly, grey appearance. I have never been so terrified in England since as I was that night by the sight of that pale image of death.[22]

This intensely registered figure of otherness, of separation from the mother and motherland, is both an abjection of male Anglo-British whiteness and an acknowledgement of its symbolic power.

At this point it is useful to recall the figure of the Polynesian women waving at the liminal American quayside created by Priestley in *Faraway*. That image of a sexually voracious, sexually diseased and dying female was the Englishman's racialised and gendered Other at its most abjected: 'He did not really see her as a person at all, only as a dread symbol'.[23] Dabydeen's middle aged figure of death is a similarly unexotic self, an externalisation of the strangeness experienced at a cultural frontier.

Within the unaccommodating, racist culture that misrecognised and marked out this young migrant from the South American continent as a 'Paki' to be bashed and abused, Dabydeen's secondary school offered an empowering reversal. His achievements in the English class were better than those of his white, culturally insular peers who 'showed little curiosity about the world outside England, but were quick to invent derogatory names to call foreigners'.[24] The colonial motherland and its culture – the English imaginary as coded by English Literature – grew in importance as the Kristevan maternal guarantor of identity, a surrogate for the new distant familial mother.

Dabydeen helped himself to the cultural capital of the English, accumulating the literary and artistic currency of national identity faster than his white working-class peers, and used it to access higher education. His investment in a process of re-articulation, rather than opposition or assimilation, is a good example of the 'resemblance and menace' that Bhabha identifies as anti-colonial mimicry.[25]

'You had to take what was defined as English high culture ... [and] insert your blackness there'.[26] The fatalism of Hardy's peasantry, Lawrence's attention to pre-Columbian culture and aspects of Strindberg's metaphysics were all read in ways that valorised and reconnected with traces of Guyana. 'Reading Sir Gawain was a startling moment', he remembers. 'The sheer energy and nakedness of the dialect instantly recalled the "pre-civilised" language of Guyanese Creole'.[27]

In 1978, soon after he graduated, Mrs Thatcher drew on the still vibrant resources of Powellism to warn against the swamping of British culture by black migrants, spelling out the threat to law, democracy and international relations that any further growth in the scale of this abject represented. After her election victory of 1979, this figurative exclusion from citizenship was converted into a programme of sustained indifference to the black experience of mass unemployment, low pay, poor housing, unresponsive schooling and hard policing.

That form of the settlement between the white Anglo-British nation, its resident commonwealth citizens and their children could not last. A year after the Brixton riots of 1981 forced an end to its most unresponsive phase, Dabydeen helped to organise an important conference of antiracist education professionals. Although multiculturalism had become the new discourse of the inner city educational establishment, institutional and curricular change had proved to be lamentably slow. As always, real change lagged well behind the modernising rhetoric of the Anglo-British. Dabydeen quickly dismissed the reforms that had taken place as a 'flurry of conscience'.[28]

The early 1980s, after all, had also seen the success of Thatcher's military adventure in the Falklands. This was a conflict which was amplified into a reaffirmation of Anglo-British supremacy – 'the nation still has those sterling qualities which shine through our history' – that unnerved the nation's black community. Dabydeen pointed to the consequences: 'There has been a hardening of attitudes to black demands, a regrouping of the forces of security and a resurgence of imperial emotion'.[29]

Again, his response was to urge a revision and re-articulation of the canon. The challenge was how to modernise the reading habits of the Anglo-British and the aspiring postcolonial reader, liberating them from procedures which failed to acknowledge the black presence in British culture, and which reproduced the white English imaginary. This could be done, he suggested, without abandoning the imperial library and its adjoining art gallery. The books which sat on the nation's shelves and the paintings which adorned its walls had a multi-cultural content and import that had been unacknowledged for too long. 'It was merely a matter of making the black man visible'.[30]

Dabydeen's contribution to the publication which came out of the conference was an essay on how eighteenth-century British writers had reconciled their notion of commerce as a civilising activity with the barbaric realities of the slave trade. Morality was subordinated to profit-seeking but it had been protected nonetheless by the construction of Africans as sub-human. According to its philosophical overseers, slavery had successfully introduced the virtues of labour into a primitive, non-scientific and pre-commercial society.[31]

The identifications of Anglo-British whiteness were particularly difficult to escape. Even the counter-knowledges produced in the metropolitan centre were unable to extricate themselves from the colonial relations of power. Dabydeen reported on a tradition of writing against slavery that included Swift, Johnson, Defoe, Wordsworth, Blake, Southey and Cowper. He also mocked it for devoting little time and no funding to the cause of abolition. The credit for ending the trade is attributed to slave revolts.

Dabydeen's historical narrative contained an implicit apologia for the contemporary violence of the ghetto. 'The sword was mightier than the pen ... The irrationality of whites, their refusal to be persuaded by reasoned and moral arguments, forced blacks into violent behaviour.'[32] It was a valuable if daunting essay, implying that violent confrontation might once again be necessary if the structures of Anglo-British whiteness were to be dismantled rather than reproduced.

HOGARTH AND SOCIAL INCLUSION

Dabydeen first contrasted dominant and subordinate Anglo-British identifications, and supplied another divergent articulation to the colonised other, during his re-visioning of Hogarth's work.

Hogarth's Blacks, a version of the doctoral thesis Dabydeen completed at the University of London, was published in 1985.[33] The opening lines, in which he cites an early eighteenth-century newspaper report of a fear that London might be swamped by black people, signals his continuing engagement with contemporary cultural politics. Within a few pages he had rescued a black eighteenth-century wit, handy with his fists, from obscurity. Francis was nominated a precursor of the Brixton insurgents, anticipating by two centuries 'the barbed and witty curses, and the broken pavement stones, hurled simultaneously at police in retaliation against their bullying, in the Brixton Rebellion of 1981'.[34]

The 1980s were the years of 'black as a political colour', a period when 'black' as a shared social identity operated as a temporary unifier of the diverse black diasporas present in Britain.[35] This identification was perhaps at its strongest at the time of the death of thirteen young black people in Deptford in 1981, an incident which become known as the New Cross Massacre. It was consolidated in opposition to the dominant Anglo-British response, which Dabydeen characterises as 'the apathy of the majority white population to the death of fellow citizens and human beings'.[36]

In *Hogarth's Blacks* Dabydeen offers a counter-reading of the canon that both helps to delineate and to unfix whiteness. Hogarth was the 'most prolific painter and engraver of blacks' in the eighteenth century, but there had been virtually no recognition of this in the extensive archive of commentary on his work.[37] Alert to the depersonalisation and damage caused by the cash nexus, Hogarth had developed 'a compassion for the fate of the common people'. They crowd into his paintings and engravings, violating the decorum of the age. Dabydeen suggests that Hogarth had extended his compassion to black people by representing them as full participants in the subculture of the English lower classes.[38]

In eighteenth-century artefacts, black servants are usually represented as forms of property with a physical affinity to animals, the abjection which also served as a justification for the slave trade. Refiguring his own isolation at Cambridge, Dabydeen attributes a sense of loneliness and humiliation to these black subjects who had been inserted into white aristocratic culture 'merely to reflect upon the superiority of the white'.[39] This aspect of his argument develops into an important account of the corruption of religious iconography by the West, including the redeployment and transformation of images of the relationship between madonna and child by a white imperial imagination seeking to naturalise the relations between 'mother country and child colony'.[40]

In art-historical terms Hogarth's caricatures of libidinal black men with white women allude to Titian's Venetian paintings of dark satyrs embracing pale nymphs.[41] These figures of violated white womanhood are generated by the white fear of miscegenation and failed reproduction, persistent aspects of the English imaginary.

Fundamentalists might take this as evidence of Hogarth's complicity with the colonial imagination. However, Dabydeen demonstrates that Hogarth uses the 'satiric device of the superior alien' to provide a critical perspective on the white Anglo-British aristocratic life and morals represented in his work. Honest black people, usually associated with libidinal and bestial appetites, are placed in white contexts – a cockpit here, a brothel there – that are saturated with vice. Although they remained contrasted others, and reminders of what had been abjected in order to establish Anglo-British identifications, these black figures began to accumulate new associations of honesty and openness, even on occasion becoming 'the norm against which the inadequacies of his masters are measured'.[42]

In Dabydeen's reading of the *Rake's Progress*, interracial sex – a white man's liaison with a black woman – expresses the unconscious appetites of the civilised Briton, namely 'a desire for retrogression, for the dark animal sensations symbolised by the black woman'.[43] According to Dabydeen, this was one manifestation of Hogarth's wider message that: 'Instead of civilising, money degrades, instead of progressing men regress into a state of primitivism'.[44]

In *Hogarth's Blacks* Dabydeen identifies the racial binaries that structure Anglo-British development and its representation. But he also deploys racialised abjections of his own, particularly in his mobilisation of a number of normative notions of heterosexuality and race in the account of the 'seedy' and 'deviant' white Anglo-British desires to which he contrasts a black vitality, conscripting Hogarth in his support.[45]

Dabydeen celebrates the redefinition of blackness that results from Hogarth's technique. But this transfiguration is, at least in part, based on a reaffirmation of the original racial polarities and racialised national identifications of the Anglo-British, albeit through their satirical reversal. To this extent Hogarth and Dabydeen both adopt a form of opposition that Spivak calls 'repetition-in-rupture'.[46] They are caught inside the logic they contest. An idealised disembodied whiteness – moral, honest and free – is preserved as an aspiration by Hogarth's carnivalesque representations of white eighteenth century mores as blacker than black. The artist's motivation was not an egalitarian deracialisation, but an improvement in white Anglo-British behaviour that would subsequently improve its chances of reproduction.

Dabydeen goes some way towards acknowledging this in his conclusion:

> Hogarth consciously employs current myths and stereotypes about blacks, relating to their sexuality, paganism, primitivism and simian ancestry, so as to comment on the morality of the English aristocratic class [...] The black is used as a yardstick, as well as a stick with which to beat the whites. In incorporating gross notions about blacks in his art, he has however put himself in a precarious position in relation to eighteenth century realism. Whilst we may allow for the fact that his contempt was intended for the whites, and that the black was merely being employed as a satirical device to achieve that end, nevertheless Hogarth exposes himself to the charge of the perpetuation of racism.[47]

Dabydeen's final verdict is ambiguous. Major aspects of Hogarth's work could be decoded 'in accordance with the worst conventions of English racist thought'.[48] *The Rake's Progress* and *The Harlot's Progress* were, after all, purchased and displayed by an owner of slaves. But Dabydeen's account also demonstrates that many positive and creative readings are possible, and that some of these might make Anglo-British elites strangers to themselves, or even subject to change from below.

REVERSALS THAT ILLUMINATE WHITENESS

Dabydeen's work doubles the colonial imaginary by revealing that it is based on a dynamic of complementary abjections and utopic longings in which Anglo-British whiteness and colonial blackness differentiate, attract and destabilise one another. He calls this transaction 'a criss-cross of illusions, a trading in skins and ideals' and maps these exchanges in his poetry.[49]

In the late sixteenth century Elizabethan pirates serving under Raleigh thought they had discovered an utopic alternative to England in Guyana's El Dorado. That culture, itself transformed by Empire, would eventually locate its own utopia in a vision of England. 'In the moment of our rawness, there is recoil, the cry for transfiguration is heard which to the Guyanese is the cry for "whiteness", for the spiritual qualities of Raleigh's Elizabethan Empire. "England" is our Utopia, an ironic reversal' (*SS* p9).

The complementary reversals – yet another form of 'repetition-in-rupture' – install a mutual craving for an exotic alterity which is distant from the abjected present. This exotic alterity is imagined as a condition of comparative ease, in which desirable commodities and sexual gratification, even the illusion of the chora, are freely available. Pirates, travellers, slaves, migrants and planter families, dislocated strangers all, are emissaries from that other place. This is the burden of *Slave Song*, a collection of poems written by Dabydeen while he was still an undergraduate at Cambridge. It explores the 'erotic energies of the colonial experience' (*SS* p10), in a moment and an imaginary which is clearly not yet over. Dabydeen's texts are produced within a diverse Caribbean literary diaspora, and more specifically within an Anglo-Guyanese literary formation whose British-based contingent has hosted both the historical realism of Edgar Mittelholzer, Jan Carew and Roy Heath, and the narrative innovations of Wilson Harris. The creole political engagement of Linton Kwesi Johnson, and the Guyanese creoles that appear in the work of John Agard, E.R. Braithwaite and Fred D'Aguiar, further delineate the inter-textual space in which he writes.

The voices constructed by Dabydeen's poetry are often territorialised, and frequently located in the Indo-Guyanese plantation village. The language is highly specific too, a 'made-up, interlanguage of Guyanese Creole and Hindu symbolism, cut with medieval and eighteenth century English phraseology'.[50] This is akin to Vivienne Westwood's use of tartan, a hyperbolic reworking of a historical fiction. Dabydeen does not offer an authenticated Guyanese language or identification as a counterpoint to Anglo-British values and practices. Instead his work is based on an awareness of the constructed nature of identities within relationships of power and distinction that valorise and abject skin colour, language and culture in different and mobile permutations. As Sarah Lawson Welsh has pointed out, 'there are no originary voices in *Slave Song*, only reconstructed, represented, mediating ones'.[51]

Dabydeen constructs creole as the linguistic other to the Queen's English, a physical, less abstract, broken and non-elocutionary discourse. It is 'a natural gush from the gut, like fresh faeces' (*SS* p13). This attempt to refound language in the body is a defiant celebration of the Anglo-British abject. Even for Dabydeen, to write in creole –

which involves 'an unsheathing of the tongue and ... contact with raw matter' – is described as 'painful, almost nauseous' (SS p14).

One of the recommendations of the Scarman Report, following the Brixton Riots, was the greater dissemination of normative English in the migrant community and this has been an obsession of all government schemes to increase the employability of the poorest of Britons ever since. However Dabydeen has defended and celebrated Black British creoles on the grounds that a linguistic community that excludes white listeners is 'an assertion of self sufficiency and spiritual independence'.[52] In the English imaginary, creole is a paradoxical, lawless symbolic in which Anglo-British whiteness cannot be reproduced. As such it is revalorised by Dabydeen.

Much has been written about the satirical reflexivity and parody of western critical procedures involved in Dabydeen's decision to illustrate Slave Song with engravings, as if it were a colonial primer, and to include English translations and explanatory annotations for its simulated creole. The effect is to create a multi-tiered intertextuality which questions the authority of western criticism and which also establishes that the relationship between black writers, the academy, British artists and plantation-derived capital, past and present, is one of changing yet enduring colonial articulations of power.

While Mark McWatt sees the ambiguous metacommentaries of Slave Song as a 'technique of masking' that is both an expression of the complexity of migrant identity, and a defensive move,[53] Dabydeen prefers to emphasise his comic purpose.[54]

For the white Anglo-British intellectual, however, the basic point is clear: our institutions of cultural power taxonomise difference and are an attempt to manage the anxieties stirred by the abject by drawing the English away 'from the point where meaning collapses'.[55] They distinguish black representations as subordinate and insubordinate, as restricted and unrestricted, and ultimately as containable threats to Anglo-British order and reproduction.

It is a project doomed to fail. The language of the Other can't be successfully mediated, its difference must be recognised as must our own. As Dabydeen suggests, 'Creole choreography becomes lame in translation' (SS p65). These texts ask us to reconsider the terms of our membership of the western, Anglo-British 'congregations of the educated' who listen politely as the black, supplicant poet entertains with lurid sexual confessional and tales of the Guyanese peasantry (CO p13). If we accept the proposition that to be British is to be

Caribbean and Guyanese, for we were formed and distinguished simultaneously and relationally, in unequal interdependence, then these poems are about ourselves too.

As we have seen in the normative sexuality informing his discussion of Hogarth's carnivalesque exploration of whiteness, Dabydeen's is a gendered subaltern voice. The opening poems of *Slave Song* are crowded with images of violated, abused women, figures of abjected Oedipal desire and the pain of separation. Dabydeen vocalises the destruction of black female bodies just as vividly as his simulated canecutter fantasises the rape of white women. 'For Mala' is an angry Indo-Guyanese lament for the victims of an Afro-Guyanese pogrom in the early 1960s, the very wave of violence which forced Dabydeen's family to flee New Amsterdam in 1962 (*SS* p19-20). 'Canecutters Song' explores interracial sexual desire and the imagined rape of a white female (*SS* p25-6). A violent coupling with a white woman is also prominent in 'Slave Song', a celebration of an insurgent black male sexuality (*SS* p29-30). 'Nightmare' burlesques a white female fantasy of gang rape and cannibalistic murder (*SS* p34). The defilement of white beauty also figures in 'Servants Song', a poem in which a white woman's ring is recovered is from a duck's arse (*SS* p23-4). In these poems woman is not so much an object of patriarchal exchange as the site of racialised plunder and revenge.

'Love Song' vocalises the utopic vision of a canecutter, in which the love of a white woman and a release from toil, dirt and abjection are conflated. The elevated, redeeming white woman is both a product of and a differentiation from the colonial abject, which also figures male slavery and indentured labour as a feminisation, the result of an imaginary castration by the colonial patriarch: 'Dut in e soul, in e battie-hole ... Cutlass slip and cut me cack' (*SS* p32).

'Two cultures' deals with the return of an Anglicised Dabydeen to Guyana where his elders are sceptical of his cosmopolitan, cultural hybridity: 'An a who pickni yu rass?' His elders attempt to preserve an imagined pure white Englishness – and their own black daughters – from defilement by this young man rendered indeterminate of race by the English cultural capital he has accumulated. In the colonial imagination, the cultures of coloniser and colonised must remain pure and distinct, and reproduce themselves.

In Dabydeen's second collection of poems, *Coolie Odyssey*, the migrant has taken the canecutter's transgressive, utopic longing to the metropolitan centre of the colonial formation. In 'Miranda', the narrator's quest for redemptive sex with a white woman is reflexive and self consciously aware of the colonial formation of desire: 'the sun shook with imperial glee at the fantasy' (CO p33). The sexual relations of a black migrant with a white woman can be a 'song of bursting chain' (CO p36). But the transgressive encounter also generates the images of violence, pain, retribution and death found in 'Rebel Love' (CO p35).

In Dabydeen's work interracial sexuality is a process capable of stimulating new and mobile identifications. 'I endured your creation' and was 'reborn to your desire', the lover reports (CO p34). But the transitions are partial, and unable usually to escape the colonial imaginary. Images of impotence proliferate, reminiscent of the stutter of Townshend's young mods. The Anglicised black migrant male does not take full possession of the speaking position offered by the Anglo-British discourse into which he has entered. He remains a stranger to himself. The incompleteness is signalled in the 'stalk of blighted cane' in 'Miranda'(CO p33), the 'flaccid black' of 'Seduction' and the 'finger of feeble ash' in 'New World Words' (CO p37). In Dabydeen's poetry impotence is a figure for 'the failed insurrection' against Anglo-British colonialism, but it also references the failing potency of an English culture that has proved unable to modernise itself (CO p29).

The white lover, after all, fails to shed her whiteness. A 'longing for rebirth' is dismissed as naivety (CO p32). Dabydeen suggests that the transformation of whiteness would require a recapitulation of the trading, suffering and othering of the colonised, the recognition that to be fully British involves being Guyanese. But his formulation – 'She could not endure the repetition/Necessary for new beginning' (CO p32) – also leaves open the possibility that it might involve conforming to sexual fantasies of the kind vocalised throughout Slave Song.

The poem also references the self dissatisfactions, self perceived strangeness and divided nature of white Anglo-British identities. Discontented with the 'dull plumage' of an 'elderly civilisation', Englishness still associates jouissance with primitivism, the 'longing to be startled into primeval flight' (CO p37). The black migrant's nagging question – whether a desire which, as we have seen, takes the form of 'rupture-in-repetition' will leave him 'forever imprisoned in a Romance of History' – cuts both ways, also putting England's capacity to decolonise its imaginary in doubt (CO p36).

'Burning Down the Fields' is a characteristically Dabydeenian burlesque of white Anglo-British fears about black defilement.

Parodying the Powellite imaginary, and all its assumptions about white ethnicity and the continuity of Anglo-British political institutions and culture, Dabydeen revels in the abjections constitutive of the dominant form of English nationalism, yet also preserves his own distinction by resorting to the third person:

> They will encrust the Shiny Monuments,
> They will besmirch the White Page with their own words,
> They will cremate their relatives on the Riverbank
> And the Tiber will foam with halal blood
> And the Maidens will faint, or bear bastards
> If the Lion lies down with the woolly-headed beast (CO p24).

Later in the 1980s Dabydeen surveyed the postwar history of black migration into Britain and concluded that the Labour and Conservative parties had both passed measures redefining nationality and resticting immigration. To be British was still, most definitely, not to be black. Black migrants 'came with a sense of cultural identification with the motherland', he wrote, but 'the journey to Britain ... was a journey to an illusion, for the West Indian immigrants faced the reality of rejection by the motherland. They may have believed passionately in their closeness and affinity to Britain and possessed a sense of belonging, but the British were equally convinced of their alienness, their otherness'.[56]

He produced genealogies of the racialised tropes of the Anglo-British colonial imagination, drawing attention to its most enduring fears, assumptions and strategies in the selection of racialising narratives, from Shakespeare to Conrad, which was published as *A Reader's Guide to West Indian and Black British Literature*. In the rogue's gallery he placed the moral and physical blackness of Aaron in Shakespeare's *Titus Andronicus* and Othello's decline into savagery. Caliban was 'the native colonised and dispossessed by the European'. Crusoe's rescue of Friday was a 're-enactment of the myth of salvation' that justified master-slave relationships. Conrad's *Heart of Darkness* explored the vulnerability of European civilisation to the 'swamping forces of savagery'.[57] Buchan's adventures demonstrated that white solidarity emerged at moments of crisis.[58]

His conclusion remains a salutary warning to the cheerleaders of Cool Britannia and the power brokers of multiracial England:

What emerges from such a study is a realisation of the ways in which black people have been fodder for white conceptualisation. Their social, personal and historical realities are constantly ignored or denied. They are instead creatures of myth, the demons or buffoons of the white imagination, the personification of notions of savage or exotic 'otherness'.[59]

Dabydeen's work up to this point had been characterised by a gendered hyperbolisation rather than a transformation of the figures of the colonial imaginary. Benita Parry suggests that the poems in *Slave Song* 'condense the internalisation of colonialism's institutional and psychological violence'.[60] She argues that 'pain, frustration and anger is spoken by the native positioned as the very figure of phobic white fears and desires'.[61] As we have seen, however, this limitation did have a tactical strength.

Dabydeen's reversals highlight – indeed exacerbate – the anxieties of Anglo-British whiteness, disclosing England's own social and psychological contribution to its emerging crisis of identity. His writing stirs and provokes the enduring colonial fear of white non-reproduction and the damage that has resulted from the dissociation of whiteness from the body, making this strangeness public. The price of Anglo Britain's self image as the bearer of modernisation when its social structures and social imaginary now block modernity becomes more apparent. Dabydeen's work suggests that inherited Anglo-British identifications are unsustainable not for external reasons – Americanisation, Europeanisation, migration, globalisation – but because of their self divided incompleteness.

It's no surprise, then, to hear a wise black voice suggest that 'white people don't want to heal their own scar or hear their own story' (CO p40-1). But until that past is reprised and understood, the problem of national identity will not recede, even temporarily. The contemporary crisis of Anglo-British whiteness will simply be displaced by – or much worse, will fail to be engaged by – political injunctions to adopt a new purpose, new direction and new leadership, to look forward rather than back, and to think of ourselves as a young country.[62]

IN AND AGAINST THE WAXWORKS MUSEUM

Black British writers have long had to deal with the racialised figures that populate the slow moving English imaginary 'almost as rite of passage', says Dabydeen.[63] He prefers to renegotiate the terms of subsequent black settlements, disconnecting from the original templates. 'Fuck the "masterscripts" ... let me write instead to Harris and Naipaul, write back, quarrel with, borrow from, love, praise, worship them'.[64] This rewriting of the rewrite – like Westwood's reworked tartanry – deconstructs and marginalises the original mythical figures. 'After a while', Dabydeen claims, 'the canonical texts will disappear'.[65]

In *The Intended* Dabydeen was still negotiating an intertextual rite of passage by settling his accounts with Conrad. The novel recounts the sexual discoveries, the rivalries and the tensions between the material and cultural aspirations of four Asian teenagers – 'the regrouping of the Asian diapora in a South London schoolground' – and a Black British Rastafarian (*TI* p5).

The themes of Dabydeen's poetry persisted into *The Intended*: the Anglo-British pressure for blackness to become invisible is shown to generate migrants' unease with signs of their difference. Colonial proscriptions elicit shame as the accompaniment to lust for a white girl. A failed sexual encounter with a white woman becomes a figure for the narrator's anxieties about his entry into English culture.

In this heavily autobiographical *bildungsroman* the narrator tells of his journey from the rum, cane and creole culture of Indo-Guyana, to London, the heart of whiteness. At Battersea he supervises the World Cruise Ride, a funfair attraction decorated with stereotypical colonial images of other cultures and abjecting racist graffiti. The novel ends as he waits in the South London darkness for a taxi that will take him to Oxford University, reflecting on the taunts of friends that he wants to become white, and newly separated from his white girlfriend; he is the counter-colonial inversion of Kurtz's Intended in *Heart of Darkness*. Englishness is his intended destination. But at Oxford he rediscovers blackness by articulating the remembered creole of his friends and the medieval English of his colonial family.

Language and representation are the shifting, unstable ground of the narrator's subjectivity. He is only residually a creole-speaking subject. The four young black men are involved in an intensely Anglicising school-based study of Conrad's *Heart of Darkness*, and the pre-modern language of Milton, as they develop their new identifications. Their informal bedsit debates and amateur filmmaking explore how far 'black people must have black words' (*TI* p148).

En route to Oxford, the petitioner-narrator of *The Intended* rarely doubts the primacy of English learning. As a child he used his superior mathematical ability to cheat an Afro Guyanese peer in the village market. As a teenager in London he used his superior facility in English, the language of power and administration, to distract an Asian shopkeeper, and win space in which to shoplift.

Once installed in the heart of enlightenment, the narrator's memory and subjectivity are reconfigured: 'We are mud, they the chiselled stone of Oxford that has survived centuries and will always be here' (*TI* p198). *The Intended* tracks the itinerary from the colonial abject to the qualified and precarious assumption of the position of Anglo-British speaking subject. 'I am no longer an immigrant here, for I can decipher the texts, I have been exempted from the normal rules of lineage and privilege' (*TI* p195). By contrast, the Rastafarian Joseph, whose film-based creole renegotiations of Conrad are haphazard episodes of jouissance, and whose itinerary leads from prison to suicide, figures the inauthenticity of all identification, the acknowledgement of the self as stranger pursued to the point of delirium and loss of meaning: 'He was telling me ... the quest for completion was absurd' (*TI* p196).

For everyone else, the process of identification continues, with differing degrees of dislocation, racialised distinction and reflexivity. In *The Intended*, a self improving and materialistic Asian entrepreneur characterises the white working class as 'walking banknotes', locked into a culture of prostitution, pub violence, drug and video consumption. This act of Anglo-Asian distinction signals the disappearance of the inclusive participatory community – and also, perhaps, of the very possibility of a singular, alternative national popular – that was still figured as a possibility in Dabydeen's account of Hogarth's representation of English plebian culture.

The stability of the Anglo-British culture that paved the way to Oxford, does not endure into *Disappearance*, published two years later. There, Anglo-British culture is figured as shrinking, decrepit, corrupt and self divided. It can no longer sustain or reproduce itself, and therefore matters no more: 'To smash up England would be no more than going beserk in a waxworks museum' (*Disappearance* p179).

In *Disappearance* the condition of Anglo-Britain is figured as a white woman who has spent time in Africa, living in a south coast retirement cottage which is doomed to fall into the sea. Mrs Rutherford's anticolonial attitudes and points of equivalence with the black Other – a tactical commonality made possible by a shared history of subordination to the white Anglo-British male – are reawakened by the arrival of a Afro-Guyanese engineer who lodges with her while he works on the sea wall that is intended to save her village and all that it represents in the colonial imagination. The cliffs, at once a defence and a vulnerability, are a figure for that constant erasure of Anglo-British identity by renegotiations with its alterities, deliquescing abjects and new configurations of power and knowledge.

As Dabydeen renegotiates earlier anticolonial texts, Englishness becomes a mystery and a disappearance. Englishness is Jack, the husband who has left Mrs Rutherford, his name a trace and a contrast to Naipaul's representation of his own encounter with Anglo-British rurality.[66] The condition of post-imperial English masculinity is also figured in Mrs Rutherford's reclusive lover, Curtiss, who is not vocalised and never appears directly. Curtiss deploys a series of resonant Anglo-British tropes one after another – nationalist, imperial and Churchillian – in the campaign for state action to save the clifftop village. These are turned back against him as rumours of scandal and his own status as a second generation immigrant develop. Like his namesake Kurtz in *Heart of Darkness* – the literary precedent for Jack's reported rapacity in Africa – Mr Curtiss is, symbolically at least, dead. As such he joins the emissary of Anglo-British enlightenment who trained the narrator as an engineer in Guyana, Professor Fenwick, who is later revealed as corrupt. Their Anglo-Britishness is fictional, duplicitous and has lost its authenticity.

Mrs Rutherford's cottage is a hybrid but nonetheless Anglo-British space, traditionally English in its appearance, book lined and adjoined by a carefully cultivated garden that was once tended by Irish labour. It houses a colonialist collection of African masks once used in circumcision rites. Once the home of Jack, it is also a place of fetished savagery, a figure for the imaginary, a shrine to the moment of racialised gendering and loss of the chora. The rural idyll is recorded as the locus of contemporary dissatisfactions and renegotiations. As Dabydeen later said, comparing the white clifftop Brittannia and the Guyanese contract engineer, 'She is the creole character, and he's not'.[67]

An elderly white woman, like Nancy Cunard suspected of drunkenness and promiscuity by her neighbours, Mrs Rutherford suggests the possibility but also the high price to be paid for pursuing desires which jeopardise the reproduction of Anglo-British whiteness. A critic of England's myths and inflated sense of its own worth, she gained her freedom from her husband on the same day as Guyana was given national independence.

Dabydeen develops a critique of the English pastoral which, as we have seen, serves as the residual home of an imagined white nationhood and as a brake on modernity. As in his later poem *Turner,* the rural village settled in its practices, affirmations and exclusions is a figure for the dominant English imaginary.[68] By contrast, the narrator offers the city as a space of possibility, for new non-racialised identifications: 'random, chaotic places, allowing people to dissolve into each other. Cities contained little memory of the past ... Nor were the rituals of nationhood enacted in cities, apart from the odd procession put on for sheer pageantry' (*Disappearance* p131). A new Anglo-British modernity, if such a formation is possible, will be urban.

As Mrs Rutherford explains the history of her African pots and masks to her diasporic lodger, it is impossible not to remember Nancy Cunard berating Henry Crowder, and all Black Americans in general, for their indifference to the 'blood nationality' of their African roots. Whiteness itself is based on this relational, primitivising distinction, whether it is constructed in biological or cultural terms. Black modernity – in the figure of the engineer – collapses these primary distinctions and consequently threatens older Anglo-British distinctions and identities.

Disappearance is about the fraught and ultimately doomed attempt to escape from the racialised scene of history, identification and colonial truth. At the start of the novel the nameless narrator has 'no sense of the past, no sense of ruptured innocence' (*Disappearance* p10). An Anglicised engineer, wedded to Anglo Britain's version of the civilised ideal, he insists that 'What happened long ago was not of my making and didn't make me' (p16). He prefers to look ahead, not back, and to engage with the timeless, transhistoric colonisation of the land by the sea. 'I'm me, not a mask or a movement of history. I'm not black, I'm an engineer' (p102).

It is his role to contain the sea, a place of unfixing and transformation, a relentless resurgence of abjects, a space of mobility and modernity, which transforms identity. In this respect, Dabydeen's seas – even more so in the later case of *Turner* – are kin to Gilroy's *Black Atlantic.*[69]

> I was seduced by its endless transformations, which promised me freedom from being fixed as an African, a West-Indian, a member of a particular nationality of a particular epoch ... And yet I wanted to be somebody, not anything, and resisted the sea's indiscriminateness ... I knew a dam was my identity, an obstacle I sought to put between shore and sea

to assert my substantialness, my indissoluble presence, without reference to colour, culture or age (*Disappearance* p132).

The engineer is not threatened by this encounter and welcomes the chance it appears to offer. But the Anglo-British, no longer rulers of the waves, fear the erosion of their being.

In answer to the recurring question of why he is an engineer, the narrator replies 'the sea'. But his recollection tells a very different story. His career choice was the result of his disenchantment with the dreamers and the drunks of Guyanese village culture and a determination to be better than the coolie. It is the empowering and apparently deracialising otherness of engineering – 'an engineer is a man of grammar whereas you speak waywardly like the nigger you are.' (p60) – which explains his occupational 'rupture in repetition'.

Like the narrator the English also try to retreat from history and neo-colonial operations of desire and knowledge, in their several disappearances. Take the example of Mr Curtiss, crusader for the village: 'After the collapse of his mission he withdrew into a private space, wanting to forget the history that had awakened huge ambition in him' (p178). And Mrs Rutherford, who absconds from marriage and her colonial role into the African desert: 'I really longed to be alone, colourless and invisible, but I couldn't escape being English ... So I fought against myself' (p102-103). At the end of the novel she 'twitched constantly with anger, unable to emancipate herself from history', but she is ready for her rural winter solitude. The narrator intends to disappear too, and will act on his 'desire for obscurity' by returning to Guyana, to where 'there was space to forget' and begin anew (p179).

In Dabydeen's account the deracialising flight of the English from history and representation takes the form of territorialisation, of refuge in monocultural villages and racialised locales, even if coastal erosion – the displaced figuration of the contraction of Empire, the ceaseless surge of the abject and the forces of globalisation – forces them to reappear, and name themselves, even if only to resist further encroachments.

The utopic wish to disappear from history and racialised culture is a measure of the enduring strength of the Powellite imaginary of white nationhood, which obstructs the modernisation of Britain, constricts the nascent urban ideal of multicultural and participatory democracy, and extends the life of the colonial imaginary. Life without this imaginary is unthinkable, but life within it is unsustainable. This is our moment. Reassured by the image of a reawakening Bulldog, ready to guard the cliffs of Dover, the anxious southern England of *Disappearance*, for years a core constituency of Thatcherism, has been incorporated into the bloc assembled by New Labour. Dabydeen's novel discloses its anxieties and incoherences, and implies that the racialised sea walls of England will not hold.

TURNER

Of course Dabydeen knows the impossibility of disconnecting from contemporary struggles over historical forms of knowledge. In the 1990s, nearly 160 years after its abolition, and along with Fred D'Aguiar, Caryll Philips and Barry Unsworth, he is still writing about the slave trade.[70]

The experience of slavery and the formation of the colonial imaginary which both made it possible and evolved within its 'porno-tropics' remains the defining moment in the relationship between Anglo-Britain and the black peoples of the world. The inequalities and human commodification manifest in the slave trade still provide the strongest available metaphor – and historical explanation – for the continuing subordination of black peoples in Britain. The poem *Turner* is the high-point to date of Dabydeen's complex renegotiation of colonial forms of representation, disorganising racial binaries and the subjectivities associated with them. This time the nameless narrator is the almost wholly submerged black figure in Turner's 1840 painting 'Slavers Throwing Overboard the Dead and Dying', an image that has prompted a series of Black British commentaries.[71] The painting was in fact a post abolition critique of the slave trade and an act of Anglo-British modernisation. Colley calls it 'a study of the past giving way.'[72] However the most famous Anglo-British commentary on the picture, by John Ruskin, dwells on the painterly representation of the sea and the sky.

Dabydeen suggests that the break with the recent past was not clean and that the excitations of the colonial imaginary endured in the painting. 'The intensity of Turner's painting is such ... that I believe the artist in private must have savoured the sadism he publicly denounced' (*Turner* px).

In *Turner* an unstable, paedophile white masculinity is offered as a figure for colonial identity, its expulsions the occasion for the narrator's presence in the sea and for his coaxing awake of the black unconscious, an unwanted mixed race child tossed into the water alongside him 'salt splash burning my eyes awake' (*Turner* p11).

The manacled black foot suspended above the waves in Turner's painting is a manifestation of the uncanny, a reminder of the subject's formation by an imaginary that is sundering, and a symbolic field that is racialised and gendering.The submerged head, Dabydeen writes, 'has been drowned in Turner's (and other artists') seas for centuries'(pix). That sea is also what Spivak calls the 'enabling violence' of colonial representation. For Dabydeen it contains 'the memory of ancient cruelty' (*Turner* px). The narrator, like all speaking subjects, is therefore 'too trapped by grievous memory to escape history ... The desire for transfiguration or newness or creative amnesia is frustrated' (px). Although this human fragment is bleached of colour and of ambiguous gender in the poem, no subject can fully escape its difference, its gendered ethnicity, and remain a subject.

As the young child hits the water alongside the narrator this offspring of master and slave is 'Stillborn from all the signs'. The punning opening line of the poem suggests something that is both dead and alive – still born, after all – generated and suppressed by colonial discourse. The dead child brings double consciousness and strangeness to the narrator. Its first word is an act of abjection, a founding separation that creates an identification and an Other into which its own anxieties are externalised: '"Nigger" it cries, sensing its own deformity' (*Turner* p28).

No subject position is untouched by the operations of the colonial imagination. 'Neither can escape Turner's representation of them as exotic and sublime victims ... Neither can describe themselves anew but are indelibly stained by Turner's language and imagery' (*Turner* px). However, abjected uncoded material, like these two floating corpses, will force itself into representation. The narrator has 'words of my own dreaming and those that Turner primed in my mouth' (p14). Here, perhaps, are the grounds on which black Anglo-British culture will find common cause with Townshend's punk with the stutter: tongue-tied foreignness in the dominant discourses of Anglo-Britain.[73]

Turner abandons the territorialised tropes of *Disappearance*. There is no dam but language to shore up a temporary identity. The threatened black subject has only one way to maintain itself and reaffirm distinction. Like Joseph in *The Intended*, he is expected to sink into abjection and delirium, 'and come to rest on the sea's bed among/ The dregs of creatures without names/Which roamed these waters before human birth' (*Turner* p21). Instead he was saved by 'hate hardening my body like cork' (*Turner* p21).

Turner ends 'on a great note of pessimism'.[74] Meaning has, and has not, been recovered in this encounter with the past, indeed with the unconscious.[75] As the dead child tries to dive below signification and die once again the narrator realises that without this interruption of colonial representation, s/he would have been 'nothing and a slave to nothingness, to the white enfolding Wings of Turner brooding over my body' (*Turner* p39). His interlocutor, his unconscious, and the prospect of jouissance depart and he is left dead and adrift in colonial representation once again, aware only of his separation and his strangeness.

> There is no mother, family,
> Savannah fattening with cows, community
> Of faithful men; no elders to foretell
> The conspiracy of stars; magicians to douse
> Our burning temples ... (*Turner* p39)

In the poem all the white colonial figures, dead or alive – the pederast captain of the slave ship, drowned women, the new arrival – are named Turner. Karen McIntyre argues that these 'competing alternative Turners' assist a process of creative decolonisation by preventing the formation of fixed and essential identities.[76] This is certainly one of the unsettling effects the writing strategy has on the process of reading. But it simultaneously offers a composite Turner, a white cultural coalition, that is all pervasive, dangerous, and not self aware. As a result of this uncomfortable doubling a space opens – and a demand is made – for Anglo-British whiteness to redefine itself, and to develop a new positionality.

The poem *Turner* operates as a literal embodiment of its title, enforcing a constant and dizzying change of direction, meaning and identification. Anglo-British whiteness, based on fixed racialised concepts of truth, knowledge and power, is one of the polarities its narrative seeks to escape.

The challenge which Dabydeen leaves the white Anglo-British reader is whether he or she can relinquish a fixed vantage point as Turner and instead become a Turner in a mobile process of identification. In this process the Anglo-British colonial imaginary – and perhaps any notion of national identity – would be left far behind.

COUNTING HOUSE: THIRD WORLD FIRST
Counting House, Dabydeen's third novel, deals with the Middle Passage of indentured labour from India to the Albion estate in

Guyana, and the vortex of identifications, abjections and resistances that informed Indian peasant and British colonial cultures, the traces of which persist in our time.

The novel is a development and renegotiation of the historical narratives characteristic of an earlier Guyanese writer from New Amsterdam, Edgar Mittelholzer.[77] Dabydeen, however, introduces textual strategies intended to double Englishness and unfix identification. These include his naming of the plantation as Albion, and of its owners, and colonial practices in general, as Gladstone. By establishing this link to England and to the liberal Prime Minister of late Victorian Britain – whose father had indeed opposed abolition but derived his wealth, via the city, from the plantation system – Dabydeen enfolds the contemporary culture of the Anglo-British in his critique.

In *The Counting House* Dabydeen offers no unitary subaltern identity for reader affiliation. Anglo-British codes increasingly structure the indentured Indo-Caribbean imaginary. 'To be something you had to be like Gladstone,' thinks Vidia, a labourer satirically named after V. S. Naipaul. 'Gladstone was the science that invented the machines ... To be a Gladstone-coolie was the first stage in becoming Gladstone himself.'[78] The utopic longings of Vidia's wife, Rohini, are also shown to contribute to 'the sickness of greed' that characterised plantation culture (*TCH* p70).

Neither does early nineteenth century India provide a homogeneous community or stable point of identification. Village hierarchies and the ethnic cleansing of Muslims by Hindus during the long conquest by Britain, are shown to be a major stimulus to the flow of indentured labour.

The erotics and brutalities of colonial differentiation and attraction are revisited. But the priority of any Gladstone in Albion is the reproduction of colonial society and the maintenance of white distinction. 'For all the appeal to spirit', Dyer argues, 'if white bodies are no longer indubitably white bodies, if they can no longer guarantee their own reproduction as white, then the "natural" basis of their own dominion is no longer credible.'[79]

An older Gladstone, at the time of emancipation, had lost his wife. Her death and the new laws issued by the imperial centre removed his ability to reproduce colonial society and sustain 'order in the bush' (TCH p119). His atrocities were an expression of his impasse. He executed his slaves and then killed himself.

As Dabydeen shows, the cornerstone of plantation culture, and

Englishness, is white desire. Desire for money, for power, for reproduction and for the alterities and abjects which fascinate and stir its
imaginary. But when white subjectivities enter erotic relationships with
black women, Dabydeen suggests that this cornerstone begins to
loosen. Interracial sex, a black house servant observes, has the effect of
'putting ideas into nigger people head that they beautiful – that's why
whiteman desire them – so why can't they have this right and that right
and more wage'. An acknowledgement of black beauty, and worse, the
practice of miscegenation, could lead to a chain of demands for land,
for the vote, and for power, jeopardising Albion's reproduction. 'All
because Gladstone weak in flesh', the house servant reflects. 'Imagine,
a piece of sugar-cake the size of his palm can change the whole course
of the colony and make a nigger king, a coolie governor' (*TCH* p143).

In *The Counting House* white degeneration and the threat to the
reproduction of colonial structures – including the vested interests of
the black house maid – are thwarted when one black female servant
forcibly aborts another. In Dabydeen's vision, such force can check the
momentum, but not change the dynamic. 'Is 1860 but wait till 1960,'
Dabydeen vocalises, ironically, on behalf of the servant. 'Who will
force me to scrub floor then ... when I have freedom?' (*TCH* p124).

Colonial identifications structure the forms of resistance available to
those who wish to challenge Anglo-British power. Miriam, the house
servant of Gladstone, adopts a strategy of collusion, granting the white
planter the erotic pleasures of the black sublime and then living on the
proceeds of his penitence. Her lover Kampta, non-indentured, property-
less and of mixed race, is a figure of resistance who escapes planter regulation and moves between Guyana's many non-white cultures. But their
relationship is another example of Spivak's 'repetition-in-rupture': 'He
loved her only because she belonged to Gladstone. She could tell from
the way he insisted on taking her at night to the cemetery, always beside
or on top of old Mr Gladstone's grave' (*TCH* p111). In a trope by now
familiar in Dabydeen's work, at the close of the novel Kampta wishes to
escape the racialised identifications and relationships of colonial history,
to 'escape from hatred and shame' (*TCH* p146).

The Counting House is a reflexive and open-ended representation of
a colonial past and a racialised and inegalitarian present. Instead of a
closure, the house servant Miriam offers speculative itineraries for
three of its main characters. In this historical novel, history is evanes-
cent. As Mrs Rutherford observes in *Disappearance*, 'Everything is
reported story. You can't know anything for certain' (*Disappearance*

p157). These are created rather than discovered Anglo-British and black identifications. They suggest a creatable and different future.

FOREIGNERS TOGETHER

As Anthony D. King points out, 'The first globally multiracial, multi-cultural, multicontinental societies on any substantial scale were in the periphery, not the core.'[80] Guyana has hosted a particularly complex and volatile nexus of power, ethnicities and creolised representations for a century and a half.[81] In England of course, this has only been the case since the 1950s. Guyana has also experienced, and attempted to overcome, the problems of ethnic communalism.[82] 'Let white people make the effort to be mongrel!', Dabydeen urges, suggesting that whiteness has not yet been made strange to its bearers, and that Cool Britannia is therefore a configuration of Anglo-British power, a convolution but not a departure from the English imaginary.[83]

Many white Anglo-Britons 'don't want to heal their own scar or hear their own story' (CO p40-41). But for those of us that do, exposure to Dabydeen's work helps to disperse racialised national identifications, begins to reveal the 'incoherencies and abysses' that mark our constitution, and helps to prepare us for 'the togetherness of those foreigners that we all recognise ourselves to be.'[84]

NOTES
1. Frantz Fanon, *Black Skin, White Masks*, Pluto Press, London 1986, p231.
2. Anne McClintock, *Imperial Leather: Race, Gender and Sexuality in the Colonial Context*, Routledge, London 1995, p22.
3. Richard Dyer, *White*, Routledge, London 1997, p14.
4. Karen Patricia McIntyre, *Creative Decolonisation: A Study of the Writings of David Dabydeen*, PHD thesis, University of Bristol October 1996, p137.
5. Trevor Jones, *Britain's Ethnic Minorities*, Policies Studies Institute, London 1993.
6. Wolfgang Binder, 'Interview with David Dabydeen, 1989', in Kevin Grant (ed), *The Art of David Dabydeen*, Peepal Tree Press, Leeds 1997, p174.
7. Richard Dyer, *op.cit*, 1997, p4.
8. Wolfgang Binder (ed), *op.cit.*, 1997, p161.
9. David Dabydeen, *Disappearance*, Secker and Warburg, 1993, p178. Further references to this title will be marked in the text as *Disappearace* followed by page number.
10. Wolfgang Binder, *op.cit.*, 1997, p164.
11. Kevin Davey, 'Mongrelisation is our original state: an interview with David

Dabydeen' in Mark Perryman, (ed), *Altered States: Postmodernism, Politics, Culture*, Lawrence and Wishart, London 1994, p186.

12. Ralph Premdas, 'Race and Ethnic Relations in Burnhamite Guyana' in David Dabydeen and Brinsley Samaroo (eds), *Across the Dark Waters: Ethnicity and Indian Identity in the Caribbean*, Macmillan, London 1996, p44.

13. David Dabydeen, *The Intended*, Secker and Warburg, London. 1991, p179. Further references to this title will be marked in the text as *TI* followed by page number.

14. Kevin Davey, 1994, *op.cit.*, p188.

15. Wolfgang Binder, *op.cit.*, 1997, p165.

16. *Ibid*.

17. David Dabydeen, *Coolie Odyssey*, Hansib/Dangaroo Press, London 1988, p10. Further references to this title will be marked in the text as *CO* followed by page number.

18. For contemporary accounts see Cheddi Jagan, *Forbidden Freedom: The Story of British Guiana*, Lawrence and Wishart, London 1954; and Ashton Chase, *133 Days Towards Freedom in Guyana*, New Guiana Co, Georgetown 1953.

19. Dabydeen has retold some of his biography in the essay 'From Care to Cambridge' in Kirsten Holst Petersen and Anna Rutherford (eds), *Displaced Persons*, Seklos, 1988, pp137-141. See also the interview with Frank Birbalsingh, 'David Dabydeen: Coolie Odyssey' in Frank Birbalsingh (ed), *Frontiers of Caribbean Literature in English*, Macmillan, London 1996, pp167-182.

20. David Dabydeen, in Kirsten Holst Petersen and Anna Rutherford (eds), *op.cit.*, p139.

21. Fanon, *The Wretched of the Earth*, Grove Press, New York, 1968.

22. David Dabydeen, in Kirsten Holst Petersen and Anna Rutherford (eds), *op.cit.*, pp137-141.

23. J. B. Priestley, *Faraway*, Mandarin, London 1996, p168.

24. David Dabydeen, in Kirsten Holst Petersen and Anna Rutherford (eds), *op.cit.*, p138.

25. Homi Bhabha, 'Of Mimicry and Man: The Ambivalence of Colonial Discourse' in *The Location of Culture*, Routledge, London 1994.

26. Wolfgang Binder, *op.cit.*, 1997, p164.

27. David Dabydeen in Kirsten Holst Petersen and Anna Rutherford (eds), *op.cit.*, p140.

28. David Dabydeen (ed), *The Black Presence in English Literature*, Manchester University Press, Manchester 1985, pix.

29. *Ibid*, pvii-ix.

30. *Ibid*, pix.

31. David Dabydeen, 'Eighteenth Century English Literature on Commerce and Slavery' in *Ibid*, pp26-49.

32. *Ibid*, p46.

33. David Dabydeen, *Some Aspects of William Hogarth's Representation of the Materialism of His Age*, PHD dissertation, University of London, 1982; *Hogarth's Blacks: Images of Blacks in Eighteenth Century English Art*, Dangaroo Press, Coventry, 1985.

34. David Dabydeen, *op.cit.*, 1985, p21.

35. A. Sivanandan, *Communities of Resistance*, Verso, London 1990.

36. David Dabydeen and Nana Wilson-Tagoe, *A Reader's Guide to West Indian and Black British Literature*, Hansib-Rutherford Press, London 1988, p154.

37. David Dabydeen, *op.cit.*, 1985, p9.

38. *Ibid*, pp37-8.

39. *Ibid*, p30.

40. *Ibid*, pp33-36.

41. *Ibid*, p51. See also the account of Nancy Cunard's *Black man, White Ladyship*, in this volume, pp35–38.

42. David Dabydeen, *op.cit.*, 1985, p74.

43. *Ibid*, p97.

44. *Ibid*, p100.

45. *Ibid*, p64.

46. See Bart-Moore Gilbert, *Postcolonial Theory*, Verso, London 1997, pp97–106.

47. David Dabydeen, *op.cit.*, 1985, pp130-131.

48. *Ibid*, p131.

49. David Dabydeen, *Slave Song*, Dangaroo Press, Coventry 1984, p9. Further references to this title will be marked in the text in brackets as *SS* followed by page number.

50. Sarah Lawson-Welsh, 'Experiments in Brokenness: The Creative Use of Creole in David Dabydeen's Slave Song' in Kevin Grant (ed), *op.cit.*, p31.

51. *Ibid*, p37.

52. David Dabydeen and Nana Wilson-Tagoe, *op.cit.*, 1988, p171-172.

53. Mark McWatt, 'His True-True Face: Masking and Revelation in David Dabydeen's Slave Song' in Kevin Grant (ed), *op.cit*, pp15-25.

54. Wolfgang Binder, *op.cit.*, 1997, p169.

55. Julia Kristeva, *Powers of Horror: An Essay on Abjection*, Columbia University Press, New York, 1992, p2.

56. David Dabydeen and Nana Wilson-Tagoe, *op.cit*, 1988, p81.

57. *Ibid*, 109.

58. *Ibid*, p111-116.

59. *Ibid*, p86.

60. Benita Parry, 'Between Creole and Cambridge English: The Poetry of David Dabydeen' in Kevin Grant (ed), *op.cit*, p52.

61. *Ibid*, p54.

62. Tony Blair, *New Britain: My Vision of a Young Country*, Fourth Estate, London, 1996, pix-x.

63. Wolfgang Binder in Kevin Grant (ed), *op.cit*, 1997, p173.

64. Kwame Dawes, 'Interview with David Dabydeen, 1994' in Kevin Grant (ed), *op.cit.*, 1997, p210.

65. Kevin Davey, 'Mongrelisation is our original state: an interview with David Dabydeen', *op.cit.*, p189.

66. V S Naipaul, *The Enigma of Arrival*, Viking, London 1987.

67. Kevin Davey, 'Mongrelisation is our original state: an interview with David Dabydeen', *op.cit.*, p185.

68. David Dabydeen, *Turner*, Jonathan Cape, 1994, p25. Further references to this poem will be marked in the text in brackets as *Turner* followed by page number.

69. Paul Gilroy, *The Black Atlantic: Modernity and Double Consciousness*, Verso, London, 1993.

70. Fred D'Aguiar, *The Longest Memory*, Chatto and Windus, London 1994.

71. Dabydeen's *Turner* was preceded by Paul Gilroy's reflections in *Small Acts*, Serpents Tail, London 1993, pp81-84 and followed by Fred D'Aguiar's power-ful novel *Feeding the Ghosts*, Chatto and Windus, London 1997.

72. Linda Colley, *Britons: Forging the Nation 1707-1837*, Pimlico, London 1992, p350.

73. Chantal Mouffe, 'Hegemony and New Political Subjects' in Cary Nelson and Lawrence Grossberg (eds), *Marxism and the Interpretation of Culture*, Macmillan, London 1988, p199.

74. Kwame Dawes, 'Interview with David Dabydeen, 1994' in Kevin Grant, (ed), *op.cit*, p199.

75. *Ibid*, p200.

76. Karen McIntyre, 'Necrophilia or Stillbirth? David Dabydeen's Turner as the Embodiment of Postcolonial Creative Decolonisation' in Kevin Grant, (ed), *op.cit.*, pp141-158.

77. See Edgar Mittelholzer's *Children of Kaywana*, Secker and Warburg, London 1952 and *Kaywana Blood*, Secker and Warburg, London 1958.

78. David Dabydeen, *The Counting House*, Jonathan Cape, London 1996, p147. Further references to this title will be marked in the text in brackets as TCH followed by page number.

79. Richard Dyer, *op.cit.*, p25.

80. Anthony D King, 'Introduction' to Anthony D King (ed), *Culture, Globalisation and the World System*, Macmillan, London 1991, p8.

81. See the impressive account provided in Brian L Moore, *Cultural power, Resistance and Pluralism: Colonial Guyana 1838-1900*, University of the West Indies and McGill-Queen's University Press, Jamaica and Montreal, 1995.

82. See Ralph Premdas, 'Race and Ethnic Relations in Burnhamite Guyana' in David Dabydeen and Brinsley Samaroo, *Across the Dark Waters: Ethnicity and Indian Identity in the Caribbean*, Macmillan, London, 1996, pp39-64. In 1992 the first free and fair elections for forty years propelled the late and long-standing leader of the Indo-Guyanese majority, Cheddi Jagan, into the president's office, where he initiated a programme of economic reforms and multi-culturalism. Dabydeen was a prominent supporter of the PPP/Civic government. See David Dabydeen (ed), *Cheddi Jagan: Selected Speeches*, Hansib, London 1995.

83. Kevin Davey, 'Mongrelisation is our original state: an interview with David Dabydeen', *op.cit.*, p182.

84. Julia Kristeva, *Strangers to Ourselves*, Columbia University Press, New York 1991, pp2-3.

7

Mark Wallinger: the lost horizon of the English studfarm

In 1997 a Union Jack transformed by the colours of the Irish Tricolour flew over the impoverished and ethnically diverse streets of Brixton in inner London. Mark Wallinger's *Oxymoron* was a joke and a challenge, the national flag inverted into the colours of its historic republican opponent. It wasn't so funny when I took a smaller version across the Irish channel, as the peace process stumbled. In one Belfast street it was seen as a symbol of national unity, corrupted by its loathsome abject. In another it was an offensive appropriation of Irishness, and further evidence of Anglo-British arrogance and insensitivity. If nothing else, young British art (yBa), at least in the North of Ireland, had proved it did possess the capacity to shock.

In the mid-1990s cabinet ministers, business leaders, night clubbers and unemployed youth jostled in the long queues which formed for exhibitions of work by the young British artists. A new aesthetic formation had been defined through a combination of self promotion, dealer packaging, patronage, public gallery endorsement, the manipulation of broadcast and print media and British council promotion overseas.[1] In a final homage to its dominance, yBa became the target for acts of iconoclasm, including attacks on Damien Hirst's entropic animal sculptures and his West End restaurant Quo Vadis, on Rachel Whiteread's *House* and on Marcus Harvey's painting of Myra Hindley.

In a powerful critique of the yBa formation, Mark Harris argues that the artists were being used to revalorise an anachronistic idea of Britishness, and that 'the artists themselves offer no lucid critique of this use to which they are being put'.[2] Stuart Home argues more generally that the institutions of art invariably serve 'the interests of a narrow-minded nationalism' and 'retrench class divisions'.[3] Harris overlooks, and Home underestimates, the work of Mark Wallinger, one of the more significant figures in this much hyped but disparate group of artists.

George Stubbs, the eighteenth century equestrian painter, remains one of the nation's most revered artists. His pictures still command prominent gallery space and huge prices at auction. In 1997 the National Gallery celebrated its purchase of Stubb's *Whistlejacket* with a laser projection of the image in Trafalgar Square.[4] In the 1990s, by repainting and reconfiguring the work of Stubbs, and more generally by using film, video and performance as a means to analyse the breeding and racing of horses as an important nexus of sport, power and Anglo-British national identifications, Wallinger destabilised the fields of sport and of art, and by doing so contributed to the process of making the English strangers to themselves.

Wallinger has contextualised his own practice: 'The first work I showed had to do with national identity and its iconography', he recalls.

> I started working after two key events, the Falklands war and the miners' strike. The war stirred up a lot of ugly jingoism. The Right hijacked patriotism and the 1983 election campaign became a victory march for the Tories. Nationhood and ideas of Englishness were invoked with unquestioning authority and subsequently wielded against the miners. Curious and archaic laws dating back to the seventeenth century were used to incarcerate 'the enemy within', which paved the way for sweeping anti-union legislation. This led me to think about what constituted nationhood and Englishness ... I was personally angry.[5]

Wallinger poked a finger in the Anglo-British eye formed by national painting traditions, sporting distinctions and the burgeoning heritage industry.[6] Duchampian and socially engaged, working at the interface between the popular and the national-popular, Wallinger disorganised the notions and representations of national identity that came to the fore during the Thatcherite period.

Although his work in and beyond the gallery complemented some of the connections being made in the field of politics, it is hard if not impossible to assimilate his work to the pragmatic anti-Thatcherism of New Labour. New Labour frequently resorted to the inherited forms and narratives of English nationalism, not least in its eventual political settlement with the interests of the City of London, its ambivalence over European integration, and its use of the national flag, Fitz the bulldog, and the white cliffs of Dover in its electioneering imagery.

Although Black British artists like Eddie Chambers and Keith Piper have long reworked the icons of Englishness and questioned false assumptions about the homogeneity of Anglo-British culture, the importance of Wallinger's deconstruction of English iconography is that it is a complementary response to this critique from within white Anglo-Britain. It led him to resuscitate figurative oil painting – an activity marginalised by conceptualism's long ascendancy in the visual arts – as a hybrid historico-conceptual practice.

Every community – and perhaps more significantly, every non-community – in the United Kingdom has its betting shop and satellite link to the nation's racecourses. Wallinger's equestrian paintings, video installations and performances are therefore part of the 'open confederacy with popular pleasures' identified by John Roberts as a key feature of 1990s art.[7] More significantly, however, they are a critical engagement with the processes constructing and changing Anglo-British identifications. Wallinger's work suggests that the notion that 'sport has become a national unifier rather than a source of conflict' is far from the truth.[8]

As with Nick Hornby's bestselling *Fever Pitch*, which signalled a major crossover between the fields of literature and sport, Wallinger's installations, particularly those involving trainsets, tabletop football and memories of televised horseracing, produce a distinctively gendered exploration of Britain's evolving national identity. This is perhaps why Waldemar Januszczak has mistakenly dismissed him as 'half a New Lad'.[9]

Reacting against American minimalism and conceptual art, which was seen to threaten the demise of painting, the Continental European art practices of the 1980s were profoundly concerned with questions of painting and national identity, exploring mythological narratives, collective memory and recent history. These concerns were particularly central to German neo-expressionism, in which Kiefer, Lupertz and Baselitz re-articulated the symbols and mythology of German nationalism – in Kiefer's case, from the restaging of Hitler salutes, to paintings of Operation Sea Lion (Hitler's plan to invade England by sea) and to reworkings of the Siegfried and Brunhilde myth. A painterly counter-American national reflexivity also characterised the work of the Italian transavantgardia of Chia, Cuchi and Clemente, which revived the conventions of interwar painters like Sironi and the late

works of De Chirico. Chia in particular reworked, quoted and paro-
died classical myths. This practice was sustained in the postmodern
Pittura Colta artists who followed, most obviously in Mariani's imita-
tions of Raphael, Reni and David. In France a similar practice can be
found in the work of Tibor Czernus and Garouste.

Britain accepted the form but not the potentially destabilising
content of these European developments. The 1981 Royal Academy
exhibition, *A New Spirit in Painting*, was an important attempt to
revive British figurative oil painting. Co-curator Christos Joachimides
argued that minimalism and conceptualism were 'devoid of all joy in
the senses' and based on a 'thoroughgoing prohibition on subjective
experience'.[10] The German neo-expressionist painters were feted as
exemplary and a London School – of Freud, Bacon, Kossoff and others
– was celebrated as the indigenous correlate. The case was reaffirmed
even more pointedly in the *Zeitgeist* exhibition held in Berlin in 1982.[11]
This led to the rather ridiculous claim that the new School of London
was the real historical successor to American Abstract Expressionism.[12]

The London School was in fact a disparate mix of artists and styles
of painting. A contemporary survey confirms the comparative lack of
focus in British art during the 1980s: 'In most countries it has been rela-
tively easy to point out the specific groups of artists who constitute the
New painting. It is not so in England'.[13] Much more significantly, the
London School did not share in the European mood of national reflexivity. Indeed, the British moment was marked by Peter Fuller's uncritical celebrations of a Deep England whose landscape was a 'sustain-
ing mother'.[14]

Wallinger's re-performance of Stubbs and the Grand Style in the late
1980s trod where Fuller forbade and where the London School feared
to go. It was an unsynchronised and idiosyncratic tracking of the foot-
steps of his continental elders, unconstrained by the conventions of
neo-expressionism, of which Wallinger was highly critical. Of the
belated arrival of this reflexivity in British art, it is not enough to say
better late than never. Its tardiness was an index of the English imaginary's propensity to resist modernisation.

BRITAIN'S ART SENSATION!

An artist casts the space beneath his seat. He then casts portions of his
body in green wax. He devises anagrammatic and punning titles for his
work, like *Eat/Death*. Later in his career he creates hybrid animals
from dismembered body parts.

Question: which young British artist does this describe? Answer: none of them. Second answer: nearly all of them. The pieces described are all by Bruce Nauman, an American post-minimal and conceptual artist who has been producing work of this kind – to international acclaim – since the 1960s.[15]

In 1966, reflecting on the purpose of the artist alone in his studio, Naumann made casts of the spaces beneath his seat, beneath his wall shelves and between two boxes on the floor of his empty workspace. In the 1997 *Sensation* exhibition at the Royal Academy the work of Turner Prize winning artist Rachel Whiteread was represented by 100 casts of the spaces beneath chairs, a cast of the space beneath a bath and another of a whole room. Her work was clearly derived from Nauman, but on a larger scale.

The art-historical plinths for Damien Hirst's entropic sharks, sheep and cattle are also easy to identify. Joseph Beuys produced vitrine displays of unstable materials for two and a half decades. Jeff Koons did the same with consumer goods, suspending some in liquids. It would be easy to go on, explaining how the post-feminist works of Tracy Emin and Sarah Lucas, or the Chapman brothers' genitally mutated mannequins take their cue from artists already well known in the global art market like Louise Bourgeois, Annette Messager, Robert Gober and Kiki Smith. To a great extent, the yBa have simply appropriated the neo-conceptual techniques of American art from the 1960s and 1970s, returning to Duchampian practices with a little bit of Arte Povera, minimalism, Fluxus, process and body art thrown in for good measure. Impressive as the resulting metacommentary is, this facet of Cool Britannia is based on borrowings and translations, and is not a major aesthetic departure unique to Britain.

Only in exceptional cases – in the textile based historical paradoxes of Yinka Shonibare, in the Afropsychedelia of Chris Ofili or in Mark Wallinger's subversion of Stubbs and transgression of the boundaries between the fields of mass spectator sport and art – did the artists included in the yBa showcase exhibition, *Sensation*, directly address the divisions and anachronism of Anglo-British national identifications, and the past and future of Englishness.

If we are looking for creativity and relevance – rather than a burgeoning celebrity which politicians can piggyback while trying to develop a national popular – it is to these three artists, and to Wallinger in particular, that we should turn. But first we must understand the formation of which they are a part in a little more detail.

THE GOLDSMITHS GENERATION

With the rise of the young British artists some cultural momentum returned to the British fine arts from popular music. The rise of this predominantly Goldsmiths College trained group of artists – a 'neo-conceptual bratpack'[16] – can be tracked through a series of exhibitions, from the self-organised Freeze to the series of shows of Young British Artists at the Saatchi Gallery from 1992 onwards, consolidated by the British Art Show 4 (1995-6). *Brilliant!* at the Walker Art Gallery (1995-6), *Life/Live* at the Pompidou Centre (1996) and *Sensation!* at the Royal Academy (1997) confirmed their ascendancy.

To a great extent, the young British artists have adopted the neo-conceptual themes of the American postminimalist art of the 1960s and 1970s, itself a return to Duchampian values after the long domi-nance of abstract expressionism, colour field abstraction and Pop art. Minimalism and Arte Povera from the 1960s have influenced the choice of materials and conventions. To these traditions they have added a greater interest in the body and in identity, although this too owes a great deal to the work of Nauman, the new body art of figures like Richard Gober, and 1980s developments in American neo-conceptualism.[17]

Consolidated by public galleries and the British Council, yBa was initiated and sustained by the patronage of Charles Saatchi, who was an art collector-dealer and the joint owner of the advertising agency that was once the largest in the world, and was retained by the Conservative Party during its period of Thatcherite hegemony.

It is through Saatchi that the formation of young British art is linked to the long Conservative hegemony. After the advertising agency he ran with his brother – which owed its distinction and success to tech-niques imported and cloned from the United States – was listed on the stock market in the mid-1970s, Charles began to invest in modern European and American art. His collection grew, fuelled by his share of the proceeds of the agency's contracts with Silk Cut and British Airways and the political campaigns that lambasted the Labour Party on behalf of the Conservatives. 'Labour isn't working' helped to in-augurate Thatcherism in 1979.[18] Charles Saatchi's high profile collec-tion of contemporary art helped to brand and position his agency as innovative and leading edge in its field.

Of the nationally reflexive European painters of the 1980s, Saatchi collected Clemente, Chia, Baselitz and Anselm Kiefer, the latter of whom was exhibited at his gallery in a powerful, paired contrast with

the work of the conceptual minimalist Richard Serra.[19] Kiefer's combination of text and German national iconography, his practice of inter-
textual historical painting, predicated on an understanding of national
identifications as the precipitate of historical representations, were an
important tributary for Wallinger's work.[20]

These were the halcyon years of the art market.[21] After the recession, oil crisis and inflation of the mid-1970s, investors started to
shift their assets into the art markets, a move which soon led to speculative purchasing and a boom which lasted until late 1989. A small
number of contemporary artists secured celebrity status and high
incomes – the most prominent example was that of the young
American neo-expressionist Julian Schnabel – shaping the aspirations of
contemporary art students in British schools and universities.[22] There is
still a buoyant if speculative global market in contemporary art.

Some argue that Saatchi's enormous collection is a form of speculation, that in the art market value is added to works simply as a result of
the distinction bestowed by his purchase. 'Charles is a commercial
creature', his friends acknowledge. 'He is aware of the marketability of
art.'[23] Saatchi's high profile investments did have the effect of turning
the artists he favoured – Schnabel, Twombly and Kiefer, for example –
into celebrities. As a result their work had a high resale value during the
art boom that accelerated just as the Saatchi and Saatchi agency first hit
financial difficulties.

Within four years of the stock market crash of 1987 Saatchi and
Saatchi shares had lost 98 per cent of their value. It would not be long
before the brothers were to lose control of the company altogether.[24]
Charles Saatchi resold most of the works he had collected in the 1980s
at great profit through the New York outlets of Larry Gagosian and
Sotheby's. But the deals were also completed at some cost to his reputation as a collector.[25]

In the purchasing policy that he adopted after 1989 – particularly in
his growing partiality to a punning and post-minimalist Anglo-British
conceptualism – Charles Saatchi seems to have fostered an aesthetic
that has much in common with the advertising innovations which he
and his brother had imported from the USA a decade and a half before.
These were once summarised by Maurice Saatchi as: 'If you can't
reduce your argument to a few crisp words and phrases, there's something wrong with your argument'.[26] At first Saatchi had endorsed the
disparate London School of Freud, Kossoff, Rego and Kitaj. He also
purchased the work of the British sculptors who had engaged with

conceptualism and minimalism, for example, Tony Cragg, Richard Wilson and Bill Woodrow.[27]

Then his attention was caught by the Goldsmiths generation. From 1990 he started purchasing the work of Goldsmiths College graduates, among them Damien Hirst. Two other dealers – Jay Jopling and Kartsen Schubert – operated in the same market. But it was Saatchi's investment of the proceeds of M&C Saatchi accounts maintained by Dixons, Gallaher Tobacco and the Mirror Group, together with the profits he made from the rescue of sportswear business Adidas, that were decisive in shaping the new British art scene. By the late 1990s Saatchi had purchased a total of 875 works by young British artists.[28]

The work of these artists was valorised at a crucial moment in the evolution of Anglo-British art institutions. Changes in government and Arts Council criteria for the public funding of galleries had made attendance figures central, sensitising directors and curators to the news values that the new artists were adept at manipulating. Young British art also became a cultural complement to a wider initiative – which includes the construction of the new Tate Gallery of modern art – to maintain London's standing as a world class financial centre.

Despite its emergence from the state higher education system and its promotion by public agencies like the British Council and the Arts Council, some commentators have seen the yBa's art as a wholly subsidiary formation of Thatcherism – 'Margaret's children, deeply motivated, multiskilled risk takers'.[29] Certainly as self-employed artists they frequently relied on the enterprise allowance scheme introduced by the Conservative government as self-employed artists. They were also able to negotiate the temporary usage of vacant industrial premises created as a result of the Thatcherite neglect of manufacturing, and inner city decline. But Stuart Brisley overstates the case when he argues that contemporary British art 'has a particular energy because we have been moving from the welfare state to the free market. It doesn't suffer from the constraints of state patronage. There is an atmosphere of libertarianism and a release from social responsibilities.'[30] Young British art depended, and still relies heavily, on two important state funded networks: the art colleges at home and the offices of the British Council abroad.

Although Sarah Kent insisted that the artists whom Saatchi had begun to collect 'do not form a group or a school', the market and the media usually thought otherwise.[31] Stuart Morgan attempted to provide a unifying account in an overview written for an American audience:

In much recent British art, coding has replaced singular meanings. Polylingual, new British artists draw not only on what used to be known as high and low cultures – only the stratification of a single culture, after all – but also on the process and qualities of daily life. Detachment has lessened, distance has been replaced by involvement, and privacy by the public, difficulty by a kind of obviousness so blatant that it sends the viewer away confused. The recrudescence of a Situationist stance, the accent on comedy rather than tragedy, the use of simple materials or easily understood proposals all distinguish an art that thumbs its nose at authority. If it (paradoxically) accepts that authority, whether in reverence or for the purposes of undermining it, this should come as no surprise in a country where an insult need not take the form of a punch on the nose when a raised eyebrow might achieve the same result, a country where irony can be the most powerful of weapons.[32]

Morgan represented the movement as a form of traditional but populist English eccentricity. No one disputes that the yBa formation was simultaneously adversarial, media friendly and culturally ascendant. But when Morgan cites Situationism as source of its practice – a claim also made by Neville Wakefield – this outrages contemporary guardians of the Debordian flame.[33] Simon Ford, for example, argues that today the artistic and political mainstream requires and depends on the existence of an avant-garde, and actively exaggerates its subversiveness. 'Recuperation is seeded within every act in advance', he claims. 'The yBa represents the precuperation of an aesthetic avant garde'.[34]

Mark Harris also insists that an outdated discourse on the avant-garde survives in much writing on the yBa's.[35] In fact he accuses the Chapman brothers, Sarah Lucas, Damien Hirst and Chris Offili of 'atavistic avant gardism'. Their work is marked by 'a vestigial offensiveness that designates participation in a broader submission to abrasive imagery and language, especially in current advertising where, in order to promote commodities, these devices are developed most effectively.' Instead of challenging or 'reframing' the art world, their activities help the galleries to prosper. Harris accepts that yBa is carnivalesque and a source of anti-authoritarian laughter but insists it lacks any serious engagement with major social issues. He also points out, with much justification, that its conventions are not exclusive to Britain.

These concerns are framed by a more widespread and traditional anxiety, that the yBa formation has had 'a less-then-healthy effect in the relentless search for the newsworthy rather than the artworthy'. This view is beginning to influence the programming of galleries.[36] The spectre of a dumbing down of the Anglo-British is increasingly invoked. At this point it is salutary to recall Gramsci's injunction 'not to be afraid of innovations and audacities'.[37] The young British artists have pulled down the fence that once separated the fields of art and popular culture. Their work can be articulated with a progressive modernisation of Anglo-Britain, or it can simply be co-opted into a rebranding exercise for the capital. The choice is ours.

ENGLISH MODERNITY AS A LOST HORIZON

Wallinger's place in these events was contradictory, a fact which may explain his omission from the largest international touring exhibitions and his virtual invisibility in *Blimey!* – Matthew Colling's anecdotal account of the movement.[38] Wallinger's early work challenged the Conservative English nationalism that Saatchi and Saatchi had helped to hone and project during the Thatcher years. Nevertheless, he became a beneficiary of the Saatchi regime and also made an important contribution to the renaissance of Anglo-British historical painting.

From the early 1960s to the mid-1980s the assertion that painting was dead was a recurrent feature of artistic and critical debate. Critics suggested that painting was exhausted as a form and that the palette and the spraycan should give way to photography, sculpture and video. Many leading European artists of the 1970s opposed the practice of painting as much as they opposed the boundaries set by the American traditions of abstract expressionism, Pop Art, minimalism and conceptualism. In this respect Beuys, Merz, Kounellis, Broodthaers and Buren were engaged in an artistic detraditionalisation and de-Atlanticisation that sought to undermine the distinctions which had formerly sustained European cultural elites.

Painting survived. As we have seen, throughout the following decade there was a co-ordinated attempt to revalidate figurative painting, while simultaneously valorising European practices over American. In Britain this was spearheaded by R.B. Kitaj, and accelerated by the 1981 *New Spirit in Painting* exhibition at the Royal Academy.[39]

Marxists and radicals resisted the return of figurative painting at the time, with the notable exception of Gerhard Richter.[40] Contributors to the journal *October* were appalled by the re-emergence of notions of the painter of genius. They saw figuration as an aesthetic which complemented neo-conservatism, re-affirming the myths of bourgeois humanism and succumbing to the art market.[41] But neo-expressionists knew that a figurative re-engagement with national identity was cultural-political dynamite as the pace of European integration increased. As Nicholas Serota said at the time, 'In the best European art, there's an awareness of the ebb and flow of history, of culture and politics'.[42] The widespread reworking of national myths and symbols was a controversial, painterly engagement with national-populars. This is the practice that Wallinger brought into British art and into the cultural politics of English nationalism during the 1980s.

Wallinger's training and earliest years as a professional artist co-incided with the period of untrammelled Thatcherism. He attended the Chelsea School of Art from 1978-81 and Goldsmiths College from 1983-85. From 1985 Wallinger's work was sold through the Anthony Reynolds gallery, which was based in the East End of London until 1991. He appeared in Saatchi's second young British artists' exhibition in 1993.[43]

A highly skilled, figurative oil painter, his work is not merely a regression, a return to the archaic or a concession to heritage. His oil painting is a performance that throws up crucial questions about the social and historical value and role of this form of representation. The Art and Language group set the scene for Wallinger's historical and equestrian paintings with their recognition that 'The *culture* of painting ... could now be critically addressed *by* painting'.[44] Wallinger's parodic re-examination of Anglo-British national traditions and canonical painting conventions has much in common with Komar and Melamid's straight-faced burlesques of the socialist realism which had defined their Soviet homeland's dominant aesthetic.[45] But in Anglo-Britain it was the eighteenth century Grand Style and the work of George Stubbs which had to be interrogated.

An early work, *Stately Home* (1985), a 'bogus blue-blooded thing', was a careful reproduction of a watercoloured engraving of the eighteenth century seat of a family with a similar name to the artist.[46] Its suggestion of the deep and civilised continuity of the landed settlement was undermined by his insertion of a cartoon dinosaur, the very same trick that Komar and Melamid had played on Stalinist icono-graphy in *Bolsheviks Returning Home After a Demonstration*. In Wallinger's case it was a way of asking how far back the Anglo-British intended to project the notion of their blood line and historical roots.

An early solo exhibition, *Hearts of Oak*, at the Anthony Reynolds

Gallery in 1986, showed the influence, despite Wallinger's misgivings, of the German neo-Expressionists. The works were Anglicised Kiefer, rough assemblages of quotations from paintings by Gainsborough and Stubbs with text from Morris, Blake and Clare. They were mounted direct on the wall and then spraycan graffitied with the words Albion and Jerusalem. These works hosted a clash between received represent-ations of national identity and urban modernity, questioning the stabil-ity of the speaking positions available in hegemonic and counter discourses of Englishness.

Wallinger's most significant early painting engaging with the cacophonous process of modernisation and English national identifica-tion was *Lost Horizon* (1986). The painting was a landscape in the genre of equestrian portraiture, but the thoroughbred horse and owner required by convention were replaced with representations of a porce-lain shire horse, an ornamental dress soldier, and the names of the four Beatles and the 1960s Labour prime minister Harold Wilson, the distri-bution of the text reproducing the distribution of the figures in an iconic 1960s photograph. John Roberts correctly points out that *Lost Horizon* is an exercise in the interchangeability of signs.[47] This has implications for the process of identification, individual and national, that Roberts fails to pursue.

In one sense, the substitutions in *Lost Horizon* evoke the melan-choly of commodification and representation, the spectre of a Baudrillardian implosion of meaning, that we have already encoun-tered in Pop Art and the songs of Pete Townshend.[48] The singular vantage point characteristic of high modernism is forfeited. Images that are neither representational nor fully simulacral are deployed, register-ing 'a dimension of anxiety, melancholy and loss'.[49] These are not random signs; this painting addresses the lost horizon of the collective Anglo-British imaginary described by Laclau.[50] It suggests that England is neither intelligible nor authentic, nor a space in which its subjects can operate without a reflexive sense of their own strangeness.

The horse and the soldier are cheap, kitsch reproductions of the type that cluttered many a 1960s mantelpiece. They occupy the lost horizon of an Anglo-British childhood. As figures of the uncanny they recall the moment of entry into language and the inaugural loss that consti-tutes subjectivity. That this loss is replicated in the process of national identification is suggested by the gathering storm clouds and the dying oak tree in the foreground; but this is also an emblem of Thatcher's destruction of the nation, and a gendered and Dabydeen-like figuration of the impotence and incompleteness which accom-panies entry into the symbolic order.

A living oak thrives in the background. The possibility that tree, horse, soldier and stump are representations of the individual Beatles is not foreclosed. In its citation of popular modernity, the painting provides a comic, reflexive contrast to paintings like Kiefer's *German Line of Spiritual Salvation* in which the names of Hegel, Feuerbach and Marx accompany a rainbow which arches over the horizon of a German landscape, as the names of German psychoanalysts float on a river pass-ing through it. Wallinger's words and images speak of the lost horizon of a national, non-commercial high culture – usually formed by the abjection of kitsch and popular culture – and therefore of a reactionary market-led Anglo-British modernisation, an imaginary which cannot provide an identification.

Lost Horizon is an accumulation of signs which have lost their meaning, hollow representations of Anglo-British national identity and modernity, melancholy reminders of the lost promises of popular music – the irretrievable chora – and the Labour governments of the 1960s. Lord Wilson of Rievaulx is named, and shamed, at the very centre of the picture, above a stately home and alongside a symbolic carthorse – a familiar caricature of a dilatory labour movement origi-nated by the cartoonist David Low between the wars, here ossified and ornamental. Wilson, the modernising socialist who had threatened to sear the landed establishment with the white heat of technology, has been accommodated in the House of Lords and given a new – in fact a pre-modern – identity, confirming the ability of the Old England of the stately home to continue to reproduce itself.

The work is one of the most important produced by the young British artists, putting yBa formation and its later political appropria-tion into question at the moment of its birth, thus unsettling the discourses of art, Labour-led modernisation and Cool Britannia. *Lost Horizon* sets the scene for Wallinger's subsequent enquiry into repre-sentation and English national identification.

Lost Horizon was followed by works based on Wembley stadium; Stonehenge; boys' toys and the kitsch of Empire; his secondary school; passport imagery; the British racecourse; and the art gallery. Wallinger's conceptualism focused on the sites in which the national imaginary is created, amended and disseminated. It was complemented by a degree of personal introspection.

A Model History (1987) consists of a miniature Stonehenge

constructed from house bricks. If this post-minimalist reproduction of a monument central to England's foundational myths – Britain's symbol of autochthony, continuity and territorialised ethnicity – was a joke at the expense of Carl Andre and the English imaginary, it was also formally reflexive, reprising the moment of transition from minimalism to conceptualism.

Booty has uncanny and melancholic links to *Lost Horizon*. It is a bricolage of late imperial kitsch: a trophy elephant's foot; the British umbrella often stored within it; a train set recalling the rail arteries of Empire and British childhood play; and a velvet draped pub table over which the loss of Anglo-British distinction was frequently mourned. These resurrected memories of the 'enabling violence' of colonialism serve as a complex emblem for post-imperial Britain and the artificiality of representation, parodying the residual and inauthentic codes of the colonial imagination.

In *Passport Control* (1988) Wallinger doodles on a range of enlarged photobooth self-portraits, producing a series of mug shots in which he mimics identification with a number of non-European stereotypes, including those of Jew, Arab, Indian and negro. Although many assumptions of Anglo-British whiteness are made explicit and ridiculed by this work, the series demonstrates that an Anglo-British identification can not be easily disguised or discarded.

These explorations of Anglo-Britain's relation to its others were complemented by another figure of arrested modernisation. *They Think It's All Over ... It is Now* (1988) is a work whose title cites the famous remark made by Kenneth Wolstenholme during his television commentary on England's World Cup triumph. Tabletop football players set on a fake marble plinth freeze the moment at which Anglo-Britain's global dominance was briefly re-established, albeit in and on the field of mass spectator sport. As Wallinger has said, 'My last sense of patriotism being innocent was the 1966 World Cup when England beat West Germany, although two world wars provided a pretty obvious subtext'.[51] In this work a lost childhood chora signals the presence of a traumatised post-imperial nation.

In the collection of drawngs known as *School* (1989), Wallinger explores perspective as a regime of truth, and the relationship between institutional space, power and subjectivisation. In these studies of his own secondary school, Wallinger quite literally tries to throw light on the relationship between Anglo-British institutions and the process of identification. In each of these projection drawings of his old gymnasium, assembly hall and classroom, drawn in chalk on blackboards, Wallinger drilled a hole and placed an electric light bulb at the perspectival point – usually the spot where a clock was fixed or where teachers had stood. Unpeopled, the disciplinary purpose of the school was made clear. But we all know that schools are sites of indiscipline, play and resistance. Ultimately the works that comprise *School* must be seen as maps of an authoritarian but failing technology, spaces in which white Anglo-British identifications are meant to take shape, but cannot be determined. Composed of chalk and light, these drawings embody the instability and fragility of identification.

The first shots fired in this assault on the English nationalist discourse of the Thatcher years were confined to the gallery, but Wallinger's equestrian and footballing art in the decade that followed was a major rendevous of popular and national-popular representations, suggesting the outlines of an art practice that might begin to transform Anglo-British national identifications.

THE PEDIGREE HORSES OF A PEDIGREE PEOPLE

According to the proverbial wisdom of gamblers: 'On the turf and under it all men are equal'. In an important series of paintings, installations and performances that made the reproduction of inequality clearly and simultaneously visible – through horseracing, discourses of breeding and a related tradition of British painting – Wallinger demonstrates the lie of the proverb. Horseracing both encodes and contributes to the reproduction of inequality. His equestrian art renegotiates the distinctions and connections between the fields of sport, politics and art that are crucial to the reproduction of an already beleagered Anglo-British establishment.

In fact it is J.B. Priestley, another Anglo-British moderniser dealt with earlier in this book, who best characterises this nexus of culture and power.

> In England there are only three national spheres of interest, namely, the political, the financial, and the sporting, and if you can cut a dash in all three, if, for example, you are a rich political peer whose horse has won the Derby, then you are indeed a representative national figure.[52]

Apart from a few telling comments on the cultural politics of sport, however, Priestley left the configuration that produced this authority alone.[53]

185

Thoroughbred horseracing has always been accompanied by a tradition of oil painting. For two centuries this genre celebrated ownership and genealogy, both of the horse and the painting.[54] For many decades it was possible to purchase both horse and representation at the same place: Tattersall's bloodstock auctions at Hyde Park Corner. John Wootton (1678-1764), who also painted country seats for the same patrons, is usually acknowledged as the first artist in the Anglo-British tradition of proprietorial horse portraiture.

Representations of equestrian sport in paintings have had a complex evolution and relation to national identifications. This has ranged from an early celebration of royal prowess or distinction, the King leading the hunt or hosting the race, through to a later affirmation of country values against those of the court, involving sober landowners and well managed estates. Representations of hunting, shooting and fishing deployed finely calculated codes of social and national distinction. These were evident during the period of hostile public reaction to the Game Laws that forbade plebian hunting; in the time of the Whig ascendancy, characterised by notions of rural backwardness; and during the periods in which invasion threatened, when they often codified Anglo-Britain's military vigour, the stability of its pre-industrial structures and a social inclusiveness that contrasted to figures of abjected, revolutionary France and the threat of modernity.[55]

The changing modes of equestrian painting were therefore closely articulated with the changing hegemonies of Anglo-British history. The genre developed a notion of pedigree horses for a pedigree people and attempts were made to manage the rudimentary and restricted national-popular.

John Sparrow celebrated sporting art in the 1920s because it 'illustrates those qualities which make and preserve a colonising people'.[56] In the mid-1980s Wallinger deconstructed this equestrian art of social and national distinction, replacing it with a modern, democratic and postcolonial practice which reconfigured mass spectator sport and the domain of politics, troubling the English imaginary. Wallinger doubled as a heretic and a disciple: 'I use racing as a metaphor for class, identity, heredity, but I am also a fan', he confessed to a bemused *Sporting Life*.[57]

The anti-modern equestrian tradition was re-asserted as a form of Anglo-British distinction during the Thatcher years. In the wake of the miners' strike, the Falklands war and the second Conservative electoral victory, and while a crisis over the future of painting raged in Europe and in America, sporting art resumed its traditional responsibility for providing a sense of English national purpose and distinction, confirming the pedigree and probity of the people figured in, owning and appreciating, the works. In 1984, as Wallinger completed his training at Goldsmiths, a major Stubbs retrospective opened at the Tate Gallery. It was complemented by a Wootton exhibition at Kenwood.[58]

Almost since its inception in the seventeenth century, racing has been the preferred sport of the British monarchy, its court and the landed aristocracy. Charles II constructed a palace at Newmarket in 1671 that was later rebuilt by Queen Anne – who founded Royal Ascot in 1711. Today the House of Windsor remains an important owner and racer of thoroughbreds and a champion of the sport. For the whole of the period in question, royalty has been a major patron of equestrian art.

In the late eighteenth century the first president of the Royal Academy insisted that history painting in the Grand Style was the highest form of art. Wallinger, by renegotiating those conventions, has embarked on a postmodern masquerade as Sir Joshua Reynolds. But Reynolds regarded animal painting as a lesser art, one of the 'humbler walks of painting'.[59] As its subsequent history revealed this humble art was to play a major part in the reproduction of the nation.

ART AND ENGLISH BREEDING

In the eighteenth century the horse portraiture of Stubbs, Seymour, Wootton and Gilpin celebrated breeding and proprietorship. Although Whig hegemony meant that during the first half of the eighteenth century 'sporting pictures placed gradually less weight on the role of possessed land' – previously indexed by a representation of the relevant country seat – equestrian pedigree continued to serve as a metaphor for the social distinction of the owner.[60]

This Anglo-British painting tradition involved a double erasure, for most thoroughbred racing horses were in fact hybrids, English animals crossbred with Arab imports.[61] The painting techniques of Wootton and Tilleman in particular were also derived from Flemish artists like Jan Wyck and van der Meulen.

These are the paintings discussed by Dabydeen in *Hogarth's Blacks*, where he remarks on the frequency with which, in the eighteenth century, black servants were displayed alongside livestock as the property of the white master and mistress, implying a continuity between the physiognomy of black people and animal species – the very dehumanisation and abjection which served as a justification for the slave trade.[62] In these paintings the notion of thoroughbred became a human attribute, more specifically the condition of the white Anglo-Briton, as well as an equine trait.

The elision of the codes of bloodstock and social breeding, horse-racing and national pre-eminence is best figured in John Herring's *Cotherstone and his Forebears*. In this ornately framed series of oils, now in the Queen Mother's art collection, the 1843 Derby winner is surrounded by six separate portraits of the animals which constitute his blood line. More mirror than painting, it is a thoroughbred equine family tree that appears to naturalise the elevation of the Royal family.

Although there had always been a plebian attendance at race events, during the nineteenth century a number of improvements in transport – first turnpike roads, and later the railways – made racetracks accessible and racecrowds more socially inclusive. Representations of racecourses, and the shared experience of gambling, risk and exhilaration, as in Rowlandson's cartoons and watercolours, became opportunities for the construction of more inclusive national identifications at the beginning of the nineteenth century. This was particularly evident in John Nixon's watercolour *Brighton Races* (1805) in which a merry multi-class British day at the races is protected from French threat by a naval warship on the horizon.

An inclusive Anglo-British national identification, this time in an era of peace, was sustained in Williams Frith's *Derby Day*, whose prosperous social panorama, from rural labourers to dukes, was first exhibited in 1858. The painting formed the template for a mass-produced print, providing an early example of a modern cultural nationalism disseminated to the middle classes by new print technologies and the market. The inclusive Victorian nation was a managed hierarchy and this was clearly communicated in the tiered viewing platforms emphasised in Herring and Pollard's painting of the Doncaster Gold Cup 1838. The social pyramid, formed by the towering coaches, middle-ranking traps and pedestrian poor of the racegoing crowd is depicted in Henry Alken Jnr's *The Road from Tattenham Corner, The Epsom Derby 1879*. The boisterous multivocal and heterogeneous crowds of Rowlandson's representations of race day no longer figured in the English imaginary.

Racing tended to figure an inclusive image of nation and as such was susceptible to the tensions and discourses of regional geo-politics. The mid-nineteenth century saw the first major outburst of racing xenophobia, following the racetrack success of a French stable owned by

Comte de la Grange. The historian of Newmarket recalled that: 'The French horses and their connections were unpopular both with the English owners and with racegoers in general ... It became very much the thing to do to object to a French winner on any conceivable pretext and the crowd could always be relied upon to give a successful French horse a pretty rough passage to the winner's enclosure.'[63] French success on the turf unleashed Anglo-British abjects: the turbulence of modernity and republicanism; aristocratic decadence; Catholicism; and the slaughter of war. American owners arrived in significant numbers during the same period. Tension again increased when the number of French stables in Britain multiplied after the outbreak of the Franco-Prussian War.

The internationalisation of breeding and racing had implications for the forms of representation deployed in equestrian and sporting art, which in turn modified national identifications. In France it was the Impressionists – Manet, Degas and Dufy – who recorded the encounter between French high society and the racecourse. The construction of the Longchamp racecourse in Paris in the mid-nineteenth century sparked this new direction. French dominance of the field of art slowly transformed British equestrian painting conventions. Sir Alfred Munnings reconciled the English genre with French impressionism early in the first half of the century. Later, as President of the Royal Academy from 1944-49, he was a fierce opponent of artistic modernism and any further Europeanisation of Anglo-British painting. The work of the leading mid-century practitioner, John Skeaping, also confined itself to the interface of impressionism and racing. The English imaginary firmly arrested the aesthetic modernisation of equestrian painting.

ENGLAND'S RACE AGAINST TIME

Breeding and racing came under government scrutiny in the post-war period. The sport's close connection to the residual nexus between the landed gentry and the Anglo-British state, and an articulation with popular modernity mediated by gambling, and later by television, made the cultural and economic circuits of racing hotly contested in the middle years of the post-war settlement. The increased domestic regulation and taxation of the industry and its extensive gambling hinterland accompanied the globalisation of racing and breeding. France, Ireland and America came to dominate British horseracing and international exchanges of bloodstock proceeded at an ever increasing rate.[64] Racing Britain was simultaneously cosmopolitan, aristocratic and plebian. It was a culture which hegemony could not afford to ignore.

Off-course betting and gambling was legalised and a betting levy was introduced in the early 1960s. But a modernising government expected greater revenues from the sport. In 1967 a long battle for authority over racing and its profits commenced between George Wigg, chair of the levy board and Wilson's former paymaster general, and the Jockey Club. The struggle over the industry, its revenues, its global circuits and its relationship to Anglo-British modernisation and identity is still being fought. As we shall see, it became as much the context for Wallinger's work as the gallery.

WHO ARE THE ENGLISH?

Breeding has now become a vast international market, which already embraces Europe and North America, and is spreading worldwide.[65] Although wealthy Arab owners rescued the British sector of the industry by investing in stables in large numbers after the oil price rises of the mid-1970s – just as others turned to the art market – their recent departure has been a cause of concern. Horseracing itself is still a crucial, if impoverished, sector of the British economy, employing around 100,000 people, and contributing £350 million in betting duty to the exchequer each year. But its reproduction, like the reproduction of Anglo-British cultural distinction, for which it is a metaphor in Wallinger's work, is in jeopardy.

The Britain of breeding, racing and gambling is being supplanted by global markets, the national lottery, and the priorities of a new generation of politicians who tend to identify modernity and national distinction with the specialist engineering workshops and racetracks of the sports car industry.

Racing is in economic crisis. The prizes available in the United Kingdom are half the level of those offered in France and as little as one tenth of those that are awarded in the United States. So it doesn't come as a surprise to discover that British racehorse owners recorded a total combined deficit of £152 million in 1990 and that the numbers of trainers and horses in Britain are steadily falling. In addition, most racecourses have a lingering culture of amateurism and snobbery, reflecting their origins as the leisure pursuits of the landed gentry. They do not cover their costs, and they are dependent on subsidy and a share of the betting levy raised by the Tote. But this form of betting is contracting, hit by a people's lottery that distributes gambling revenues to other causes. Horseracing, a condensation of successive Anglo-British hegemonies, now operates as a figure for national decline. It therefore compels attention from government.[66]

Disputes over the future of racing, and the conflicts over country sports, are belated battles over who the English are and want to be. These new divisions between the countryside and the city, and the popularity of heavily marketed sports like football, are forcing a re-articulation of Anglo-British national identifications. In the early 1990s horseracing therefore offered a strong subject for Wallinger's historico-conceptual, nationally reflexive art practice.

The technique was first honed in *Capital* (1990), a series of paintings of his friends, figured as impoverished and indigent in the City of London. Wallinger employed the Grand Style that had been imported into eighteenth century English portraiture by Reynolds. Wallinger describes the images as 'paintings of the homeless in the grandiose manner of the boardroom portrait'.[67] The *Capital* series consists of ambivalent images that, while paying homage to the painting techniques of Reynolds and Gainsborough, also put into reverse the genre's contribution to the reproduction of an unmodernised, City-dominated and socially unjust Anglo-Britain. It was a political, indeed national-popular, sharpening of a practice deployed in the paintings of the Italian artist Carlo Maria Mariani, who also inserted his friends into simulations and transformations of classical paintings.

The City was fair and easy game. But Britain's racetracks and stud farms were to provide the space in which Wallinger, by renegotiating the work of George Stubbs, brought the nationally reflexive examples of the German neo-Expressionists, the Italian Transavangardia and Komar and Melamid fully to bear on the English imaginary and its reproduction.

RADICAL HORSEMANSHIP

Wallinger's equestrian paintings, videos and performances ignore the action of the race and attend instead to the stage management of meet-ings and the action taking place in the racegoers' processes of identifi-cation. Contemporary sport is mass sport, and Wallinger's achievement was his reconnection of equestrian art to the realm of the modern national-popular. He unsettles sporting and aesthetic discourses of distinction, and the reproduction of national identity.

The middle class arbiters of quality within the arts find the attribution of aesthetic, symbolic and political virtues to mass spectator sports troubling, because it threatens their patrician view of culture.[68]

Wallinger's conceptual equestrian art detournes the naturalism of George Stubbs, the genealogical mapping exemplified by Herrring's *Cotherstone*, and the representations of national community found in the work of John Nixon and William Frith.

George Stubbs himself re-articulated the fields of sport, art and politics in the mid-eighteenth century. As Stephen Deuchar argues:

> Stubb's sporting pictures, regardless of whether or not it was their primary purpose, did constitute a remarkably convincing visual counterweight to the developing belief that sportsmen were ignorant, behaved excessively and irresponsibly, gambled away their fortunes, demeaned themselves socially and morally, jeopardised their political standing, and corrupted those to whom they were supposed to set an example.[69]

Stubbs' anatomical studies and naturalistic representations of the selectively bred body of the horse – at least in the standing position – separated the sport from rural rusticity and connected racing to science.[70]

Wallinger is not the first artist to emulate the technique of Stubbs. In the second half of the eighteenth century the copyist John Best made his living this way, as did Edwin Cooper in the early nineteenth century.[71] But Wallinger is not a mannerist nor simple plagiarist: his work reclaims the lost meaning of the equestrian tradition. He changes its articulation to social and political discourses.

Wallinger's paintings are of horses without riders. The muscular presence of the animals is the effect of the absence of a human master. In *Race Class Sex* (1992) the hands holding the reins of the four lifesize and naturalistic representations of horses – each one a descendant of Eclipse, once painted by Stubbs – are beyond the frame and anonymous. The same is true of the paired genealogical portraits of *Fathers and Sons* (1993). The horsemen of Wallinger's Anglo-British apocalypse have no name and only an implied presence; his equestrian images lack the traditional accompaniment of a landscape. By the 1990s his Anglo-Britain had truly become a lost, if white, horizon.

As a result the only images in the British equestrian tradition to which Wallinger's paintings have any real resemblance are Stubbs's *Rufus* and his unfinished painting *Whistlejacket*, to which a rider –

possibly George III – and a background were meant to be added. By accident, therefore, *Whistlejacket* figures the absence of both a monarch and a territorial nation. It was particularly apposite that the recent celebration of the purchase of *Whistlejacket* by the National Gallery – a representation of an incomplete nation – co-incided with major difficulties for the House of Windsor, a new crisis of succession, and the growing affirmation of national-popular as opposed to monarchical inflections of sovereignty and national identity.[72] For one night, as *Whistlejacket* was projected above the traffic and onto the side of the National Gallery extension, Trafalgar Square really did become home to the English imaginary and its major anxiety.

Wallinger's ownerless and groom-free mounts found absent riders in *Brown's* (1993), a series of 42 oil paintings of the multicoloured jockeys' silks belonging to racehorse owners called Brown. These unfilled vests are uncanny, the strictness and artificiality of racing codes suggesting the shared trauma of the partial and gendered entry into the disembodied language of the nation.

In Wallinger's *Half-Brother* paintings (1994-95) he fully detournes Stubbs, mimicking the choices made by the bloodstock agents who engineered the horses that Stubbs' paintings naturalised and incorporated into the eighteenth century national landscape. Wallinger's life-size hybrid paintings patch together the back and front halves of horses that derive from the same dam. These oil-based metaphoric disclosures and deconstructions of Anglo-British processes of distinction and reproduction were complemented with a disturbing documentary video of men assisting stallions to service mares in *National Stud* (1995). Through its voyeurism and manhandling of the bestial, the video resurrects material abjected by Anglo-Britain's natural, familial Union and makes Englishness strange to itself.

The relationship between the two forms of reproduction, of managed racialised bloodlines both in the society and the stables of Anglo-Britain, is underlined in the installation *Royal Ascot*, which involves the simultaneous screening of four different televised processions of the monarch along the racetrack. The construction of a national identification by a contrived articulation of monarchy, sport and broadcast communications is made reflexive, returning the viewer to the ambivalences and strangeness of the English imaginary. The degree to which contemporary Anglo-British subjects have an allocated and chora-disrupting place from which to act and speak – in contrast to the heterogeneity of Rowlandson's racecrowds, but in direct continuity with the Victorian regulation of crowds – is revealed in *Race, Sex, Class II* (1994). This is a three screen video of the class stamped enclosures provided for racegoers, whose title explicitly aligns Wallinger's account of the reproduction of horses with the racialisation, gendering and stratifying of a people.

The lifesize scale of these neo-Stubbsian paintings, and the hyper-realist rendering in oils of the body of the animals suggests the possibility that for Wallinger the horse operates as a significant self contrasted other, through the eye of which his own identity is partially constructed. At the risk of offending the kind of deep green ecologist who advocates species equality, I'd suggest that in these post-colonial equestrian paintings the signs of excessive physicality and bestiality are separated from the colonised and returned to where they belong: the animal world. However, for Wallinger, the thoroughbred racehorse is a contradictory alterity. It is a commodified body harnessed and restrained like the abject. But it is also a metaphoric place of reproduction, a source of power, speed and excitement. As such the horse provides excess and jouissance over and above the codes of national identification offered at racetracks.

Behind You (1994), in which buggery is simulated in a pantomime horse, can be interpreted as Laddish homophobia, camp humour, or a joke at the expense of Anglo-Britain's fear of sexuality. One of the figures is of ambiguous gender and both are anonymous. If Wallinger's lifesize horses are a place of excess and renegotiation with the abject, then *Behind You* figures the imaginary itself, a place where anxiety and strangeness reside, where identification is threatened and reproduction ends.

THE DEATH OF WHITE NATIONHOOD

By acknowledging the multivalency of the figure of the horse as it appears in Wallinger's work, and attending to the narratives of reproduction and identification associated with it, Anglo-Britons can become strangers to themselves, capable of the ethical action and tolerance required in a modern pluralist culture. Late Powellite discourses of Anglo-British national purity, ethnic absolutism and respect for traditional institutions will find it difficult to recuperate the practice of this young British artist. Wallinger, after all, is not Stubbs: there is no white horse in his back catalogue.

In this extended reflexive encounter with processes of reproduction, alterity and identification, the fixity of gender is finally questioned. Fittingly, this occurs in a piece which addresses not only the linkage between racing and the surrogate nationalism figured by the monarch, but also the popular democratic means by which the nation is made inclusive. In *Self Portrait as Emily Davison* (1993) Wallinger had himself photographed in suffragette-coloured jockey silks at the spot where Emily Davison, campaigning for the right to vote, died under the feet of the King's horse eighty years earlier. Wallinger had planned to further complexify the gendering of the image by including the name of the felled rider in the title as well, making the piece *Self Portrait as Emily Davison and Herbert Jones*. At a first glance, the photograph offers a hybrid figure, establishing and acknowledging, through mimicry, the strangeness of gender, of racing, even of the popular in the national imaginary. To that extent, it reprises *Capital* in front of a camera. The photograph is an affirmation of the uncoded insurgency that helped initiate Anglo-British civic egalitarianism and the universal franchise. But there is an anxious, tragic undertow to the jouissance in which Wallinger is here engaged: the death of the abjected female is the price paid for his gendered entry into the national symbolic. Her resurrection in this photograph is but a trace of what has been lost, a measure rather than an overcoming of alterity.

The contemporary racing artist Peter Curling once had a horse in training.[73] He linked the fields of sport and art in a way that accorded each their distinctions, jeopardising neither. When Wallinger purchased a racehorse, he destabilised the reproduction of both fields, demonstrating the artificiality of representation and the provisionality of the cultural distinctions on which national elites depend.

In 1994 Wallinger established a consortium of gallery owners, curators and collectors who joined him in the purchase, training and racing of a chestnut filly which he named 'A Real Work of Art'.[74] After all, weren't dealers already involved in the business of establishing lineages, picking winners, taking gambles and collecting cash prizes? And weren't studfarms the studios of racing, the parade rings their galleries? The very knowledge of 'A Real Work of Art's' existence, disseminated in the sporting and the art media, unsettled the traditional meanings of Anglo-British racing and of art. Every race became an open-ended piece of performance art, securing the participation of other owners, punters and bookies. The Italian Arte Povera artist Kounellis once placed eleven horses in a gallery. But to see Wallinger's work, collectors and viewers had to visit a lifeworld, the racecourse or the stable rather than the managed and aestheticised spaces of the art world. Wallinger's carefully bred Duchampian ready-made, a living contradiction, was returned to its sporting habitus, reconnecting art to the national-popular in a mutually reflexive encounter that briefly erased distinctions central to an older English imaginary and vital to the reproduction of Anglo-British elites.

A 'Real Work of Art' engineered an evacuation of the gallery, as did Wallinger's other joke at the expense of the incorporated commodity producing descendants of Duchamp, the 'Fountain' (1992), which poured water (or pissed, as the artist prefers) through the window of the Anthony Reynolds Gallery and into the street. London's drains and reprocessing by Thames Water would eventually return it to the tap in a reproductive cycle on which the gallery would parasitically subsist.

The interrelated processes of individual and national identification, assisted by the codes of sport, were explicitly engaged in a photographic self portrait taken in 1994. The title of the work is a childlike address that positions Mark Wallinger somewhere in the universe, naming all the tiers that intervene; from the solar system to Camberwell. In this image Wallinger holds a Union Jack, emblazoned with his own name, in the middle of the crowded approach to the home ground of the England football team, Wembley stadium. Where the title was a painstaking and detailed attempt to describe the location of the artist, the flag offered no mediation between the name of the individual and the representation of the nation, between personal and national identity. It was a figuration, in effect, of the Thatcherite notion that there is no such thing as society. As Wallinger says, 'nobody would normally put their own name there because it is really too terrifyingly lonely'.[75] The flag, conceived as a question about identity and the nature of the crowd, triggered a performance that offered an answer, an ethnic grounding with his sport loving brothers, who, untroubled by the neo-conceptual and counter-hegemonic nature of the photo opportunity, began to chant Wallinger's name as they marched into the stadium.[76]

Despite this brief resurrection of the chora, the resilience of the fields of art and sport and the persistence of an older English nationalist imaginary appear to have taken their toll on Wallinger's confidence that artists can help to reconfigure social codes, institutions and identifications. He has spoken of:

The haplessness of the radical impulse in any art form faced with the implacable forces of the establishment. How a work whose intent is subversive only further re-inforces the status quo.77

What Do You Expect to Get Out of Me? Wallinger asked the viewer in *Q3* (1994), a handpainted text panel. In *Regard a mere mad rager* (1993) he returned to materials provided by the popular culture of his childhood. The video installation replayed old footage of the television comedian Tommy Cooper, dressed in the helmet of a British policeman but debunking authority. A mirror reversed the image, to match its palindromic title. The copying and framing, mimicry and simulation, was distancing and disturbing. Were the young British artists merely mad ragers provoking utopic longings but failing to deliver change?

Apart from *Oxymoron*, Wallinger's recent work establishes few direct connections to the discourses of sport or national identity. A longstanding concern with 'the inevitable artificiality of representation' has led to works of punning and reversal. This is a Derridean register that is more questioning, but less socially embedded, than Wallinger's work of the early 1990s – it is more reminiscent of the melancholy of *Lost Horizon*.78

Upside Down and Back to Front, the Spirit Meets the Optical Illusion (1997) consists of a bottle of clear spirit fitted with an optic on a mirrored surface. The bottle bears the personalised label of the artist. It is reversed, readable only in the mirrored table on which it stands. But the transparent spirit escapes reflection and representation. It is a figure for that which lies beyond the signified, that for which there is no proof, the unameable and the unrecognisable. Too pure for the abject, it must be the chora. It is also tempting to read this 'Spirit' as an ironic comment on the repeated sightings and unfulfilled promise of a new spirit in British painting.

The video *Angel* applies a similar principle of punning reversal in order to question a faith. The artist, using a white stick and dark glasses to code himself as blind, is at the foot of the Angel underground station escalator in north London. He is talking while walking against the upward movement of the steps. The video is played back in reverse but Wallinger's speech is comprehensible because he was speaking backwards and phonetically when the performance was filmed. *Angel* figures the unfulfilled promise of communication, the primacy of representation and the difficulty of entering the symbolic order. He is reciting a biblical passage (John 1.1-1.5) which deals with this inaugural

moment: 'In the beginning was the word, and the word was God'
When this chewed and unaspirated speech ends Wallinger stops walking, and the uncanny stranger he has created recedes up the escalator to
the sound of Handel's *Zadak the Priest*, leaving us to ponder on *Angel*'s
similarities to Townshend's punk with a stutter or Dabydeen's description of creole.

Dead Man's Handle (1997) consists of four circular tables, each
beneath unsynchronised numberless clocks around which a second
hand sweeps. On each table there is a circular model railway on which
two stationary trains are set to follow each other. Have the dead man's
handles already been activated, killing all prospects of movement? For
each table there is a biblical label: Matthew, Mark, Luke and John.
Dead Man's Handle is a figure of melancholy aspiration replicated four
times. The trains also carry political freight. The installation, first
exhibited at the foot of that temple of reactionary modernisation,
Canary Wharf, is parodic' of Christianity and notions of a new British
momentum, both central to New Labour's discourse.

Dead Man's Handle, apart from being a safety device on a train, is
also a colloquial pun that refers to the name of the deceased. The
impossibility of English authenticity has made the artist a corpse and
no longer a subject in the national narrative. But a look at the form-
book suggests that Wallinger is a good middle distance runner, and will
survive. No, the figure dying in the Anglo-British gallery has got
another name: vestigial white nationhood. Its passing has been painful
and protracted, and it is not over yet.

*An early version of this chapter appeared as 'Mark Wallinger: un
farceur post-imperial' in Liber: Revue Internationale des livres no 32,
September 1997 pp14-15.*

NOTES

1. For overviews see Andrew Renton and Liam Gillick (eds), *Technique
Anglaise: Current Trends in British Art*, Thames and Hudson, London 1991;
Shark Infested Waters: The Saatchi Collection of British Art in the 90s,
Zwemmer, London 1994; *The British Art Show 4*, The South Bank Centre,
London 1995; *Brilliant! New Art from London*, Walker Art Centre, Houston
1995; Matthew Collings, *Blimey! From Bohemia to Britpop: The London
Artworld from Francis Bacon to Damien Hirst*, Cambridge 1997; *Sensation:
Young British Artists from the Saatchi Collection*, Royal Academy of Arts,

London 1997; and Louisa Buck, *Moving Targets: A User's Guide to British Art Now*, Tate Gallery Publishing, London 1997. Three broader ranging surveys of contemporary work which include but go beyond the London YBA scene are *Life/Live: La Scene Artistique au Royame Unie en 1996 de Nouvelles Aventures*, Musee d'Art Moderne de la Ville de Paris, Paris 1996; *Full House: Young British Art*, Kunstmuseum, Wolfsburg 1996; and *Pictura Brittanica: Art from Britain*, Museum of Contemporary Art, Sydney 1997. The first extended critical study of the formation is provided by Duncan McCorquodale, Naomi Siderfin and Julian Stallabrass in *Occupational Hazard: Critical Writing on Recent British Art*, Black Dog Publishing 1998.

2. Mark Harris, 'Putting on the Style', *Art Monthly* 193, February 1996, p5.

3. Stuart Home, 'The Art of Chauvinism in Britain and France' in *Disputations on Art, Anarchy and Assholism*, Sabotage Editions, London 1977, pp4-10.

4. '£11 million Stubbs bought for nation', *The Guardian*, 20 December 1997.

5. Sarah Curtis, 'Blood Lines', *World Art*, no2 1995, pp70-75.

6. The main overview and catalogue of his work to date is *Mark Wallinger*, Ikon Gallery and Serpentine Gallery, Birmingham and London 1995.

7. John Roberts, 'Notes on 90s Art', *Art Monthly* 200, September 1996, p3.

8. Mark Leonard, *Britain*™, Demos, London 1997, p31.

9. Waldemar Junuszczak, 'His Sporting Life', *The Times*, 4 June 1995.

10. *A New Spirit in Painting*, Royal Academy of Arts, London 1981, p15.

11. *Zeitgeist*, George Braziller, New York 1982.

12. Alistair Hicks, *The School of London: The Resurgence of Contemporary Painting*, Phaidon, London 1989.

13. Tony Godfrey, *The New Image: Painting in the 1980s*, Phaidon, London 1986, p89.

14. Peter Fuller, 'The Hayward Annual', *Artscribe* 53 1985, p55.

15. Nauman exhibited at the Whitechapel Gallery in London in 1986 - during the higher education of many of the Young British Artists.

16. Sarah Greenberg, *Artnews*, September 1995.

17. Michael Archer summarises what young British artists learnt from the American neo-conceptualists of the 1980s - including Nauman, Ruscha, Wegman, Ruppersburg, - in 'Reconsidering Conceptual Art', *Art Monthly* 193, February 1996, pp12-16.

18. See Alison Fendley, *Saatchi and Saatchi: The Inside Story*, Arcade Publishing 1995; and Kevin Goldman, *Conflicting Accounts*, Simon and Schuster, New York 1997.

19. For Saatchi's holdings in the early 1980s see *Art of Our Time: The Saatchi Collection* (4 vols). Lund Humphries, London 1984.

20. The best account of Kiefer's practice is to be found in John C. Gilmour,

Fire on the Earth: Anselm Kiefer and the Postmodern World, Temple University Press, Philadelphia 1990. Michael Rosentahl's *Anselm Kiefer*, Prestel-Verlag, Munich 1987 is also invaluable.

21. See the accounts in Irving Sandler, *Art of the Postmodern Era*, HarperCollins, London 1996, pp425-455; and in Christopher Watson, *The Art Boom 1970-97*, Art Sales Index Limited 1997.

22. Schnabel exhibited at the Whitechapel Gallery in 1987.

23. Victoria Miro quoted in 'Charles Saatchi: the man and the market' in *The Art Newspaper* no 73, September 1997, pp20-21.

24. Fendley, *op.cit*, 1995, pp95-149.

25. Peter Watson, *From Manet to Manhattan: The Rise of the Modern Art Market*, Vintage 1993, p434. For the reactions of one of the artists whose works Saatchi disposed of, see Sean Scully's angry comments in Stephen Warr, 'Saatchi accused over art sale', *The Times*, 24 November 1989.

26. Quoted in Fendley, *op.cit*, 1995, p61.

27. See Alistair Hicks, *New British Art in The Saatchi Collection*, Thames and Hudson, London 1989.

28. 'Charles Saatchi: the man and the market' in *The Art Newspaper* no 73, September 1997, pp20-21.

29. John Harlow, *The Sunday Times*, 17 December 1995.

30. Stuart Brisley, *The Guardian*, 7 October 1995.

31. Sarah Kent, 'Introduction', *Shark Infested Waters: The Saatchi Collection of British Art in the 90s*, Zwemmer, London 1994, p6.

32. Stuart Morgan, 'Briller a Tawdry Flickwort!', in *Brilliant!*, *op.cit*, 1995, p6.

33. *Ibid*; Neville Wakefield's comments appeared in *Tate*, winter 1995.

34. Simon Ford is the author of *The Realisation and Suppression of the Situationist International: An Annotated Bibliography 1972-1992*, AK Press, Edinburgh 1995. His comment appears in 'Myth Making', *Art Monthly*, March 1996 pp3-9.

35. Mark Harris, 'Putting on the Style' *Art Monthly* 193, February 1996 pp3-6.

36. Editorial, *Art Monthly* 193, February 1996, p18.

37. Prison notebooks Antonio Gramsci, *Selections from Cultural Writing*, Lawrence & Wishart, London 1985, p51.

38. Matthew Collings, *op.cit*, 1997.

39. *A New Spirit in Painting*, *op.cit*, 1981.

40. See the account in Brandon Taylor, *The Art of Today*, Weidenfeld and Nicolson, London 1995, pp51-2.

41. For the American debate see Irving Sandler, *Art of the Postmodern Era*, HarperCollins, London 1996, pp222-229.

42. Quoted by Brigid Grauman in 'Inside Europe:The Temperature is Lower',

Art News, April 1988, p115.

43. Sarah Kent, *Young British Artists 2: Rose Finn-Kelcey, Sarah Lucas, Marc Quinn, Mark Wallinger*, Saatchi Collection, London 1993.

44. Charles Harrison, quoted in Taylor, *op.cit*, 1995, p56.

45. Komar and Melamid, The Fruitmarket Gallery Edinburgh and MOMA Oxford, 1985.

46. Sarah Curtis, 'Blood Lines', *World Art* no2, 1995, p71.

47. John Roberts, *Selected Errors: Writings on Art and Politics*, Pluto Press, London 1992, p220.

48. See this volume, Chapter 4.

49. Andreas Huyssen, 'Popart Retrospective' in *Documenta X*, Cantz Verlag, Kassel 1997 p399.

50. Ernesto Laclau, *New Reflections on the Revolution of Our Time*, Verso, London 1990, p64.

51. Curtis, *op.cit*, 1995, p70.

52. J.B. Priestley, *Rain Upon Godshill: Further Chapter of Autobiography*, Heinemann, London 1939, p204.

53. For example J.B. Priestley, *Out of the People*, Heinemann, London 1941, p101.

54. See John Fairley, *Racing in Art*, Rizzoli, New York 1990.

55. Stephen Deuchar, *Sporting Art in Eighteenth Century England: A Social and Political History*, Yale University Press, New Haven and London 1988.

56. Walter Shaw Sparrow, *British Sporting Artists*, John Lane, The Bodley Head, London 1922, p88.

57. Andrew Sim, 'A Real Work of Art', *Sporting Life*, 29 January 1996, p19.

58. The relevant catalogues are Judy Egerton, *George Stubbs 1724-1806*, Tate Gallery, London 1984; and Arline Mayer, *John Wootton 1682-1764: Landscapes and Sporting Art in Early Georgian England*, Iveagh Bequest Kenwood, London 1984.

59. Robert R. Wark (ed), *Sir Joshua Reynolds, Discourses on Art*, 1975, p50.

60. Deuchar, *op.cit*, 1988, p75.

61. Fairley, *op.cit*, 1990, p9.

62. David Dabydeen, *Hogarth's Blacks: Images of Blacks in Eighteenth Century English Art*, Dangaroo Press, Coventry 1985, p28.

63. Richard Onslow, *The Heath and the Turf: A History of Newmarket*, Arthur Barker Ltd 1971, p63.

64. P. Willett, *The Thoroughbred*, Weidenfeld and Nicolson, London 1970, p273.

65. Christopher R. Hill, *Horse Power: The Politics of the Turf*, Manchester University Press, Manchester 1988, p212.

66. The Conservative government took horse racing seriously. It reduced betting taxes, provided VAT relief on training and bloodstock sales, permitted Sunday racing and established a new British Horseracing Board to take over many of the functions of the Jockey Club. That board is now investigating alternatives to the betting levy, with the intention of introducing a new form of funding for the sport. Labour is divided over whether to privatise the Tote. In July 1997 a new chair, Peter Jones, was appointed to make the organisation efficient and more profitable.

67. Curtis, *op.cit*, 1995, pp73.

68. *Ibid*, p74.

69. Deuchar, *op.cit*, 1988, p107.

70. *Ibid*, p67.

71. Sally Mitchell, *The Dictionary of British Equestrian Artists*, Antique Collectors Club 1985, p119 and p168.

72. '£11 million Stubbs bought for nation', *The Guardian*, 20 December 1997.

73. Mitchell, *op.cit*, 1985, p180.

74. Andrew Sim, 'A Real Work of Art', *Sporting Life*, 29 January 1996, p19.

75. *The Football Supporter*, The Football Supporters' Association, no 6 1996, p21.

76. *Ibid*, p21.

77. Mark Wallinger, 'The Pygmalian Paradox', *Art Monthly*, July-August 1998, p4.

78. Quoted in Curtis, *op.cit*, 1995, p72.